KISS MYSELF GOODBYE

The Many Lives of Aunt Munca

Ferdinand Mount

BLOOMSBURY CONTINUUM
LONDON · OXFORD · NEW YORK · NEW DELHI · SYDNEY

BLOOMSBURY CONTINUUM
Bloomsbury Publishing Plc
50 Bedford Square, London, WC1B 3DP, UK

BLOOMSBURY, BLOOMSBURY CONTINUUM and the Diana logo are
trademarks of Bloomsbury Publishing Plc

First published in Great Britain 2020

A catalogue record for this book is available from the British Library

Library of Congress Cataloguing-in-Publication data has been applied for

ISBN: HB: 978-1-4729-7942-1; eBook: 978-1-4729-7943-8;
ePDF: 978-1-4729-7940-7

4 6 8 10 9 7 5 3

Typeset by Deanta Global Publishing Services, Chennai, India
Printed and bound in Great Britain by CPI Group (UK) Ltd, Croydon CR0 4YY

To find out more about our authors and books visit www.bloomsbury.com
and sign up for our newsletters

In memory of Georgie

Birth, and copulation, and death.
That's all the facts when you come to brass tacks.
T.S. Eliot, Sweeney Agonistes

CONTENTS

1   Angmering-on-Sea   1

2   Georgie   26

3   Buster   57

4   Charters   86

5   Brightside   115

6   Crawford Mansions   162

7   Eileen and Elizabeth   183

8   W. F.   216

9   Brightside Revisited   246

10   Seven Hills   251

Thanks   259
Picture and Text Credits   260

This is not a Life. It isn't a nice rounded biography nestling in the reliable recollections of friends and family. In this book, nobody's recollections are reliable. It is a personal memoir that turned into a quest while I wasn't looking, a frustrating sort of quest in half a dozen separate stages which at first didn't seem to connect, not least because each stage was criss-crossed by false trails and blocked off by outright lies.

It's my own quest entirely, and any errors or misunderstandings are mine and nobody else's. I can only say that I have tried to uncover the truth as far as I could retrieve it from the corrosions of time. The truth turns out to be painful – well, that's no surprise – but I didn't expect how gay the lies would be.

F. M.

Angmering-on-Sea

Sometimes, even now, I try to get to sleep by recalling, in the right order, the houses where my Aunt Betty lived. There is, to start with, Blue Waters, Angmering-on-Sea, in West Sussex, a low-slung added-on-to white cottage with blue shutters that seems to have sunk below the level of the garden. The lawn behind the house runs down or rather up to the sea wall. Beyond the sea wall you can just see the heads of the taller passers-by stumbling along the pitiless shingle. In the middle of the lawn there is a small round pond with stone steps surrounding it and a lead cherub that dribbles water onto some dozy goldfish. Nearer the house there are rose beds that my aunt prunes so hard I cannot imagine them ever flowering in the summer, though they do, big cabbagey blooms in violent reds and oranges, to be deadheaded just as hard as soon as they show the first sign of being over. If it is hot, she wears a strange playsuit knitted loosely like a string bag for the deadheading; it looks out of place and childish on her leathery limbs. Along the side of the garden a line of conifers – pines, I think, they smell piney – swish gently in the sea wind and confer a quiet you do not expect so close to the sea.

When my sister and I first go there in the summer of 1945, there are concrete tank barriers ranged across the middle of the garden, like the teeth of some underground giant who has been munching up the lawn. I am six and Francie is four. I like to think of the German tanks smashing through the garden wall and then getting stuck on the tank barriers, giving us time to arrest the crews and give them cups of tea while we wait for the police to arrive. But then the Panzers might never get this far. For if you open the gate in the wall, there in front of you are the tangled, already-rusted girders of the tank traps that are the first line of our anti-tank defences, and running in and out of them the restless, milky sea that sweeps beyond them up to the top of the shingle at high tide. The traps linger on for years after the barriers on the lawn have been removed. They are encrusted with barnacles and dried seaweed, and it is easy to bark your bare legs as you climb through them on the way down to find a patch of sand. Only at low tide is there any real stretch of sand, and then the sea is too shallow to swim in without wading out miles.

I like to think of Angmering as eternally menaced by invaders. My uncle insisted that this was probably where Julius Caesar came ashore in 55 BC, though the history books I read all agreed that the

Georgie, FM, Francie at Blue Waters, summer 1945

2

Romans waded onto the shingle miles along the coast at Pevensey. I loyally stuck, however, to the Angmering theory, in my dreams seeing the Roman chariots with knives sticking out of the wheels creaking up the beach, and then falling foul of the great concrete blocks that, in the dream anyway, were already in place.

At first my uncle and aunt rent Blue Waters. Then, when the owner wants it back, they rent the place next door, White Wings, a larger affair with Dutch gables painted pink and a pillared loggia. After White Wings they move inland, to Castlewood House, Englefield Green, Surrey, a white stucco mansion also with blue shutters, more of a turquoise blue, and lovely gardens stretching down the slope to the edge of Windsor Great Park. There is a little gate into the park at the end of the garden and you can walk across a narrow plank bridge over the ditch beyond the fence and through the forest to Virginia Water. If you go around the left-hand side of the lake, you come to an artificial waterfall known as the Cascade, and beyond the Cascade you come to the Roman ruins brought from Leptis Magna near Tripoli to amuse George IV and re-erected here, rather inaccurately, by Sir Jeffry Wyatville, his court architect. At times during the bombardment of Libya in 2011, it looks as though these may be the only ruins of Leptis Magna to survive, although NATO assures us that their commitment to avoid collateral damage includes the great archaeological sites. It is a strange place for them to land up, though, within earshot of the traffic from the A30.

Castlewood is the sort of house described as imposing, and years later Prince Andrew and Fergie take a lease on it, from 1987 to 1990, which is about half of their brief and stormy marriage. At Castlewood, for the first and perhaps only time in my life with them, my uncle and aunt entertain on quite a scale. Their guests are mostly showbiz people who have alighted in the neighbourhood, which is handy for the film studios and for the West End too.

Aunt Betty has the dining room redecorated for the entertaining. A fashionable painter-designer called Arthur Barbosa is commissioned to do *trompe-l'œil* landscapes round the walls. Barbosa specializes in the Regency style. He is the illustrator whom Georgette Heyer prefers for her dust-jackets of Regency bucks handing dangerous ladies out of curricles, and the Castlewood murals are in this line. He also does theatrical designs and he decorated the inside of Richard Burton and Elizabeth Taylor's yacht. Sometimes the dining-room door is left open and I can peer in and watch him at work on his stepladder. It is exciting to watch his brush moving steadily over the plaster. To me Arthur looks infinitely dashing with his mustachios and his piercing eyes, just like an artist should. Apparently he thinks so too, because when he does the colourful jackets for the first Flashman novels, he models the figure of Flashy on himself in a dashing blue uniform, which does not entirely please their author, George MacDonald Fraser. On the dining-room walls Arthur is painting only in black, grey and white, and I wonder why because I am too young to have heard of grisaille. Anyway, it is piquant to think of the Duke and Duchess of York 30 years later having their stonking rows there while the phaetons and curricles trot on along the walls with their ladies and bucks on top.

To this elegant dining room comes, among other stars, Mary Martin, who has rented nearby while she is singing 'I'm Gonna Wash That Man Right Outa My Hair' in the West End production of *South Pacific*. A couple of times she brings over her teenage son, Larry Hagman, who is going to be an actor too and later reaches superstardom as JR in *Dallas*. Closer and more permanent friends are Nanette Newman and Bryan Forbes, who is a bit like my Uncle Greig in looks – the wavy hair, the smiley eyes – though in nothing else. To me, easily the most thrilling neighbour is Diana Dors, who lives in the village and often rings up for a chat. There is nothing like the shock of hearing her voice when I happen to answer the phone. She was born in Swindon and her husky voice still has a touch of Wiltshire in it: 'Hi, this is Di Dors, and who am I speaking to?'

Aunt Betty loves shows as well as show-people and she takes Francie and me up from Castlewood to the new American musicals in the West End: *Damn Yankees*, *The Pajama Game*, *Kismet*, *Daddy Longlegs*. She gives us high tea at the Causerie in Claridge's before or after the show, depending on whether it is a matinée. My uncle and aunt have a suite permanently reserved for them at Claridge's, which they call The Pub. They say this is a cheaper arrangement, although I don't see how it can be. Sometimes we go up to the suite for a rest before the show or have our tea brought to us up there. I don't think I've been to a proper hotel before, and I am awed by the silence and the thick carpets and the soft clunk of the lift. Inside the suite, there is a French rococo clock on the mantelpiece and eighteenth-century-style furniture in matching green brocade and fruit in Chinese porcelain bowls. I can see that it's all meant to look like a grand person's drawing room, but somehow it doesn't and I feel uneasy, more like I feel in a dentist's waiting room.

In my perverse puritanical way, I also find the actual shows rather noisy and unconvincing. Just as I remember the gothic-style cinema in Salisbury better than the films my mother and I see there, so it is the journey up to town that sticks in my mind: the Rolls gliding with its faintly sick-making motion through the Surrey woods past the fantastical salmon-pink and white pinnacles of Royal Holloway College, then on up the A30 to where it meets the Great West Road and those amazing Art Deco factories – Gillette and Beecham and, best of all, the

Jantzen swimwear sign with its ever-diving lady in whose glow
the narrator first kisses Jean Duport in Anthony Powell's novel
The Acceptance World.

Aunt Betty loves nightclubs and dancing too. At home
she will often sketch out a few steps of the Charleston while
dusting and plumping up the cushions, which she can't refrain
from doing although she has a perfectly good maid called
Mabel. When we are older, she takes us to the nightclubs that
she knew in the 1930s and that have survived the war – the
Café de Paris, the 400 – and I sit glum and ungrateful while
she clicks her fingers and sings along to the music of Harry
'Tiger' Roy, who winks and tips his baton to her as an old
friend. Harry is getting on a bit and so are his bandsmen. The
numbers they play have a pre-war swing to them. There's
one that stuck in my mind, though I have not heard it played
anywhere else since:

> I'm gonna kiss myself goodbye
> Oh goodbye, goodbye
> I'm gonna get my wings and fly
> Up high, up high

It is at the Café de Paris that Aunt Betty takes us to see Sophie
Tucker sing. By now 'the last of the Red-hot Mommas' is long
past her best, huge and rouged and powdered and monstrously
corseted, none of which stops my aunt whooping with delight
when she wheezes, scarcely pretending to sing, 'Nobody Loves
a Fat Girl, But Oh, How a Fat Girl Can Love'. After the show
we sit on velvet banquettes in the foyer and Sophie Tucker
comes out to say hello. The foyer is really only a narrow passage
and it seems even narrower as she graciously inclines to greet
us, depositing a faint dusting of powder on the shoulders of my
new, first grown-up suit.

FM, Uncle Greig, Francie, Georgie – waiting for Sophie Tucker,
Café de Paris 1957

'This is my nephew,' Aunt Betty says. 'He's going to be a writer.' I don't know how she knows that this is my ambition because I myself am not at all sure about it. I certainly do not remember telling her, and if I ever did, I now wish I hadn't. Aunt Betty is not keen on books, and having your head stuck in one is not something she approves of. It is the opposite of living and having a good time.

'That's swell,' Sophie Tucker says, giving me a puffy grin. 'I've always had a lot of time for the guy with the pencil.'

It is about this time – no, it must be a few years earlier – that Uncle Greig and Aunt Betty tell us that in future we are to call them 'Unca' and 'Munca' after the two mice in Beatrix Potter. We don't like this at all. It seems a childish idea, all the more inappropriate because it is the adults who have thought of it. I do not much care for Beatrix Potter anyway and prefer Little

7

Grey Rabbit. Also, I cannot resist pointing out that in *The Tale of Two Bad Mice* there is only one relevant mouse, not two, and it is called *Hunca* Munca. But we fall in line, and I'll fall in line here too, having registered my protest. For this is to be Munca's story, and quite a lot of it will be about the right to choose what you are called, so we had better start as we shall be going on.

Most of the showbiz characters disappear off the radar when Unca and Munca leave Castlewood and briefly return to Blue Waters. It is as though my aunt only has to be in Surrey for a year or two before she hears the slap and surge of the tide on the shingle and has to up sticks and get back to Sussex by the sea – although she never does anything seasidey like swimming or sailing. Nor does Unca, except that about once a year he takes a boat to go mackerel-fishing. The second spell at Blue Waters cannot have lasted very long because I am still at school when they are back in Surrey again, this time on the other side of the A30 in a house on the Wentworth Estate called Holthanger. For Munca's dissatisfaction works in reverse too. After a couple of years by the sea, she yearns for the Surrey heathlands where she can grow azaleas and rhododendrons and see some showbiz people again. The only show-people we know of in Angmering are several members of the Crazy Gang; not Bud Flanagan himself but Chesney Allen, I think, and possibly Nervo and Knox. But whichever they are, Unca and Munca don't actually know them, although Munca does take us to see them at the Palladium. In fact, apart from that star-studded flurry at Castlewood, my aunt and uncle lead a rather quiet life and don't appear anxious to make new friends. Certainly they don't seem to have many old friends. It is as though by these frequent changes of residence they are making a conscious effort not to put down roots, as though they too were part of the floating population of actors and tycoons who come and go around them. The other reason Munca keeps on moving house is that she likes doing them up, although the interior of the new home always ends up looking much like the interior of the old one, which is the case with most people because, after all, they still have the same furniture and pictures.

Holthanger is a peculiar dwelling, built of muted brick but mostly painted white and shaped like a ship with portholes along one side. It is moored by the third fairway of the West Course. After the war, the West Course became known as the Burma Road, apparently not because of its notorious difficulty but because the fairways had been left to grow wild for fear that enemy planes might land on them, and in 1945 German prisoners of war were put to work clearing the vegetation, as the British prisoners had been by the Japanese in Burma, and the British officer in charge had quipped: 'Let this be their Burma Road.'

From the garden you can glimpse through the shrubbery the garish costumes of the golfers processing down the slope (this was the era when golfers still wore Val Doonican sweaters and Technicolor slacks) and hear their cries of delight as they see how far their drives have rolled down the hill. In the early morning when the dew is still on the fairways I sneak out through the gate in the rhododendrons and play a few holes free of charge until I hear the first fourball of the day approaching over the hill. Then I shrink back into the woods, intending to make out that I am just going for a walk, though I have no idea how I would explain the golf bag on my back. In the summer of 1959 Wentworth hosts the Canada Cup and I follow round the American pair, Ben Hogan and Sam Snead, both clad in dazzling white with white peaked caps that make their leathery old faces look even more ancient. How graceful and merciless they are.

For me, even then, when I was in my teens, there is a mysterious allure about these swooping fairways and dark thickets of rhododendron with the opulent villas half-seen through the gaps, the lives lived in them unknowable, impermanent like the

9

landscape they hide away in. Beyond these secret colonies of the rich, the golf course opens out towards the railway line, and you can see over to the distant high wasteland, still the haunt of Gypsies and escaped pumas. Once, not so long ago, before the railway came, these manicured swards were heathery waste too. I like the idea of the whole thing: the newness of the estate and the people who live there, their obsession with privacy, their indifference to the country beyond. There is a kind of magic about it all, a not entirely pleasant kind. This is Munca's territory, where nobody is quite at home and nobody stays very long. Even the children at the children's parties seem to change each birthday. The parents who come to collect them scarcely know each other, and exclaim with noisy delight when they recognize a face – 'Oh yes, we met at the Club, it must have been the Club.'

For Unca and Munca the golf course is just a place to take the dogs for a walk, except that Munca never goes for a walk. In fact she almost never leaves her domain except when she puts on her jewels and climbs into the Rolls to go up to London. At Holthanger the furthest she goes is to the end of the lawn to retrieve the errant golf balls that have sailed through the trees and that she then resells on behalf of the People's Dispensary for Sick Animals.

Munca believes that in most respects, animals are superior to human beings. She has a sizeable aviary in the house and spends much of the day cleaning the place out and tweeting back at the canaries and budgies and finches as they flit around her. Through the big window of the aviary I watch her dusting down the perches and seed trays, as she puckers her lips and blows kisses to the lovebirds to persuade them out of their cages so she can sweep their floors.

The rest of the house is under the control of four standard poodles, three white and one chocolate. In coffee shops today, 'standard' is a euphemism for 'small'. Here it is a euphemism for 'enormous and terrifying'. The white ones are called Zephyr, Beau and Yogi Bear, but I am so scared of them I can never remember which is which, although I know the chocolate one is called Peter. When the poodles first arrived, they were bigger than I was and their bark never lost its power to make me jump. Also on the strength is a representative of the smaller breeds, sometimes yappy, sometimes snuffly, a terrier or a Pekingese. Apart from *Country Life*, the *Pekingese Gazette* is almost the only periodical in the house and, as I am always desperate for something to read, I develop a modest expertise in the malformations of Pekes' testicles. These are due to irresponsible breeding strategies, it seems, monorchism being all too often found.

Like the birds, the dogs require a good deal of maintenance and, wherever Unca and Munca are living, there is a procession of visiting vets and poodle-clippers, varied by the occasional attendant on humans, such as a coiffeur or manicurist. In Blue Waters days, these are usually called up from Worthing, which is only a few miles away and offers a wide range of services to cater to Munca's needs, especially dentists and hygienists. Munca's favourite dentist is so highly rated that her old friend Doris McNicol comes all the way from Sunningdale to have him sharpen her teeth, not an operation I have ever heard of before. Aunt Doris, as we are instructed to call her, though we are also told she isn't an aunt at all, is a stout, friendly woman, but Munca says she is spoilt.

Once or twice Munca's favourite horoscopist, also based in Worthing, makes a house call. Munca is allergic to organized religion in any form but takes the truths and techniques of astrology for granted. Years later, she has my elder son's horoscope cast at birth and presents it to us (I had been hoping for a cheque). I meant to keep it to see how its predictions pan out, but have since lost it.

This addiction to the ancient wisdom of the Babylonians might seem to go badly with Munca's other addiction, which is to modern things and generally to be where it's at. Holthanger is a pioneering building by the modernist architect Oliver Hill, and it is chosen as House of the Year in 1936. If you look at the website of the Royal Institute of British Architects, you can still find photos of the sliding doors out to the loggia and, especially, of the great drum staircase, which is visible through the circular glass windows from the rough along the neighbouring fairway. The staircase looks a bit like a miniature edition of the Guggenheim Museum in New York. But when I think of the house, I think of the huge poodles barring the way upstairs to the children's loo, which I am desperate to get to. The poodles are the same off-white colour as the stair carpet, and sometimes I don't see them drowsing at the curve in the staircase and I retreat hurriedly when they start barking.

Holthanger, Wentworth – the staircase

The aviary and the dogs follow my uncle and aunt back down to Angmering, and once more to Blue Waters, which has just come up for sale. But then, after only a year or two, they move next door again to White Wings, which is now renamed Preston House, as though the house needs to make a fresh start under its new owners. This turns out to be their final residence. My parents never come to stay at any of these houses, although they do drive up from Wiltshire to take me out from school for lunch at Holthanger and Castlewood. The neighbourhoods that Unca and Munca like to live in are not the kind of places my parents care to frequent. There is no way of stating this without making my parents sound snobbish, because in this respect snobbish is what they are. It is odd really that Munca should have been chosen to be my godmother as well as my aunt, because she and my mother have never shown the slightest desire to be friends. Nor, as I say, is Munca in the least bit religious, although she tells us that she was brought up as a Roman Catholic, which seems to be what turned her off religion. Of course she is rich and my parents are not, so that may be the reason why they asked her to be my godmother. Or it may be simply because I was christened just as war was breaking out and it was difficult to round up anyone to be a godparent in those frantic days.

At all events, Aunt Betty is a tremendously dutiful and affectionate godmother. So she is much more than an aunt to me. This is also because she is unlike anyone else I have met, alarming and warm at the same time, in an electrifying way. I can't take my eyes off her as she skitters about the sitting-room plumping up cushions that people have just got up from sitting on. I am conscious of her generosity too. There is always a large cheque at Christmas and on my birthday, and she is lavish with every kind of treat and, above all, with her time. I suppose that in our childhood we spent more time with her than with anyone else outside our immediate family – my sister certainly did.

Looking back, I do find it strange that my sister and I should have spent so much of our holidays at Blue Waters and all the other houses that Greig and Betty lived in. It wasn't just that my mother didn't get on with her sister-in-law at all. The old affection between my father and his younger brother had also cooled with their marriages and the war. The only reason we went almost every holiday was because the seaside air was thought to be good for my asthma, which was at its most violent then. Even I could see how my convulsive wheezing alarmed my parents. By the time Greig and Betty moved inland, our staying with them had become a fixture that could not easily be broken. My parents probably also thought that Munca would show us a better time than they could afford stuck out on Salisbury Plain with a Morris Ten that didn't work. Certainly my mother never showed any resentment that Munca should play such a large part in our lives. But then she wasn't one for showing resentment at the worst of times. And I now see how desperate she must have been for any sign that my asthma was improving.

Nor did Munca's sense of obligation fade after I had grown up. Now and then, a letter would arrive from her on her distinctive blue writing paper, datelined Preston House, or sometimes Claridge's. The letters are full of affection and invitations to come and stay at whatever house they happen to be living in at the time, also joshing rebukes that I do not write more often. She signs herself 'Your old squaw Munca'. A Native American squaw is certainly what she looks like and I am surprised that she is aware of the resemblance and can joke about it. The desk at which I am writing this, a sturdy Georgian scrolled oak affair, was a wedding gift from her. So I have a solid reminder of her every time I sit down to work, and, although she professed to be uninterested in anything to do with books, I wonder if this is what she intended.

With the poodles and the birds come also the chauffeur Ron Haynes, Pam the nanny (who later marries Ron), the sisters Olive and Mabel Salmon, the cook and maid, the Rolls-Royce and the chocolate Mercedes coupé, which has the number plate URA1, not a cheap extra even at this date. Ron puts on his peaked cap to drive them up to London in the Rolls to stay the night at The Pub. When Unca drives over to the factory in Bristol, where he stays from Tuesday to Thursday or Friday, he sometimes takes the chocolate Merc instead of the Rolls. Being a good driver is one of the few qualities that my father readily concedes to his younger brother, but only on the grounds that 'Greig's got nothing else in his head to think about', implying not without truth that his own crumps and contretemps with the law are due to the fact that he is thinking of something else at the time, most notoriously when he buys a copy of the new edition of the Highway Code in Warminster and is reading it at the wheel on the way home when the police car stops him. The episode is reported in the *Daily Mirror*, which I am rather proud of.

Unca's factory is Lennards Shoes, an old-established business, started by five Lennard brothers in Leicester who later trade under the charming name of the Public Benefit Boot Company before reverting to Lennards. By the 1930s the firm has finally settled in its present headquarters in Staple Hill, Bristol, and has 250 shops all over the country selling to mid-range customers – not as smart as Dolcis or Clarks but a step up from Freeman, Hardy and Willis. Lennards is, I sometimes think, Uncle Greig's only real love. He is never happier than when browsing at shoe fairs in Rome or Bologna, or opening new branches in Ghana and Nigeria, selling to customers, many of whom have never worn shoes before and may perhaps be more easily pleased. 'Walk to success in Lennards shoes' is the jingle sung on commercial radio across West Africa. He especially enjoys the fashion side of the business, always alert to see whether peep-toe or chisel-toe will be the season's new shape and eager to experiment with new colours and combinations, such as sylvana, taupe, whisky or mahogany. His own wardrobe is full of garments I have not seen elsewhere: silk pyjamas from Sulka, cashmere boxer jackets, 1930s-style belted overcoats. Some of these come to me as cast-offs but usually don't fit very well. Unca's mellow voice and faintly confiding manner have an unobtrusive charm. He is on distant terms with his elder brother Bill, who is said to have made some unforgivable remark to him, but nobody seems to know what it was. My father for his part likes to record the fact that their mother was longing for a daughter after two sons and several miscarriages and insisted on dressing Greig in girls' clothes until he was seven.

What his brothers do not say is that Greig is the only member of the family for generations who has made a huge success of his career – the only one indeed who has actually made anything since the original Mounts stopped making maps in the nineteenth century. The mystery, though, is how he gained control of Lennards in the first place, since he started out with no more money than my father had, which was virtually nothing.

'Oh darling, my foster-father put Greig into Lennards after he was invalided out with his lungs,' my aunt would say. But who was this foster-father? Who, come to that, was her father? There was a copy of *Debrett's Baronetage* on the shelves at Blue Waters, the only house I have known to contain this esoteric volume except Kellynch Hall in *Persuasion*. There, Munca is described as 'dau. of late John Anthony Baring of New York', but she has no trace of an American accent and never speaks of the late John Anthony at all, still less of her mother, and nobody seems to have a clue who he is or was. Someone tells my parents that he had been a bootlegger who possibly traded under another name.

Munca's only known living relative is her brother Archie, known as Buster, a restless dark figure who rarely appears at Angmering, being mostly occupied in marrying and unmarrying, at least according to his sister. His only recorded achievement is to have ridden a motorcycle on the Wall of Death, but I don't know whether he ever did this for a living. Occasionally Lyn, his delightful dark-haired daughter from one of these marriages, who is the same age as my sister, stays at Blue Waters and he comes to pick her up, always appearing to be in a steaming hurry and on the verge of losing his temper. Munca's relations with her brother seem to be fragile at best, and when she refers to him, which is rarely, it is as something of a lost cause.

We are also fascinated by how old Munca is, obviously quite a bit older than Unca, even discounting his boyish looks. It is hard to tell from her face. She has a sallow complexion and bright, rather hooded eyes and a flattened aquiline nose and a wide scornful mouth that goes with her proud, flaunting way of holding her head back. She really does look quite like a Red Indian chief in a silent movie or one of those alarming Graham Sutherland portraits of famous monsters, Somerset Maugham perhaps or, when hung with jewels for a night out, Helena Rubinstein. When we ask her age, because this is a question children can ask and love to ask, she gives the classic response, 'older than my teeth and younger than my little finger'. If we press her, she admits to being the same age as my father, that is, only four years older than her husband, who was born in 1911.

It certainly came as a surprise to my mother when Betty gave birth to a daughter in October 1941, only a month after she herself had had Francie. My mother was startled not only because she thought her sister-in-law might be too old to have a child but also because there had been no word of her being pregnant. 'Betty just went off to Cornwall and came back with a baby,' my mother said to one of her sisters. But then in the middle of 1941 it was as much as anyone could manage to look after their own lives.

Georgie, as Serena Georgeanne is always known, is brought up to be something like a sister to Francie, or at least that is my aunt's intention. Francie goes to stay with Unca and Munca most holidays, even when I don't. The two girls are constantly photographed as a duo. When they are 18, Munca gives a coming-out dance for them at The Pub. More insistently, she never stops pointing out how alike they are, how alike all three of us are. 'Look, hasn't Georgie got the Mount nose' – or the Mount eyes or some other feature that we are alleged to have in common. The three of us are photographed crouching by the little round pond on the lawn at Blue Waters and the resemblance between us is commented on once more. Yet apart from having fair hair and being quite tall, Georgie does not really resemble us at all. She is far prettier, her smile more radiant, her eyes more sparkling and, in any case, her nose is not quite the one she started with, having been operated on, for reasons somewhere between the therapeutic and the cosmetic (sinuses are mentioned). Her manner too is more effervescent, her responses quicker than ours or those of our other Mount cousins. Anyone outside the family meeting her for the first time is instantly struck by how different she is from the rest of us.

At the same time, although Georgie has the best of everything, I do not think that we are envious of her. More is expected of her than is expected of us. She always has to be the neatest girl at the party, have her hair brushed a hundred times a night, display perfect manners at all times. Is this quite normal, because she is an only child and all her parents' hopes are pinned on her? Or is there something odd and heightened about the expectation?

Now and then my sister and I catch glimpses of some harsher disciplines at work: there are summonses to Munca's bedroom, and once or twice I hear the slap of a hand or the smack of a hairbrush. Afterwards Georgie seems not just tearful but baffled or distracted, as if she is still not quite sure how she was supposed to behave. Even when she is grown up and every man wants to go out with her, a kind of awkwardness clings to her, as though all this carry-on is a language she has had to be taught. I don't mean just the social niceties. She has been thoroughly schooled in all of those, just as she has been to Heathfield School, Ascot, and the best dancing class, Miss Vacani's in the Brompton Road, and the best riding school, somewhere in Windsor Great Park. It is more that she seems not completely at ease in ordinary casual conversation and has to deploy the quick wit she was born with to cover up her uncertainty and to be like everyone else. At the time, of course, none of this seems to matter a bit, because she has such amazing sparkle.

Despite her efforts to turn Francie, and to a lesser extent me, into Georgie's siblings, Munca remains dissatisfied with Georgie being an only child. I don't know whether Georgie herself ever said she would love to have a sister, but at all events, when she is eight or nine, an adopted baby sister suddenly arrives, out of the blue, like a food parcel during the war. Someone tells us she came from Canada. We wonder why she had to come from so far away, but at any rate here she is and we do our best to play with her.

We played ring-a-ring-a-roses on the soft damp grass and then sat round the pond with the cherub in the middle, splashing each other, but quite gently so as not to give the frills on her dress a soaking. Then – perhaps this was a little later, the next day perhaps – we played hide-and-seek in and out of the pine trees at the side of the garden. I remember the resiny smell and the frills of Celeste's frock – we are told she is named after Celeste in the Babar books – just visible around the leathery russet tree-trunks. It was perhaps the next day, which was calm and sunny, that we took her down to the beach, each taking an arm and swinging her over the shingle until we reached the sand. Celeste chuckled with glee. Munca watched us when we were playing on the lawn, then followed us down to the beach and watched us again from over the garden wall, as though it would spoil the experiment if she got too close.

Playing with Celeste, Blue Waters, 1950

I wondered whether Celeste was her real name, or whether that was another of Munca's inventions. I wondered too what her parents would have thought of Munca. But then I remembered that they wouldn't have been allowed to meet my aunt and uncle because the hand-over would be managed by an agency. Though I was not quite eleven, knowing about the adoption system is something children find out about very early, because the subject is so crucial to them. You cannot help imagining what it would be like to be adopted, and that's why 'you're adopted' is the worst insult you can throw at another child and why there's so much adoption in children's stories, but not so much in grown-up novels, because the fear of not having your own parents looking after you is supposed to fade along with other childish fears, to be replaced by other fears – the ones that don't fade.

What I also went on wondering was whether Georgie herself had actually asked for a little sister, or whether Munca had just presumed that this was something she ought to have, like a pony or a top-of-the-range bicycle. I didn't like to ask Georgie herself, because if she said, Yes, she had asked, that would make her sound like a spoilt child having her every wish gratified, and if she said, No, she hadn't asked, that might have cast doubt on whether she really wanted a sister. Or perhaps I didn't think those things through but just thought the subject was too delicate for me to raise.

I soon grew fond of Celeste, very fond; so did Georgie. We liked her clucks and gurgles, and applauded her first words and sentences, and we admired the way she set off after the dogs, quite fearlessly, and didn't flinch when they surrounded her, bounding along beside her while she trotted off to some corner of the garden on her chubby little legs. Her not being a bit frightened of the dogs put me to shame, but I didn't mind that. All the time we played, I could see Munca smiling her glittery smile as she pruned the bare branches of the standard roses. I felt proud to be part of this arrangement, which seemed to be going so well, although it was the last thing I had expected when I had got off the train at Angmering.

My parents too were surprised when I told them. 'Oh, adopted, really, that's nice. Does she look like Georgie at all?' My mother said. I retorted, 'No of course she doesn't, she's adopted,' I retorted. 'Silly question,' my mother agreed. I sensed some reservation, though, some unspoken thought, which annoyed me. I now considered myself as a key part of the adoption team and I only wanted to hear positive things. 'Well, I think that's lovely for Georgie,' my mother said, seeing what was expected of her.

That summer, the summer of 1951, I didn't go to stay with Munca. We went to Brittany instead, my first trip abroad and my first foreign food – omelettes at Mont St Michel, snails in garlic butter at St Malo, and my mother let me taste her frogs' legs – like chicken she said, but a very scrawny chicken, I thought. Stumbling across the stony beach reminded me of Angmering, and I missed Celeste as much as I missed Georgie. The Christmas holidays were too short that year to fit in a visit to Angmering, so it was the following Easter that I went back there again.

I couldn't wait to see how Celeste had progressed; not just how much she had grown, but how much her vocabulary had enlarged. I was a regular reader of the feature 'Increase Your Word Power' in *Reader's Digest*, which Munca subscribed to, though I never saw her reading it or anything else much. I had persuaded Georgie that it was part of our duty of care to increase Celeste's word power. Georgie didn't take much persuading, because she had a bossy streak like me, and we started writing down in a green notebook all the words we had heard Celeste use and then teaching her new ones to add to the list and how to say them properly: no, Celeste, wardrobe not warrobe. She never seemed to pay much attention at the time, but the next day she would point at the little French walnut wardrobe in Munca's bedroom and say 'wardrobe' quite beautifully. We had started teaching her French cricket too, but she didn't really get the hang of the game. What she liked doing was hiding behind whoever was batting and then popping out her dark curly head as a surprise. That's how I think of her still, the dark head darting out one side or the other of Georgie's knees and the upright bat.

That was a Gray's Junior model. For my birthday I had got a larger Select bat, and I took it with me to Blue Waters so I could practise, in the hope that I might get into the Second XI. Georgie came out to greet me; she was definitely taller now and had just gone to Heathfield School at Ascot, a posh boarding school where quite a lot of the parents were divorced and several of them lived in Switzerland.

'Where's Celeste?'

We were halfway between the front gate and the front door, and Munca was coming out of the house towards us. I could see she was in a hurry but trying not to show it.

'She's gone back to her family,' Munca said. 'They'll look after her much better than we could, now that Georgie's away at Heathfield. It was so kind of them to let us have her for so long. We really loved having her, didn't we darling?'

'But wasn't she——?'

I hesitated, not quite daring to say the word, though I think I would have in the end, if not there and then, because the question mattered so much. But Munca saved me the trouble.

'No, she was never properly adopted, darling. We just borrowed her to help her parents out. You had such fun together, didn't you?'

'Oh,' I said. 'Yes, yes, we did.'

It was true that Munca had never used the A-word before, but everything she had said since Celeste first arrived was clearly meant to make us think that she was here for keeps, that she would always be Georgie's little sister. Now suddenly she wasn't. And I knew that could not be right, because children are as clearly seized of the fundamental laws of adoption as any family barrister. After all, everyone is usually an expert in the subject closest to their heart. And what we know is that adoption is a permanent thing. You can't just send a child back like a toy you have got bored of. But it goes deeper than that. Adoption is meant to be a sort of magic, to offer a kind of rescue, salvation even, that is not to be tampered with or desecrated. The romance of Celeste's coming had taken hold of my mind. The mysterious circumstances that had stopped her parents from being able to look after her seemed all the more compelling because it was part of the rules that we should not know what those circumstances were or indeed who the parents were. Was her mother dead or drunk or bankrupt, her father in jail, or dead too, perhaps both of them killed together in a car accident? Now, suddenly, those terrible circumstances had apparently melted away, and so quickly, almost overnight.

The lawn and the shingle seemed empty without that cheerful chubby little figure stumping along chuckling at the dogs. I expected that what Munca had said was only a preliminary, that more would be said once I had settled in, perhaps by Uncle Greig, grown-up legal stuff. Once or twice, I looked at him, and I thought he was going to say something, but then Munca came into the room with her glittery look and he thought better of it. Celeste had become an unperson. I suppose it was the first time in my life this had happened to someone. Whenever it has happened since, in public or private life, I often think of how suddenly Celeste had disappeared from our conversation, as suddenly as she had gone away.

Much later, half a century later in fact, I discover that what we were told was untrue. Marguerite Celeste Mount was adopted by Mr and Mrs G. R. Mount of Blue Waters, Angmering-on-Sea, on 30 April 1950, a week after her second birthday, under an adoption order made by the High Court of Justice (Chancery Division). Celeste was as fully and legally adopted as any child ever has been. But Unca and Munca never mention her name, and we somehow know that it is not a subject to be raised. So Georgie becomes an only child again.

2

Georgie

Though Georgie is a talented and quick-witted girl, her parents, especially her mother, are strangely reluctant to release her into the world. 'I don't want Georgie to go to university, she'll only meet a lot of scruffy boys who'll make her do their washing.' Despite this, Georgie soon gets to know several of my Oxford friends, above all David Dimbleby.

In fact, they meet first, not in Oxford or London but in Florence, where Georgie is doing a course in Italian or the history of art or both and David is on holiday. A mutual friend – it must have been me, I suppose, though I do not remember doing it – says that they ought to meet and gives a description to each of them of what the other looks like. From this they somehow manage to pick each other out in the crowded streets and, like Dante and Beatrice in the same city, click instantly. Their restless, sardonic natures seem to make a beautiful fit. And over the next couple of years (unlike Dante and Beatrice who actually met only twice) they become as inseparable as Munca's relentless programme of polishing Georgie will allow.

One weekend at the end of February 1962 we all go down from Oxford to stay at the Dimbleby family cottage in Devon, at Dittisham on the estuary of the Dart. It is marvellously crisp sunny weather and David takes us out in his boat, which is a picturesque old hulk of the type once, I think, used by the local

26

oyster fishermen. We go down the river past Agatha Christie's mansion on the hill and then turn the corner to an empty bay for a picnic. The bracken on the cliff above is russet gold in the strong sunlight. We stretch out on the sand in our shirtsleeves. I have never seen either of them so relaxed. Quite instinctively they tease each other out of their habitual tensions (nobody could be quite as relaxed as David is on screen without being a tense character off it).

At the beginning of that summer they decide to get married. David, with his instinct for the theatrical as well as the romantic, chooses a night when the moon is rising over Angmering beach to ask the question and place the large aquamarine ring on Georgie's finger (he has been carrying the ring in his pocket for some time, waiting for the perfect moment).

They are young – he is 23, she is 20 – but in the early 1960s marriage is in the air. Several of my friends get married aged 21, 22, 23. This is a fashion completely out of keeping with the English tradition, which has always favoured marriage quite a bit later, at, say, 26, 27, 28 (except in upper-class families who had estates to tie up). For all classes in Britain, those early 1960s are a moment that may not come again. There is something blithe and easy about the whole thing, as though at long last we can say goodbye to the sobrieties of war and austerity. I remember wondering at how carefree it all was, and how I utterly failed to share the impulse myself.

The engagement is announced in *The Times* on 12 June 1962, and because of Richard Dimbleby being the most famous broadcaster in the country the press descends on Angmering. Georgie and David are photographed with the poodles on the lawn at Preston House.

ENGAGED YESTERDAY: David Dimbleby, 23-year-old son of Richard Dimbleby (and like him a BBC commentator). To Georganne Mount, aged 20, daughter of a shoe manufacturer.

David and Georgie with poodles

They tell their story to a reporter from the *Evening Standard*. It all sounds so blissful and such easy sailing that, to add a little salt to the tale, the *Standard* reporter asks Georgie: 'Wasn't there a suggestion a few months ago that your parents were against an engagement?' 'Absolutely untrue,' say Georgie and David together, 'We had no intention at that time of becoming engaged. It was all nonsense.' Which of course leaves the impression that there had been some opposition; that, at the very least when the question first came up, Unca and Munca had said they were too young to think of getting married.

Anyway, the wedding is scheduled for some day in the autumn. It will be somewhere in London, and it is in London – at Claridge's of course – that there is a formal meeting between the two families to discuss the arrangements. Here, unmistakable signs of trouble begin to surface. At lunch, Munca brings up the subject of what the parents are to do for the young couple. She says that they will pay for the cottage at Strand-on-the-Green that Georgie and David have already looked at (although they are dubious about it because it doesn't have the view of the river they had hoped for). Richard Dimbleby, taken unawares, says that he and Dilys had thought of giving them a washing machine. After they have seen the Dimblebys off in their Rolls-Royce outside Claridge's, Munca tells Georgie that she thinks they must have hired the car to impress them. This is an absurd suggestion, Richard being probably the highest-paid broadcaster in Britain at the time, but it is a foretaste of Munca's determination to keep on top of the situation. David, of course, relays the Rolls-Royce slur to his parents, who are naturally affronted. In the public view, if not in their own, the Dimblebys are, after all, only a step or two below royalty – who are these Mounts to give themselves such airs?

Still, such friction is not unusual in the tense days of affiancement, and David and Georgie float through the summer of 1962 on clouds of bliss and expectation. By September, David has started his first proper job in broadcasting, at BBC Bristol as it happened. Bristol is also where my Uncle Greig has the headquarters of his shoe empire, driving to and fro in *his* Roller for the main part of the week. So David suspects nothing untoward when Greig invites him to lunch at the hotel where he always stays. It is a natural sort of get-together, and the worst David could be in for would be one of Greig's homilies about the need to do snap inspections of every Lennards branch.

But the conversation begins quite abruptly, as soon as the menus have been put aside.

Greig: I have something to tell you. Georgie has decided that she's not ready to get married, so it would be better not to go ahead with the arrangements.

David is thunderstruck. In fact he bursts into tears, which startles both of them. Georgie has not given him the slightest inkling that she has any such hesitation, let alone that she has formed a firm decision to call the whole thing off. He can't stop sobbing, almost too choked to get the words out coherently.

'Can I speak to her?'

'No, I'm afraid not. We've decided that it would be best if she went back to Florence to finish her course. She's on the train up from Angmering at the moment to catch the boat train from Victoria.'

Still sobbing, David jumps up from the table and runs out of the restaurant without a single further word, certainly not a goodbye. His Mini is parked outside the hotel and he pelts off through heavy rain. The notoriously imperfect wipers of the Mini at that date make it hard to tell whether it is his tears or the rain that are misting his vision. After battering up the old A4, he arrives at Victoria. There is a train up from Angmering just arriving, and he quickly spots Georgie getting out of it, struggling with some hefty luggage, suggestive of a long stay abroad (Munca always insists that Georgie take a full wardrobe).

To his further amazement, he also sees a tall figure stepping out of the mêlée to help her with the cases. David recognizes this as Peter Snow (not to be confused with the future broadcaster), a suave City operator with impeccable manners and the polished shoes that Munca loves so much (several of my friends have already been rebuked for the scuffed and shoddy footwear they come in to The Pub). What Munca also admires about him is that he is a beautiful dancer, which none of my friends is. 'Why didn't you dance with Peter at the Arundel Ball?' I remember her chiding Georgie. 'He's got such lovely feet.' The only time he ever put a polished foot wrong was when he saw Munca wearing her immense emeralds and enquired whether they were genuine. The suggestion that there could be anything fake about her or her whole set-up was explosive.

For a moment, David imagines that this lounge lizard has supplanted him, that she is going off with him to Florence, or probably not Florence at all; Monte Carlo would be more Peter's style. But Peter with his usual suavity puts him right straight away.

'Georgie's mother asked me to come and help get her things on the boat train safely.'

Munca's fingerprints are over the whole operation. In fact P. Snow's presence makes it clear just what an operation it is. The rest of them – Georgie, Greig, P. Snow – are merely acting under Munca's orders.

David rushes forward and pleads with Georgie as best he can, but the whole situation – the clanging of trains and trolleys, the hefting of the luggage, the presence of P. Snow as bodyguard with his polished shoes – makes it impossible to have anything like a proper conversation. What Georgie does make clear is that she is going away and at this moment she wants David to go away. Which, after a bit, disconsolate and baffled, he does. He never speaks to her again, or rather she refuses to speak to him again. He remains hurt and sad, and above all mystified as to what he has done wrong.

He writes letters to her of course, but they are never answered. Suspecting that the letters are being intercepted, he gives me a letter to place directly into her hands when I next go down to Angmering. I give her the letter, but he receives no answer to that one either. I am too timid to ask her why she doesn't write back. I was instrumental in bringing them together in the first place, but I am the weakest link in keeping them together, a cack-handed Cupid quite lacking in magic power. The break is decisive and irreparable. After a slow accumulation of trust and affection over three years, the glass is shattered in a moment.

David retrieves his dignity only to the extent of insisting, over the objections of Unca and Munca, that the breaking off of the engagement too must be recorded in *The Times*. And so, on 13 October 1962, at the end of the Court Circular, there appears one of those grim little notices that in those days delighted society gossips: 'The marriage arranged between Mr David Dimbleby and Miss S. G. Mount will not take place.'

This whole extraordinary episode seems ripped from the pages of a Victorian novel, and not a late Victorian one either: a story from the period when the power of parents over their children could be questioned only with great agony and turmoil – the Barretts of Wimpole Street era.

Why and how did Munca bully Georgie to call it off and arrange for her to be transported abroad, even posting a trusty at the station to prevent David from intercepting her? At the time we all puzzled over the whole business a lot, and the general conclusion was that Munca was driven not only by a pathological reluctance to let her daughter go but also by a demented snobbery. No Dimbleby would do for her princess. Only a duke's son, a marquess's at a pinch, or perhaps an international tycoon of some description would be good enough. One early contender, the younger son of an earl, was certainly not. 'Nice boy, and lovely hair,' Munca remarked, 'but no estate, and no money either.'

Yet we soon began to wonder whether that explanation was quite enough. There was something so frantic about the calling off, such a whiff of panic, as if to allow the engagement to go on a moment longer would have terrible consequences, which might not simply be a question of Georgie's unhappiness. The question remained dark, blanked off. Yet the rainy day in Bristol left a mark that was never washed away. David never ceased to say quite openly that Georgie had been the love of his life – not the only love: he was to be happy for years in both his marriages and very happy in his four children. For Georgie, the scars were permanent.

———

I wondered whether Munca ever felt remorse for what she had done. And just as I was thinking that she almost certainly did not, it came to me that the reason she didn't was because she couldn't afford to. This was not the selfish impulse of a moment; it was the desperate measure of someone who was scared. Munca was not really scornful of the Dimblebys, she was frightened of them. She could deal easily enough with the uninquisitive upper class and their indolent children, who could not be bothered to enquire into anyone's ancestry but their own. But this family of alert, energetic reporters could pierce her disguises. Richard had been the first reporter to force his way into Belsen and had insisted that the BBC carry his harrowing report. His wife Dilys was no less sharp-eyed. David was bred to enquire and to uncover things. They would find out the truth in no time.

With her feral instinct for trouble, Munca was not wrong. Years later, David told me that he had already been puzzled by Georgie's lack of visible connection to her parents. Had I myself accidentally tickled up his suspicions by passing on to him my mother's wisecrack about Betty going down to Cornwall and coming back with a baby? I am quite capable of such crassness. At all events, David had gone so far as to pay a visit to Somerset House to look up her birth certificate, which he couldn't find. Had he then unwisely raised the subject with Georgie, perhaps in pseudo-casual terms such as 'you know you'll need your birth certificate when we get married' — which would almost certainly have led her to say to her mother, 'Mum, where *is* my birth certificate?' Perhaps nothing quite so specific happened to unnerve Munca. Perhaps there was only an accelerating dread that this marriage of all marriages would take Georgie away from her for ever, that the adoption which had been her later life's work would come unstuck as a result of it, finally and irrevocably.

Certainly the breaking off of the engagement seems to set a fractious and unhappy pattern. One after another, Georgie's courtships are scuppered by the parental veto, sometimes openly, sometimes by covert pressure. Among those who retire, sometimes hurt and a bit bewildered, are the otherwise dauntless Max Hastings; the playwright Michael Hastings, author of *Tom and Viv* (no relation to Max); Christopher Bland, later to be Chairman of the BBC and BT; the suave pop-eyed boulevardier David 'Wheeler Dealer' Wheeler; and Richard Heygate, son of the John Heygate who ran off with Evelyn Waugh's first wife. Earlier on, there is my best friend Henry Harrod, and Henry Berens — I mention their names only to remind myself that about half of my friends go out with Georgie for a bit. One or two come quite close to getting engaged to her, but years later even those who only have a fleeting walk-out never fail to ask me for news of her. When I run into Norman Lamont after he has just stopped being Chancellor of the Exchequer, it is almost the first question he asks me: 'Do you have any news of Georgie?' In later life several of these grandees still feel a twitch of jealousy when they hear for the first time that she went out with one of the others. 'Oh no, not *him*.'

For a time, each of these suitors is warmly welcomed to Angmering and Munca's suite at Claridge's, which are otherwise strangely cloistered from the outside world.

At the seaside they take the poodles for walks along the beach with Unca, and exclaim with delight over Olive's roast beef and apple pie with ice cream. In London, Unca and Munca entertain them to dinner at the Causerie, 'so much cosier than the big dining room, darling', and Munca encourages them to discuss the dishes of the day with Luigi, her beloved maître d'. After dinner, she shoos them off to the 400 or the Blue Angel, from where they are strictly expected to return at an hour that shows they have had a good time but not too good a time.

In return, Munca expects first-class manners: nicely written thank-you letters that get over the page; Georgie seen home in a taxi; proper turn-out – decent suit or dinner jacket (no question of jersey or jeans) and polished shoes. As I have said, several of the swains, otherwise given the green light as 'that charming boy', fall down on the shoes. After a bit these romances too seem to hit the wall, often quite abruptly and without warning. The parental veto comes so suddenly, which may be why the whole thing sticks so long in the mind of the victim. There seems to be an unexpected misunderstanding at work. The boyfriend imagines that Georgie is just as free as any other girl to make up her own mind. Her lively manner, her enthusiasm, her directness, all suggest, if anything, that she might be freer than most to decide for herself. But she isn't. She is not in charge of her own future. And her mother, who seems so convivial, so eager to see that everyone has a good time, who will still hoof a lively Charleston on the drawing-room carpet, who when the visitors have gone will smile her broad glittering smile and say 'now we can all fart and scratch our balls', this apparent old good-time girl turns out to be as much of a dragon as a Victorian duenna.

As the years tick on, we begin to think, more charitably, that Munca simply doesn't want to lose Georgie to anyone; she cannot bear to let go of her only child. Even this explanation, though, comes to seem inadequate. There is something darker here, something that we can sense only dimly – a feeling that things will fall apart if the engagement is not stopped before it is too late. This apprehension does not seem to be simply a question of Georgie's happiness or unhappiness. In fact Georgie herself begins to show signs of strain. The constantly renewed assault course is becoming too much for her. There's a hint of desperation about the beginning of each new affair.

In any case, Angmering was no longer the same for me, though quite what its place had been in my life I could not quite analyse, then or now. A second home? A home from home might be a better way of putting it, because it was so different from home, so warm and comfortable and yet so strange, somehow offering freedom and claustrophobia simultaneously. Anyway, whatever Munca's world had been to me, it wasn't that any more, and Georgie was no longer like a sister to me, though she had never been very like a sister, despite Munca's best efforts. And as I write that self-inflicted nickname, I wonder for the first time whether Aunt Betty had not insisted on it in the first place as a preparation for telling Georgie that she was not to call her Mum any more, and then when it came to the moment couldn't face it.

I did see Georgie now and then in the next few years. If I went into a crowded room, I would often catch a glimpse of her across it, on the arm of someone I might know slightly or know of by repute. 'On the arm' is the exact phrase, her sequined elbow tucked lightly into his, her face turned up towards his, as though even in this crowded milieu they were catching a moment of intimacy, his smile breaking out in response to hers. When we got close enough to speak, we chatted briefly with a kind of forced easiness, as though we were trying to convince anyone standing by that we were in touch every other day, although it would more likely have been months since we had last bumped into each other. 'Sweet coz,' she would say, 'I didn't know you went slumming in places like this.' 'On the contrary,' I would riposte, 'I'm amazed they let me in.' And the latest swain would smile politely, or not as the case might be, and try to move her on as soon as he decently could. 'The swains' was how I began to think of them, which made it all sound light and easy like rustic swains in a pastoral comedy, though I could see she was not really having a good time.

There is a distance between us now. I'm aware of it, and if I'm aware of it, I'm sure she is too. I've no idea any more what she is thinking, what she wants out of life. That is true of many people, I suppose, perhaps most people, but with someone so expressive, so bright, so forward, always coming towards you, it is disconcerting to realize that she is just as much a mystery as a silent brooding character who advertises their mysteriousness. But our old affection has not disappeared. And when my eldest son is born, she generously sends him a complete set of the Beatrix Potter books. Fifty years later, it is from the copy of *The Tale of Two Bad Mice* in that set that I check the details of Hunca Munca (she is pictured on the tattered jacket busily flossying with a dustpan and brush, not unlike Munca as I remember her in her heyday).

I do not mean to imply that she leads her beaus on, or that she is quicker than average to fall in love with someone new. The initiative continues to come from the other side. It is still true that you only have to see her to want to take her out. I know now that this is not always the luckiest quality to have, although it may look that way at the time. For Georgie I think that being so attractive is unnerving too, almost as though it is happening to someone else for whom she keeps on having to stand in, for reasons that are not clear to her. I am sure that she enjoys being taken to the places girls want to be taken, but she always has Munca watching her, looking critically at the sleeveless cocktail dress to see whether it is right for Quaglino's, or whether she needs to be lent a brooch. Even when Georgie is supposedly well launched, she is still expected to report back at the end of the evening and sit on Munca's bed and tell her how it went. She is like a prize greyhound with an obsessive owner, petted and groomed and trained to a hair, but never let off the leash.

By now we are all in our mid- to late twenties, but it is only now that I begin to realize (my sister is a little quicker on to it) that Georgie has somehow been effectively deprived of any will of her own. The simplest arrangement – buying a flat, booking a holiday, getting a driving licence – is managed for her by her parents. Munca is eager that Georgie and I should share a flat in Kensington – Ennismore Gardens is mentioned – because 'she can't begin to manage on her own'. When I start my first job, Munca sighs in a letter to me that Georgie 'shies away from the trivial round, the common task at the slightest pretext'. Her parents even fill in her passport application after she has signed it. This withholding of responsibility is reinforced by remarks like 'Of course Georgie would be incapable of organizing anything like that' or 'I don't know how Georgie can hope to get a job when she can't even do for herself.' Through all this Georgie remains cheerful and affectionate. Wherever I am during my twenties, she writes to me, chatty letters, full of sprightly parentheses and self-deprecating throwaways, in her instantly recognizable rectangular hand quite unlike anyone else's, always beginning 'Sweet Coz'.

So I am very pleased when she finally gets properly engaged, to Claude Johnson whom I used to know slightly at Oxford, a gentle, lugubrious, rather witty character who suffers from low self-esteem. Although Claude is not a duke's son (his father had been a captain in the Royal Navy), this time the marriage goes ahead – Munca's powers of dissuasion are waning – and there is a slap-up reception at The Pub. It is the last time that my father and his two brothers are in the same room (my father dies a month later). They look so happy to see each other again. You would not have known they had ever exchanged a cross word. To my eyes, Claude and Georgie, too, seem to get on pretty well. They share the same self-deprecating wit and they can match each other cigarette for cigarette and glass for glass. So, I thought, can I, but I realize they have moved into a different league when I have lunch with them in an Italian restaurant somewhere down the Fulham Road and finish up back at their flat at half past six that evening moving on to the second bottle of kummel and feeling iller than I can ever remember. The drink, I suppose, begins to turn their self-distrust upon each other. This is not helped by Munca's refusal to treat them as properly married, referring to Claude as though he were some faithful but low-ranking boyfriend whom Georgie could fall back on when no one better was around: 'Oh, you could always bring that Claude Johnson down for the weekend.'

Sadly, after a year or two they separate, and Claude goes over to Northern Ireland to manage the estates of Georgie's old boyfriend Richard Heygate. Neither of them drinks much less separately than they did when they were together. Not long after, they are divorced (Georgie the first Mount in our branch of the family to get divorced), and quite soon after that Claude dies. He was an extremely nice man who was not properly appreciated, mostly because he did not appreciate himself.

Georgie takes up work with a drug rehabilitation charity. She has a meticulous and efficient side to her, whatever Munca may say, and she makes a bright and enthusiastic start. But after a few months, her boss notices that she seems distracted and her work is falling off. Then she becomes decidedly unreliable, and he hears the bottles clanking in her handbag. He finds it difficult to speak to her, but when he finally gets up the courage, she says she only wished someone had spoken to her before, and she gives up drinking, I think, pretty much there and then. For someone so lively and forthright, she seems always to need guidance, and it isn't hard to see who to blame for that.

————

At around this time John Saleby, an elderly cousin of my father's whom I have not seen since I was a child, invites me down to his house outside Stroud in Gloucestershire, where he has practised as a solicitor all his life. Long divorced – his ex-wife may be dead too – he has retired to the end of one of those narrow valleys that once hummed with cloth mills but are now abandoned to sheep and straggling orchards of apple trees that people have stopped making cider out of. It is a steamy afternoon and the long rutted track seems to be drawing us into a realm of deep remoteness and obscurity. John has grown immense in old age; he looks uncared-for but undimmed, as though a malicious sense of fun is all that is keeping him warm in his draughty farmhouse. He wants to give me some family memorabilia that came to him from his Mount mother – a few early Victorian silhouettes, a silver inkstand with a Chinese mandarin penholder given to my great-uncle Francis on his retirement as vicar of Horsham in 1871, that sort of thing.

But what John really wants to do is to pass on his accumulated hoard of family gossip. He has an inside track here, because for years he used to be the family solicitor. At the same time, he always felt rather looked down on because his father was a Maronite Christian who changed his name from Saleeby to

Saleby after he became a Church of England clergyman and married my great-aunt Alice. Despite these strenuous efforts to fit in, the Salebys had not been warmly received by her family. So any beans John has in store, he is more than eager to spill.

'I used to know your Aunt Liz in the old days, you know.'

'Aunt Betty, did you really?'

'She was quite a goer. Had this hunting box in the Beaufort country; had pretty well everyone in the hunt too. She was married to Bev Lyon then of course.'

'Bev Lyon?'

'Beverley Lyon, captain of the Gloucestershire cricket team. I don't think he could handle her at all.'

I have not heard a word of this earlier marriage and I have never heard of Bev Lyon. Indeed, I have never heard cricket mentioned at Blue Waters, although Unca is a member of the MCC as he is a member of White's Club, not because he has the faintest intention of going to either place but just to show he can get in. But there he is, in Wisden's *Cricketers' Almanack* for 1931, B. H. Lyon, one of Wisden's five Cricketers of the Year, along with the visiting Australian immortals, D. G. Bradman and C. V. Grimmett. The history of Gloucestershire County Cricket Club describes him as 'a captain who will always rank among the finest in the history of the game and one who had he been able to give the time to it would have made an ideal England skipper'. Bev Lyon was a dashing batsman and a blithe, restless, inventive leader, inclined to make daring declarations, sometimes even when his team was still behind on first innings, in order to force a result. He quarrelled with the stuffy authorities at Lord's and elsewhere because he wanted matches to be played on Sundays and proposed a new knock-out competition to bring in the crowds – ideas that were unthinkable then and are taken for granted these days.

Bev Lyon at the crease

At Lord's then, at most cricket grounds in fact, the amateurs and the professionals had separate dressing-rooms and went out on to the pitch by separate gates. Bev thought this arrangement ridiculous, and playing Middlesex once, he told the professionals to meet him and the other amateurs in the Long Room, and they would go out onto the field together through the hallowed white gates. But as the professionals came up to the door into the Long Room where Bev was waiting, they were turned back. When he heard, he said, 'Well, if they can't go out this way, we will go out through their gate.' Which they did. To forestall any repeat of this embarrassment, an official compromise was reached by which the pros would in future skirt the boundary fence and join the amateurs outside the gates. Not much of a compromise really, and anyway the players went on changing in different dressing-rooms for another 30 years.

The 1930 Gloucestershire team that tied with the Australians. B. H. Lyon, front centre, and W. R. Hammond in hats

Off the pitch, Bev was always stylishly dressed, in a double-breasted suit and trilby hat, with a silk handkerchief displayed in his breast pocket. He was much admired by Walter Hammond, Gloucestershire's star batsman of the inter-war years, in fact one of the two or three best English batsmen ever. Wally, a rather rougher diamond, aspired to imitate Bev in his get-up, and in the team photo of the Gloucestershire side that in 1930, uniquely, tied with the Australians, he and Bev are the only ones wearing hats. In his typical laconic style,

Bev said of that famous match: 'Any captain can win or lose a game against the Australians but there are bloody few who can tie one.'

In another photograph in the club history, Bev is flailing with his bat high over his shoulder and looks not at all athletic with his big black specs and hunched posture. He looks more like a demented Jewish accountant. Unusually for a first-class cricketer, Bev was of Jewish descent. In fact he could claim to be England's greatest Jewish cricketer after Fred Trueman. Munca would have liked that. She had a strong affinity with anyone even partly Jewish and always spoke of this as a plus point.

Bev was also a dashing businessman. He was said to have made and lost a million pounds before he was 21 — say ten million in our money. He would disappear from the pavilion on business for weeks on end, leaving his team rudderless. He always had an eye for the coming thing and played a leading role in the formation of Rediffusion, perhaps the most pioneering company in the history of British broadcasting, though it came to a sticky end. When Bev died in 1970, his death notice in *The Times* makes no mention of any surviving wife or children, recording only that 'there will be no funeral as his body has been bequeathed to the Royal College of Surgeons'. Munca would have liked all that too: the obsession with brighter cricket and the determination that everyone should have a good time, and the dislike of funerals. She leaves instructions that there should be no funeral for her either, and there isn't.

———

Things have started to unravel a little before she dies. There is, for example, the occasion when Georgie happens to be

44

glancing through her new passport that her mother has just handed her.

'Mum, it says here I was born in High Wycombe, but you always told me I was born in Cornwall.'

'Yes, darling,' says Munca, thinking quickly as people like her learn to do, 'the High Wycombe in Cornwall.'

By now most of us have pretty well accepted the truth, but Georgie herself, at least to outward appearances, seems still to accept the story as it has been told to her. It is only when Greig dies in 1991, ten years after Munca, by which time she is nearly fifty, that she finally gets her hands on her birth certificate. She was born on 16 October 1941 (at least she had not been deceived about her birthday) in High Wycombe, Bucks, the daughter of Clare Sullivan, who is registered as coming from Northern Ireland (this is not her real name, but I have no wish to startle and distress her surviving relations if they do not know about Georgie). She was adopted by Unca and Munca the following spring, on 26 May 1942, fully and legally, just as Celeste was to be eight years later. Surprisingly Clare Sullivan describes herself as married. Georgie tries to trace her mother, who apparently returned to her native Ireland, but it is too late. Mrs Sullivan, who would by now be well into her seventies, turns out to have died a few years earlier. At least the mystery of the elaborate precautions to prevent Georgie from filling in her own documents is explained. How strange it must be to gaze on your birth certificate for the first time when you are nearly fifty, to see the unfamiliar names on it of people who might have been with you every day of your childhood and your growing up, the shapers of your adult world and your memories. But how much worse if the existence of this other world, your blood world, has been deliberately kept from you.

•

Why is Mrs Sullivan having her baby in High Wycombe?
The natural assumption would be that she has left Ireland
to give birth in some place where nobody knows her, which
many other Irish girls have done before and since. Yet she is
married. Is her husband away at the war and this child not
by him? Or perhaps she has left him and taken work in one
of the furniture factories of High Wycombe that have been
converted to make aviation parts, and her child is by a new
boyfriend, who may himself be married? Or perhaps she is still
living together with her husband, but they already have more
children than they can support and agree to give the baby
up for adoption in prosperous Buckinghamshire, where her
chances in life are likely to be better than in Fermanagh or
Tyrone. That too has happened in many families, and not just
in Ireland.

When the news of Georgie's adoption trickles through to
me, these are not my first thoughts. It is too painful to leap
into such grim speculations. I think only how sad it is that it
has taken so many years for the facts to be confirmed. If only
the conspiracy of deceit had fallen apart earlier, while Unca
and Munca were still alive, Georgie might have made her
peace with them and come to terms with the truth more easily.
Every now and then a newspaper gathers together stories of
men and women, now well into middle age, who have only just
discovered that they were given away for adoption at birth.
The older they are when they find out, it seems, the harder
they find the gnawing sense of abandonment. The growth of
the internet has filled the electronic ether with appeals for the
whereabouts of birth mothers who have disappeared off the
radar and of fathers who abandoned their children in infancy.
Their stories are no less painful than Georgie's, except in the
one respect that she was so cruelly brainwashed to believe the
opposite of the truth. But perhaps other adoptive parents do

such things too, and continue to rehearse and embroider their lies for fear of themselves suffering the intolerable loss if they should cease to be their child's only parents and the unique recipients of her love.

But this is not the only shock Georgie suffers on the death of her adoptive father. Unca and Munca had lived lavishly over the years. They had followed the maxim that there are no pockets in a shroud. The Rolls-Royce and the chauffeur and the suite kept perpetually on hold at The Pub must have eaten deep into the £7.6 million for which Unca eventually sold Lennards to Sir Isaac Wolfson's Great Universal Stores in 1973, after years of fending off the attentions of Charlie Clore's British Shoe Corporation. Even allowing for the stakes owned by the minority shareholders, Unca and Munca took the lion's share of the deal – just over £5 million, I dimly remember. What I do remember is how pleased they both were, and why not? It was the culmination of a brilliant career that nobody had predicted for Uncle Greig. The money could well have doubled in the soar-away 1980s. But it didn't. It is almost as though they wished to leave as little as possible behind them. Even so, what remains is a fair lump by most people's standards – £641,000 to be exact, according to the probate valuation. Of this not negligible sum – well over a million pounds in today's money – Unca leaves just £30,000 to Georgie absolutely, no more than a twentieth of the estate. The rest, including the proceeds of selling Preston House and such of its contents as Georgie cannot find house room for, are to go into trust. She is to enjoy the income from the trust during her life, but not a penny more. Nothing extra is to come out of the trust if she marries again or wants to buy a house or herself make a legacy to a friend. After her death, the whole estate is to go in equal shares to the local Guide Dogs for the Blind, the Donkey Sanctuary in Sidmouth and the Brent Lodge Wildlife Sanctuary of Cow

Lane, Sidlesham, West Sussex. I don't think that, deep down, my uncle really liked dogs as much as he pretended. I certainly never heard him mention donkeys. The whole will was a memorial tribute to Munca. It was also a disowning of Georgie as far as was decently possible.

Which led me to look up Munca's will, made nearly twenty years earlier. She had much less to leave, only £14,000. But the will follows much the same pattern. All she leaves to Georgie absolutely are 'my furs and my pearl necklace and earrings'. The rest is to be held on trust. Georgie and any children she might have (she was 30 at the time Munca made the will) are to have the income, but when Georgie dies, if she has had no children, all the money is to go in equal shares to Wingspan of Sheffield Park, Sussex, the People's Dispensary for Sick Animals, and a different Donkey Sanctuary, or perhaps the same one before it moved to Devon. There is a specific exclusion ruling out any adopted child of Georgie's from receiving a legacy, which I find incredible in view of her own history. But perhaps Munca felt that the adopting and unadopting had to stop.

The Trustees are empowered to advance any part of the capital of the trust to Georgie, 'but only if my Trustees are satisfied that there is a genuine need for such payment and advance to be made'. No such stern caution is attached to the power of the Trustees to pay out of the income or capital any sums necessary for keep and welfare to 'any persons who may undertake the care of my dogs'. It is clear that the animal kingdom comes first, and that Munca still does not trust her daughter to look after herself.

Georgie goes to live in Suffolk, about an hour's drive from my sister, living very quietly but remaining resolutely cheerful whenever Francie sees her. She casts off anything to do with the Mounts and no longer writes to me as 'Sweet Coz'. In fact, she no longer writes to me at all. She doesn't want to see any of us, except my sister. I often wonder whether I ought not to risk her displeasure and pay her a surprise visit, but even my sister finds it increasingly hard to maintain contact, especially after Georgie's health begins to go downhill. She has several operations for cancer of the mouth and jaw but still remains remarkably upbeat, except on the last occasion Francie goes to see her when she admits she is a bit depressed.

'My cat's just died. It's the first time in my life I've ever really grieved for anyone.'

―――――

By then she would have heard from Buster's daughter Lyn, who writes to me in January 2006 asking for Georgie's address. I have not seen Lyn for 50 years and more. She tells me she has been living in New Zealand and has just come home to England. Her letter is written on writing paper fringed with sepia kiwis foraging in the undergrowth. She introduces herself and her remarkable news a bit breathlessly (perhaps she is still off balance after hearing the news): 'My name is Lyn Gregory (née Baring), my Grandmother, unknown to me for many years always had to call her Aunt! & as you know married to your Uncle Grig Mount & she herself was Betty and adopted a daughter Georgie.'

At first reading I do not quite take in what she is saying. The words 'adopted a daughter Georgie' distract me. Although I now know the truth about this, to see it in black and white takes me aback. Come to think of it, this must be the first time I have seen it written down, and it brings home the cruel

49

finality. The new news in Lyn's letter takes a fraction longer to decode: 'my Grandmother, unknown to me for many years always had to call her Aunt!' So Buster, the much-marrying Wall-of-Death-riding brother, is in fact Munca's son. 'Was' would be more accurate, it turns out, because when I ring Lyn to give her Georgie's address, she tells me that Buster has been dead for years. In fact, he died ten years before Munca's death in 1981. Lyn says he had married again after he divorced Lyn's mother and had two more children, Sarah and Adrian, to add to Lyn and her brother Nicholas. So Buster had four children in all, and Munca had four grandchildren, none of whom seems to have known that she was their grandmother. Far from having no descendants, she has a rich progeny. How sad for her not to be able to rejoice in them openly. Buster died the year before she made the will in 1972. Perhaps it was a new will to take account of his death, but I rather doubt it. There is certainly no mention of Lyn or of Buster's other three children in the will. So she denied her real relation to them to the end.

How then was Buster brought up? Who looked after him? Munca's mother? That was and is often what happens to a child who is born out of wedlock – what a quaint clanking phrase that is now, how broken and rusty the lock. Or was he officially adopted by someone quite else – by these elusive Barings? Perhaps John Anthony Baring was indeed Buster's father, but Munca's lover rather than her father. Perhaps he didn't come from New York at all, if he ever existed. Each new piece of information seems to lead only to fresh questions and darker mysteries.

Receiving Lyn's letter was the moment when my vague curiosity began to turn into what can only be described as a quest. I didn't think of it that way. I never sat down and planned anything. Nor did I pursue the quest continuously. This was a slow-burning addiction that came and went and came again, vanishing from my screen for months on end, but always there stored in the memory and popping up often unbidden or when least expected, and not to be dismissed again until this or that piece of the puzzle had been found and fitted into what looked like its proper place. I see that more than ten years have now passed since Lyn wrote to me. I never dreamed that it would all take so long, or that I would have to reach so far back in time to get at the truth.

The first thing that struck me then was that if Buster was put out for adoption soon after he was born (whenever that was), then Munca had been involved in not one but three adoptions over her lifetime: that of Buster himself probably around the outbreak of the First World War, then Georgie in the middle of the Second, and then the short-lived tenure of baby Celeste, about forty years after Buster's adoption. This strange conjunction seems more than coincidence. And it comes to me, with a flash of what may be inspiration but may just as well be delusion, that there is some connection between the three cases.

Having given away Buster to whoever and decided to live as his sister in order to conceal the secret of his birth, Munca then secretly resolves that if she has another child or children she will bring them up with all the affection and single-minded devotion of which she is capable. But it doesn't happen. She perhaps has a string of miscarriages and is finally forced to admit that she is now too old to bear another child of her own. This is a hard thing for her to accept. And she takes a long time to bring herself to accept it. She and Greig have been married for six years before they adopt Georgie in May 1942, when she is seven months old, and it is fair to presume that Munca has been trying for a baby for most of that time.

Finally, she takes delivery of beautiful, blue-eyed, golden-haired Georgie. And she is determined that her daughter shall never know a moment's anxiety. She must never feel abandoned or estranged. Georgie's life will, so to speak, make up for Buster's. And the only way Munca can see of ensuring this is never to let Georgie gain the faintest suspicion that she is adopted. Throughout her life she must be totally persuaded that she is her mother's natural daughter. How cruel the double way we use 'natural', but what other word is there for it? 'Blood-daughter', I suppose, but that sounds too biological, and so indeed does 'biological'.

This policy turns out to be a terrible mistake, blighting Georgie's life for ever. And it may be a mistake that leads to another mistake, in the case of Celeste, whose coming and going remain a mystery.

Think of the three of us, Georgie, Francie and me, playing on the lawn at Blue Waters with little Celeste, and Munca looking across from the rose bushes she is pruning with a smile on her wide mouth. I remember how she used to watch us, but only now do I see that there was probably as much anxiety as pleasure in the smile. Celeste had been handpicked for the role of little sister. But it was up to us to do the bonding.

When Celeste is finally dispatched to Canada, I remember now that the age difference between her and us is mentioned – 'she was too young to play with Georgie'. But that gap, of seven or eight years, would have closed as time went by and we would have become bound together by the memories we shared, of afternoons on the lawn like this one.

But then I think it comes home to Munca that there is another gap that can never be filled, the gap generated by our knowledge. We shall always know that Celeste was adopted. She will always be an add-on, an artificial afterthought. Munca cannot bring off the same trick twice. Perhaps if Celeste stays, she cannot keep it up at all. Far from providing a stable family background, Celeste's continued presence may unwittingly disturb the balance. Will it really be possible to go on pretending for ever that one child is adopted and her elder sister is not, when in fact they both are? Georgie's suspicions may be aroused by the lack of any difference between her arrival on the scene and Celeste's. Why are there no photographs of Munca when pregnant? Why no photo albums at all in the house? Resourceful as she is, Munca may find this added complication too much. She has put so much into Georgie. She dare not risk it. And so, goodbye Celeste.

Even without Celeste, there is a ziggurat of lies to be propped up. To start with, the question of Munca's age. In the photo album of my parents' wedding in March 1938, there is a picture of her and Buster skipping across the pavement towards St Peter, Vere Street (the church just behind John Lewis's on Oxford Street). Munca is holding Buster's hand. In retrospect, I think this is a bit unusual for a brother and sister going to a wedding, but I did not think so before now. In the picture Buster is clearly a fully grown man, who could be aged anywhere between 20 and 30. At the very latest then, he must have been born in 1918. So Munca must have been born in Queen Victoria's reign, which would make her nearly a decade older than my father (born 1907), whose twin she claimed to be. Well, compared with her other deceptions, that is harmless enough. Not as bad as telling Buster that she is his sister. I would like to ask Lyn if she knows the answer to any of this, but she may not care to pursue such embarrassing questions. Only much later do I discover that she is as mystified and enthralled by the whole saga as I am.

Munca and Buster, arriving for my parents' wedding, St Peter,
Vere Street, March 1938

Looking back now, I realize at last that Munca never told the
truth about anything. She claimed to have borne a child whom
she had adopted. She claimed not to have properly adopted a
child whom she really had adopted. She denied the child whom
she had borne and insisted he was her brother. She blotted out
her marriage to one of the most dashing sportsmen in England.
The collateral human damage she inflicted over the years is hard
to calculate. They fuck you up, your Mum and Dad, even when
they aren't really your Mum and Dad at all.

Who then was Buster's father? Could it possibly have been
Bev Lyon? When I compare the picture in my parents' album

with the photos of Bev, he and Buster do look remarkably alike – the same slicked-down hair and beaky nose and worried eyes – but Bev was only born in 1902 and would not have been old enough, unless he fathered Buster when he was an undergraduate and Buster was not as old as he looked (always possible with men as dark as that). In that case, presumably Bev and Munca were not married, or not by then, which would explain why Munca covered up Buster's parentage. In those days subsequent marriage did not legitimize an illegitimate child. And was Bev, with his mercurial millions, also the mysterious foster-father who set Unca up in Lennards? The Gloucestershire connection looks like a pointer in that direction. Or was the foster-father someone else entirely? I worry away at the possibilities without ever coming to a satisfactory answer, moving from one hypothesis to another as restlessly as Munca moved house to and fro between Surrey and Angmering-on-Sea.

But what chutzpah she shows, dashing across Vere Street on that chilly March morning in her fur tippet, holding hands with her saturnine 'brother', ready to introduce him to a bunch of stiff top-hatted Mounts who would never have a clue what kind of life she has been leading or what lies she is capable of telling.

Blue Waters had a garage built on to its right-hand side, and there were a couple of small rooms over the garage, no more than attics. Originally, these were used as a flat for Ron, the amiable long-serving chauffeur who died young of a heart attack. In between he had married Pam, Georgie's lovely freckled nanny, and they needed a bigger place. A cottage was found for them in the village, and the two rooms were done up as a playroom and bathroom for Georgie. To celebrate the conversion, Unca bought a fine new TV, which had a faintly pink-tinted extra screen on the front of it, presumably to improve picture quality. I have never seen a similar arrangement. It must have been superseded by some other technological advance.

I had brought my new cricket bat with me to Blue Waters, and I was on my own one afternoon up in the playroom, practising strokes with it. Sketching out an over-expansive off drive, I hit the pink screen with the tip of the bat and the screen cracked right across.

My only hope, I thought in my panic, was to report this obviously expensive disaster straight away.

'The wind blew the chair over and it hit the screen,' I said.

Munca looked at me. I must have been about eight years old at the time. She did not get angry as I had seen her get angry with Georgie. On the contrary, she smiled. But it was a strange, knowing, not entirely friendly smile, a smile full of all the experience in the world.

I think what the smile said was, welcome to the great brotherhood of liars.

3

Buster

I could have left it there. Quite a lot had already come out. It would have been easy enough to call it a day. But I was not satisfied. I could see just enough through the half-open door into the next room. I was sure that there was another little room beyond that, a small and musty place that nobody had been in for a long time. I had tugged the thread and I could not resist following it to the end.

Buster, I thought. From what little I had seen of him, he sounded like a careless if not exactly carefree person. Someone who was so eager to move on to the next thing that he might not cover his tracks. Buster would surely have dropped a clue somewhere, if only I knew where to pick it up.

On the off chance, I googled Buster Baring. I couldn't think of anything else to try.

The first stuff that came up was all about dogs, mostly Staffordshire bull terriers called Buster who were reported as *baring* their teeth. Roy Hattersley had a dog called Buster, a mongrel not a Staffie, who he claimed had the sweetest nature, though it was once had up for killing a goose in St James's Park. When Buster had to be put down at the age of 15, Mr Hattersley told the *Daily Mail*, 'I merely state, as a matter of fact, that nothing has ever caused me as much pain as Buster's death. Nor have I ever behaved with such a shameless display of emotion.'

How strange, I thought, as I finished reading this distracting lament. Georgie had said that she had never felt so sad in her life as she had when her beloved cat died. Munca too preferred the animal kingdom. She expressed her love to her birds and her dogs in a way she didn't to children and certainly not to adults. The world, it seemed, was full of people who placed their own species in the number two slot. I had failed to haul in just how disenchanted many of my fellow humans were with our kind, how much easier and more rewarding they found the company of their pets.

Still, none of this was why I had logged on to Buster Baring. This was a manhunt, not pets' corner. I scrolled on, past some stuff about the Dam *Busters* and Dr Barnes Wallis, which I refused to be detained by. And then suddenly I was ankle deep in references to the human Buster. Almost all of them were about the various motor races he had driven in.

He had finished out of the money in a 1.5-litre Bugatti in the 1937 Bristol Speed Trials at the old city airport. He had finished eighth in a Maserati in the British Empire Trophy on the Isle of Man in 1948. He was sixth behind Reg Parnell and Tony Rolt in the first heat of the Zandvoort Grand Prix that year, again in the Maserati, but dropped out after 28 laps in the final, which was won by the legendary Prince Bira of Siam. He dropped out after 38 laps in the British Grand Prix at Silverstone that year, though Parnell, Roy Salvadori and the great Luigi Villoresi failed to finish too. Buster was described as 'causing something of a sensation' at the West Hants and Dorset Car Club meeting in 1949 'driving a German Veritas with its beautiful and advanced streamlined body'.

The first public appearance of his that I can trace was in a Frazer Nash at the Easter Monday meeting at Brooklands in 1932, the last nearly twenty years later when he drove the prototype of the famous HWM (standing, not so glamorously, for Hersham and Walton Motors) in several events in 1950. John Heath, who was to die in a crash in the Mille Miglia a few years later, built the HWM himself at his modest garage near the bridge at Walton-on-Thames, which still stands today, its façade scarcely altered, at a total cost of no more than £10,000 for the first three cars. The HWM recorded some good results in both sports car races and Grand Prix, while at the same time £200,000 was being poured into the notoriously non-performing but elegant BRM, the car built by British Racing Motors on which so many patriotic hopes rested. The HWM was famous too for giving the 20-year-old Stirling Moss his first break. In old age, Moss wrote lyrically of the fantastic summer he and his co-drivers had enjoyed chasing girls and lap records round the circuits of Europe. In the 1950 Prix de Mons, the four HWMs finished in a bunch; Johnny Claes (a Belgian jazz trumpeter who had a band called the Claepigeons) was sixth, Stirling seventh, John Heath eighth and Anthony Baring ninth.

Anthony/Buster was remarkable in those giddy days, not just for the variety of cars he drove – Frazer Nash, Bugatti, Maserati, Veritas, HWM – but also for the number of different names he appeared under on the track: Archie, Alistair, Anthony as well as Buster. This in-and-out running had led to a frantic fluttering among the addicts of motor racing trivia. To my amazement, I find myself in the middle of an online imbroglio concerning a driver who has been dead for 40 years and who never, so far as I can see, actually won a race of any description. How odd it feels to fall among these besotted petrolheads. They are just as bewildered as I am about who Buster really was and where he came from. It is extraordinary that Munca's machinations should, at one remove, still be baffling people who have no idea of her existence.

One of their number with the blog-name of *Rewind* appeals to his fellow bloggers:

> I listed a certain 'Archie Baring' as being born on 6 January 1912. But meanwhile I'm rather doubtful about the correctness of that entry. Should it be *Anthony* Baring instead? Unfortunately I cannot retrace my source. So I am not sure whether or not I transcribed the name correctly. Can anyone help?
>
> My suggestion would be that it is one and the same person with perhaps full name as Anthony Archibald Baring (which would explain 'Archie' if that name isn't a fault of mine). But surely there is someone out there who can confirm or deny this, isn't there?

There is a prompt response from *Marc Ceulemans*, who sounds Belgian. He is not much help to the distraught *Rewind:* 'Anthony Baring or A. A. Baring drove a Veritas and a Maserati in 1949. I don't know what the second "A" stands for.'

A new respondent, *alessandro silva*, strikes an altogether more confident note: 'He was Archie Alistair Baring. I do not know why the Anthony came out in the Black Books. Born in Manila, 6/01/1912, from Motor Racing Directory, 1955/56, Pearl Cooper Ltd.'

Rewind is poignantly grateful: 'Thank you Alessandro. I was afraid Archie was a transcription error of mine. BTW: as he was born in the Philippines – what is (or *was?)* his nationality? Do you know whether or no he is still alive?'

This new conundrum fails to dent *alessandro*'s magnificent self-confidence:

> From a personal communication Adam Ferrington I have also a switch in the names: Alastair Archibald Baring same

place and date of birth. He was known as 'Archie' in any case. Never Anthony in contemporary sources. He certainly was British, a timber merchant and farmer from Berkshire. He retired from racing in 1950. I ignore if still alive.

Adam F himself now jumps in:

Alister Archie Baring was born in Manila, Philippines on 6 January 1912. During his racing career he was sometimes known as 'Buster' Baring but usually Alister. The erroneous reference to Anthony came, I believe from a biog. in one of the contemporary race programmes. He often 'reversed' his name and was later known as Archie Alister Baring. He died on 21 January 1971, on the Algarve, Portugal.

I can scarcely resist the urge to join in this farrago of nit-picking myself and point out that the know-all *alessandro* can't be quite right about Buster never being known as Anthony, because Anthony is what he is quite often called in the results of post-war races. Sir Stirling Moss in his photo scrapbook *All My Races* calls him Anthony too, and he ought to know.

But my mind is in any case fully taken up with the news that Buster was born in the Philippines. Graham Gauld, the Scottish motor racing historian, endorses this claim in a separate article to be found on the internet about Buster's HWM, adding that 'his family moved back to England'. Can this really be true? What on earth was Munca doing out in the Pacific at the beginning of 1912? Had she gone as far away from England as possible to give birth without anyone knowing – a bizarre reversal of her flight to Cornwall in 1941?

And then there does trickle into my head some recollection I have – or, no, it is something my sister has reminded me of – that

Munca used to tell a story about being partly brought up in the
Philippines and learning to ride out there and how she once, for
a dare I think, rode her pony up the steps into the dining room.
When I originally heard the story, it did not seem very plausible. It
sounded more like an incident in an old film, a 1930s adventure story
set in the Deep South or, well, perhaps in the Philippines.

Yet now I begin to think that there might be something in
it after all. Barings Bank and the Baring family had a lot of
connections with Latin America. It was a debacle in South
America that caused the bank to suffer its first crash, in the 1890s.
Munca's father, the mysterious John A. Baring, might be some
distant cousin of the dynasty, a remittance man of sorts sent off
to manage some obscure branch of the business in Manila.

Alas, when I consult the General Register Office Index of
Overseas Births for the years 1911–15, there is no trace of
anyone called Baring at all, be he Archie, Alistair or Anthony,
being born in Manila on 6 January 1912 or on any other date
in those years. The GRO Overseas Indexes are often a bit of a
mess, with entries scrawled all over the page, often in different
hands, as reports come in from the laggard Consuls. But there
really is no Baring there, no name between Robert Barham born
in Shanghai and David Barker born in Swatow.

It is easier to trace the history of the HWM car that Buster
drove than it is to track down his own antecedents. He bought
it for £2,500 off John Heath's partner, the daredevil George
Abecassis, in 1950 and sold it a year later. Graham Gauld takes up
the HWM's after-life. It was sold on to another Scottish fanatic,
who fitted a Jaguar engine onto the Alta chassis, then thought
it would go better with an Aston Martin engine and sold the
resulting hybrid to another madman in Ireland. Through all these
metamorphoses, apparently you can distinguish Buster's machine
by its distinctive bonnet louvres. Gauld describes Buster as 'a well-
known British privateer of the time'; that is, a private owner who

pays his own mechanics instead of being financed by a garage or a motor manufacturer, as almost all Grand Prix drivers are today. 'Privateer' sounds dashing, the right sort of word for Buster. I like to think of the four HWMs zooming round the Mons circuit in a phalanx with the young Stirling in the slipstream of the leader of the Claepigeons and the doomed John Heath and the elusive Anthony/Archie/Alistair bringing up the rear.

I imagine that Munca did not approve of Buster becoming a racing driver. What mother would, even a mother who was pretending not to be a mother? And now it comes to me that when she talked about Buster and his crazy determination to ride the Wall of Death, Munca may have been referring, not literally to the Wall of Death you ride in a funfair but to the terrifying steep banking of those old pre-war circuits like Brooklands where the car is almost on its side as it corners higher and higher towards the rim.

Buster was barely 20 years old when he made his debut in the second race at Brooklands at the Easter Monday meeting of 1932. It was a gusty, rainy March day. There is a photo of the cars lining up for the start of Buster's race, the drivers in their white overalls and linen helmets. Their mechanics and helpers are wearing trilbies and tweed jackets. Behind Buster's car is a man in plus-fours smoking a pipe. Perhaps he is the starter.

Only a fraction of the banking survives today, just enough for vintage car fans to rattle up and round on trial runs. And you can still stand on the Members' Bridge and watch the cars below you as they roar up round the steepest part of the banking, 30 feet high. They crawl across the scarred concrete like flies across a windowpane. But they can no longer sweep on across the 170-foot-long Hennebique Bridge over the glassy weed-strewn River Wey and on down to the back straight with the whole of Surrey spread out ahead. The bridge was demolished years ago for safety reasons. Consequently, gone too is the infamous 'Brooklands Bump' caused by Monsieur Hennebique's piles settling into the river bed and causing the Bentleys and Bugattis to leave the ground and fly like huge beetles for a few yards. The track was broad enough for the cars to drive eight abreast for half a mile up to the Byfleet Banking at the far end of the course. John Cobb set the lap record at 143.5 mph in his brutal Napier Railton. Later he broke the world land-speed record at Bonneville Flats, Utah, and he died attempting to break the world water-speed record on Loch Ness at the age of 52. These Kings of Speed tended to be self-made men. Cobb was a fur broker, Sir Malcolm Campbell, who had just broken the land-speed record in *Blue Bird*, made money in the diamond trade. *Blue Bird* did a lap of honour that March afternoon. In the mid-1930s, when Campbell took up with Sir Oswald Mosley, *Blue Bird* flew the British Union of Fascists pennant on its bonnet. Not that Easter Monday, though.

The old Brooklands buildings survive, the clubhouse with its wooden balconies and verandas and the little garages where the mechanics tinkered with clutch and camshaft, the names of the old firms with addresses in the West End still painted on the wooden doors. It is rather touching how the people who built Brooklands mimicked the smart horse-racing tracks – the paddock, the little white starters' box, the badges and race glasses and race cards – as though the new sport was struggling for legitimacy. You can see how the whole set-up would appeal to the upper-class patrons who bombed round the track – Earl Howe, Lord March, Sir Henry Birkin, Prince Bira of Siam.

There is another side to Brooklands, a feminine, rather flirtatious side. From the start, the women drive too, often in ladies' races as they do in point-to-points, but sometimes they compete against the men, usually being given handicaps to even things up. The clubhouse is lined with pictures of the famous lady drivers like Kay Petre and Fay Taylour doing ladylike things in the driver's seat: adjusting their lipstick or fiddling with the straps of their helmets. In fact, the clubhouse now has a room named in honour of Barbara Cartland, who was a Brooklands habitué (though not I think a driver), because motor racing is a smart thing like cocktails and cigarette holders.

And there, in the middle of it all, is Buster: his family lately returned from Manila according to the petrolheads, with his dark eyes and darting gaze, levering himself into his Frazer Nash to embark on an obsession that is to consume him for the next 20 years.

But how on earth could he afford to pay for his cars? The HWM may have been cheap compared to the monstrous sums being spent on the BRM, but £2,500 in 1950 was the equivalent of well over £100,000 today, probably nearer £200,000. Where does Buster's money come from? He seems to have been able to afford the smartest wheels on the track ever since he was 20 years old. The source of his effortless wealth continues to elude me totally.

It is in 1950, or perhaps late 1949, that Buster goes into a strange sort of partnership with Charles Mortimer, a fellow racing driver almost exactly his age, who is better known for his earlier exploits on motorbikes. Mortimer has a garage in Byfleet, next door to the Brooklands circuit where he raced with some distinction before the war. Buster bought his latest Maserati off Charles, who is an experienced motor trader and loves wheeling and dealing. Charles's luscious wife Jean is also a racing driver and the belle of the circuit. Jean's father, Captain 'Mutt' Summers, was the chief test pilot for Vickers. He was the first man to take the Spitfire aloft; he also carried out the tests for Dr Barnes Wallis on the bouncing bomb (so the Dam Busters do have a tangential relevance, after all). The Mortimers' son Chas is destined to become the star of the Isle of Man TT Races in the 1970s and 1980s, winning no less than eight races. The Mortimers are bred for speed.

So Buster is mixing with the cream of the sport when he proposes his deal: that Charles should take a shareholding in Buster's timber business, which manufactures wood products from timber felled on his own farm. In return, Buster will take an equivalent shareholding in Charles's two garages. You get the feeling that the Mortimers are rather bustled into the deal and before very long are regretting it.

In his memoirs, *With Hindsight*, published in 1991 20 years after Buster's death, Charles tells an extraordinary story of their association. He was finding the expense of full-on motor racing too daunting, and he liked the idea of racing a good sports car instead. Healey's had recently produced their new model, the Silverstone, and had already raced it a few times. Buster tells Charles that he has just bought the car that the great Tony Rolt had driven in the 1949 production sports car race at Silverstone itself, and could Charles possibly go up to the works at Warwick and collect the motor? You sense that already Buster is treating Charles more like an employee than a partner.

Anyway, Charles always likes a spin and is happy to go up to Warwick. The further he drives the Silverstone on his way home, the better he likes it. He even stops for a coffee and sandwich and makes a few notes about its performance, which he thinks may interest its new owner. He arrives back at the office in Byfleet to find Buster standing on the front steps as he drives in. As Charles ruefully records, 'this particular meeting was to tell me a lot about him that, at that time, I didn't know'. For without any greeting, let alone thanks, Buster's opening words are, 'Do you think you could sell that for me. I don't want it.'

The Silverstone was an extraordinary car. It was scarlet and as low-slung as a centipede with a slanting front grille like a shark's snout. The yellow headlights were weirdly placed behind the grille, which gave them a veiled, hooded look. The wheels were set wide away from the body with bendy mudguards like on a child's tricycle. Interior space was limited, to put it mildly. The cockpit was strictly for midgets, and there was apparently no room to stow the spare tyre, which stuck out of a slot in the boot, as though about to be shot out at the car behind. It was a roadster dreamed up by a crazy child.

As it happens, Charles is so in love with the Silverstone that his heart leaps at the thought of owning one. So he asks Buster to name a price, which he does. 'No,' says Charles, shaking his head like the canny dealer he is, 'I do know someone who wants a Silverstone, but not at that price or even near it.' So Buster, feverish to be rid of this car that he has not even sat in, names another, much lower price, and Charles solemnly writes out a cheque on the spot on behalf of his mythical client. As he does so, he asks casually why Buster has made this surprising decision to sell. Apparently he has found a faster, better car, a Le Mans Replica Frazer Nash. Faster and better certainly, Charles says to himself, but at the time far, far more expensive.

From that moment on, Mortimer realizes that 'where cars were concerned, Buster was erratic and indecisive, one of those people who thought that success in motor racing was just a matter of getting the fastest possible car without even considering their ability to get the best out of it by improving their driving with experience'. A comment which, I fear, applied just as well to other departments of Buster's life.

But the saga was not yet over. Charles collected the Frazer Nash for Buster the next day, thinking it one of the loveliest cars he had ever driven. Buster then drove it in an event the following weekend with no success, and then asked Charles to return it to Roy Salvadori from whom he had just bought it. Roy took it back without question, ran it two weekends at Shelsley Hill and broke the lap record with it. In place of the Frazer Nash, Roy offered Buster in part exchange a 1.5-litre Maserati (which had formerly belonged to Mortimer). Again, Buster raced it without success, and then in turn traded that car in for the HWM, which he then drove for that season of Grand Prix races on the Continent culminating in the Jersey International Road Race. Austin-Healey, Frazer Nash, Maserati, HWM – four cars in the space of a single season. Buster's impatience is staggering. He tosses aside one car after another like a spoilt child, never dreaming that his lack of success may be due to the way he drives them.

In the case of the HWM, at the last minute Buster decides not to go over to Jersey to fulfil the engagement. 'Charles, old boy, business has escalated so much while I've been away that I can't possibly stay away any longer. Buckle has gone ahead with the car to Jersey. How would you feel about driving the car in the race?' Buckle is Maurice Buckle, Buster's faithful mechanic, a patient and easy-going young man who works, immaculately attired, on the cars one day, and then is up to his ankles in mud, hauling Buster's timber to the mill. In Charles's first book, *Racing a Sports Car*, published in 1951, there is a photo of the start at Jersey, in which you can see Buckle with his hands clasped behind his back while Jean is sitting on a railing looking glamorous and flirty and Charles is talking to a race official. The

Charles and Jean Mortimer and Maurice Buckle at the Jersey Road Race, 1950

sign above them says A. A. BARING H.W.M., but the great man isn't even on the island.

Buster's impatience has a generous side to it. He allows Charles, and Jean too, plenty of races in the HWM. When things are going well, he is a splendid companion. They jump in and out of each other's cars. There is another photo in *Racing a Sports Car*, captioned 'Buster took over in Race 8', showing Buster in driver's gear at the Goodwood meeting in 1950 studying something that Charles is holding, with Jean looking on. But from Charles's account, you could scarcely call Buster a good sport. He does not meet triumph and disaster and treat those two impostors just the same. No, he storms off.

I came across another book that Charles Mortimer wrote about his experiences on and off the track, about cars and the happy-go-lucky hucksters who race them and also buy and sell them. It's called *Brooklands and Beyond* and was published in 1974, many years before *With Hindsight*. Like the later book, it is mostly about prangs and near misses and cylinders and superchargers. Except that from time to time he breaks off and tells us, in a quite different, more agonized tone, the story of his marriage.

He first met Jean Summers when he was transport manager for Fairmile Marine, a firm that was manufacturing and distributing gunboats and rescue boats for the Admiralty during the war. Charles was lodging near the works, at the Oatlands Park Hotel, Cobham, and he and Jean both frequented the bar known as The Snakepit. Jean was only 16, ten years younger than him. All through the war, they drank and buzzed about Surrey together. It was not love at first sight, he tells us; they had very different temperaments and when they drank too much, which was often, they became carping and cantankerous to each other. It was not until the war was over, in October 1945, that they finally got married and had three children.

Then, 17 years later, in 1962, when Charles Junior is 13, Robin is 10 and Pippa only 3, Jean tells Charles that she has found someone else, someone she wants to marry but who is already married. She tells him who the other person is, but we are not told his name. Charles tells us only that he knows him and he doubts whether they will be happy together. Anyway, she leaves Charles, and the three children stay with their father, which is quite unusual then, even more than now. After a month or two completely apart, Jean comes to visit the children, and 'I was happy to notice that she nearly always sought me out too.' Charles agrees to a divorce, if only she will mark time for a year to make sure that her feelings have not changed. Presumably they have not, because in 1963 they do get divorced.

So far, so ordinary, if sad. But then a sequence of decidedly odd things happens. They remain divorced for a year, then in the summer of 1964, they remarry. This vanishingly short interval between divorce and remarriage turns out to be a catastrophe. Only three years later, Jean takes off again and preparations are made for a second divorce.

But the second divorce never happens. Before the lawyers have really got their teeth into it, Jean and Charles halt proceedings and get back together for the third time, but this time more warily. Instead of setting up again in one house, they live in two nearby cottages. 'One day, who knows,' Charles ends the story of this nerve-jangling excursion, 'we may end up sharing the same fireside.' Which, in old age, they do, as we learn from his last memoir, *With Hindsight*. Jean is at his side at last, almost as if she had never been away. It is the plot of *Brief Encounter* on speed.

You will notice, though, that there is no further mention of the lover. The Someone Else seems to have disappeared off the scene as soon as Jean and Charles are divorced. And what I cannot help wondering is whether the Someone Else is Buster. His wandering eye could hardly have missed someone as attractive as Jean. The race track, like the hunting field, is a great breaker of marriages. And Buster fits the description. For one thing, he is already married, to Philippa Cunliffe-Owen, but it is in 1962 that he gets divorced from her. Jean may well have expected that he will marry her as soon as she is herself divorced. Instead, the following year, Buster marries someone quite else, Daphne Bateman, a hairdresser from Kent, who is eight years younger than Jean and twenty years younger than Buster. That would be a shock to any woman's self-esteem, especially one who has just left her husband and three children in order to make a fresh start. A shock like that would be quite enough to drive her back to Charles and to an unwise impromptu rematch. Or perhaps it was the other way around. Perhaps Jean came quite close to becoming Mrs A. A. Baring but saw the light in time, and Buster then married Daphne Bateman in a fit of pique after being jilted. As with serial killers, serial marriers must experience quite a few near misses who live to tell the tale.

All this would certainly account for the bitterness with which the normally charitable Charles describes Buster's behaviour over cars. There is a piquant contrast between the respectful way he talks of his 'business partner Alastair Baring' in his first book and the savage portrait of 'Buster' as erratic, spoilt and a not very talented driver in *With Hindsight*, 40 years later. In both his first two books, he tells the Buster stories: about the trip to Jersey and about buying the Silverstone Healey. But he tells them in a milder spirit, commenting only that 'My business associate, Baring, tended to change his cars rather frequently.' It is tempting to guess that it is not only their business relationship that has soured. Whether this is true or not, it is strange to find the whole fraught story in such an otherwise sunny book. You do not feel that it was put in to titillate the reader, rather that the pain of the memory was so great that it forced its way into the text. If the Someone Else really was Buster, it would not be the first or last time that he left a legacy of pain behind him.

The only other thing, after all, that I really do know about Buster is that he was married several times, enough times to arouse Munca's displeasure, if not despair. This is the most promising avenue to be pursued, though one can never be sure how reliable the information is likely to be if he is anything like his mother. Anyway, to make a start on this side of his life, I begin to look out for the certificate of his marriage to Lyn's mother, which must have happened in 1939 or thereabouts, because Lyn is only a year or so younger than me. And there it comes up: 18 June 1939, Alister Archie Baring, bachelor of independent means, aged 27, marries Esmé Rose Pezaro, spinster, aged 19, daughter of Harry Pezaro, a retired fur manufacturer. The address of both the bride and the groom is Barrie House, Lancaster Gate, London W2. This does not necessarily mean, I think, that they are already living together. One or other of them may be just staying there for the wedding. The marriage must have Munca's approval, because one of the witnesses is G. R. Mount. And I know this much: that Unca would not be signing any register against his wife's wishes.

In any case, at this period Unca, Munca and Buster seem to be living all close together, like rabbits in a burrow or the original Beatrix Potter mice. In the great National Register, drawn up in September 1939 at the outbreak of war, George R. and Elizabeth (Patricia) Mount are listed at 36 Barrie House, Lancaster Gate, the very same block (perhaps it's the same flat) as Buster and Esmé put down in the marriage register two months earlier. By the time of the National Register, Buster and his bride are living only a few hundred yards away, at 10 Westbourne Crescent. What is more, Buster is listed as 'manager of joinery and cabinet works' (a profession he has presumably just taken up, for in the marriage register he puts merely 'of independent means'). In their Register entry, Munca is listed as 'director, furnishing company', and Unca, more specifically, as 'director, furnishing company (hotel supplier and caterer)'. So they are all working together in a business to manufacture and supply stuff to hotels – a continuation by other means of Unca's original plan to train as a hotel manager. Where did they get the capital to start this business? How long does it survive? Is it obliterated by the war?

What also catches my eye is that here on this certificate we have a definitive statement of who Buster's father is, inserted by Buster himself and approved by his supposed brother-in-law, Unca, and, by extension, by Munca too. And what Buster puts in the column for 'Father's Name and Surname' is 'Reginald Baring (deceased)'.

Now Baring is not a common surname in Britain. It is only because the founders of Barings Bank were so prolific in their descendants and in the number of peerages they hoovered up that the name is so familiar. Almost all the Barings you will ever come across in Britain are descended from John *né* Johan Baring, the son of Franz Baring, the Minister of the Lutheran Church at Bremen. John settled at Larkbeer, near Exeter, as a merchant in 1717 and was naturalized six years later. Forty years on, his two sons founded what became the oldest surviving merchant bank in London. Barings dominated the City landscape for more than two centuries until its second collapse, at the hands of the rogue trader Nick Leeson in 1995. Virtually all the Barings whose births, marriages and deaths are to be found in the GRO Index belong to the clan. Many if not most of them are also to be found in *Burke's Peerage* under the titles of Baring *Baronet*, Northbrook, Revelstoke, Howick, Cromer and Ashburton.

There is one and only one Reginald Baring to be found anywhere among them. And he was indeed deceased. Reginald Arthur Baring was a lieutenant in the Royal Air Force and he died in action in France at almost the last gasp of the Great War, on 9 June 1918. His father, the Rev Francis Baring, had predeceased him, shortly after the outbreak of war. But his mother Amy lived to see the deaths of four of her five sons in action: Ernest and Charles with the Australian forces in 1916 and 1917 respectively, then Christopher with the West Kents in 1918 and finally Reginald three months later. All four of them are commemorated on the war memorial at Sudbury, Suffolk, where their father had once been rector.

So poor Reginald was indubitably dead. But he could not have been Buster's father. Not because he was unmarried at the time of his death, though he was. But because he was only 19 years old when he was killed. So when Buster was born in January 1912 (a fact that Buster himself confirms on this certificate), Reginald would only have been 12. As a father, tragically, Reginald remains strictly fictional. Buster's parentage is as invented as that of any character in *The Importance of Being Earnest*. In fact, Reginald is just the sort of name Oscar Wilde might have used for the purpose.

The only real Reginald Baring being dead was obviously a big advantage. Who would bother to check his date of birth? Though if Munca and Buster were to be brother and sister, she too should have proclaimed herself the child of Reginald rather than of John A. Baring of New York. But then Munca regarded consistency as an overrated virtue. She would have liked Emerson's crack about it being the hobgoblin of little minds.

Had Buster always put Reginald in the space for father on documents? When had he first been told this untruth, by Munca – who else? It seemed like a good idea to check if there were any earlier marriages registered under some name that bore an approximation to Buster's shifting identity markings.

I went back to the beginning of the 1930s, reasoning that someone as impatient as Buster was likely to be an early starter. It was just as well I did, because it was as early as 28 March 1931 that Alistair Archie Baring had got married, at Christ Church, Mayfair, to Kathleen Dorothy Lennard. He was staying around the corner at the fine old art deco Washington Hotel in Curzon Street, and he gives his age as 21. He was in fact only just 19. Either he had lied to his new wife and family, or he did not have Munca's permission, without which he legally could not marry. Probably both. But there can be no question of this being anybody other than Buster, because in the father's column there is the one and only Reginald Baring (deceased). So the myth has already taken root before Buster has left his teens.

And Lennard? Had it been through Buster that Munca had first grafted a connection with the great shoe firm? The surname could just be a coincidence, but it is not a very common surname either, and I am learning to be wary of coincidences when Munca is around.

Leaving this intriguing question aside for the moment, what also catches my eye is that Buster, in March 1931, is describing himself as 'electrical engineer'. So not only is he a married man when he makes his debut at Brooklands the following year, he also has an educated clue about what goes on under the bonnet.

Among the three witnesses alongside the bride's father is one Nicolas Bentley. That rare spelling of Nicolas without the 'h' suggests that this may well be Nicolas Bentley, the wry and mordant cartoonist who is five years older than Buster and at this time working in the publicity department at Shell. He is about to get his first big break, the commission to illustrate *Cautionary Tales* by his father's friend Hilaire Belloc. What I am also beginning to learn is that Buster is capable of surprises.

The marriage to Kathleen is as brief as it sounds frantic. Barely two years after they walked down the aisle together, she is suing him for divorce on the grounds that 'the said Alistair Archie Baring has frequently committed adultery with divers women whose names are to your Petitioner unknown'. Even the single instance of these adulteries specified for the benefit of the Court, at the Great Central Hotel, Marylebone, on 11 May 1933, only the day before the petition is filed, is with 'a woman unknown'. You begin to get the feeling that the women were scarcely known to Buster either, being perhaps like the Unknown Soldier known only to God.

What strikes me too is the restless, unsettled nature of their life even when they are living together. The petition says that 'after the said marriage your Petitioner and her said husband lived and cohabited at the County Hotel, Chelmsford, Essex, Gorse Cottage, Churt, Surrey, and 1 Great Cumberland Place, London W.', and Buster is now said to be residing at 22 Park Lane, Mayfair. Four oddly assorted addresses in the space of two years. You never can tell where he is going to pop up next. The tenor of his life seems as mysterious as the source of his funds.

I have identified two marriages registered in the name of Alistair A. Baring in the 1930s, but there is a third one sandwiched between them: a marriage at Hampstead, to a Josephine M. Deacon, in 1935. For the sake of completeness, I order up this third entry, and cannot repress a gasp when the certificate arrives and there again is the unique fictional father 'Reginald Baring (deceased)'.

Just as there is always one more coin wedged under the cushion of the armchair, so, I am beginning to see, there is always one more marriage to be winkled out of the tightest time frame in Buster's life. If it were not for Reginald, I would be tempted to conclude that this time the groom really is someone quite different, because he describes himself as 'professional dancer', and so does his new wife Josephine. But there is no doubt that this really is Buster, because in the column for 'Condition' he describes himself as 'the divorced husband of Kathleen Dorothy Baring, formerly, Lennard, spinster'. And it is his new father-in-law rather than his first one who is in the shoe trade. Arthur Deacon describes himself as 'shoe manufacturer's agent', in other words, a shoe salesman. He sells the shoes. Josephine and Buster dance in them.

Alas, this tango does not last. Three years later, at the end Buster and Josephine are getting divorced. This time, it is he who does the suing, citing one Albert Sommer as the co-respondent. But I do not think we need feel too sorry for him because it is only three days after the decree becomes absolute on 12 June 1939 that he marries Esmé. So they must have been courting for some time while he was still officially married to Josephine, though 'courting' scarcely does justice to Buster's blitzkrieg approach to wooing.

By the time Buster is 27, he has been married three times. He has also been an electrical engineer, a professional dancer and driven half a dozen different racing cars. I am beginning to see what Munca means about his not settling down.

The years of the Second World War seem relatively placid by comparison, on the domestic front anyway. Esmé has two children, Lyn in 1940, then Nicholas in 1944 – Buster's first two children, as far as we know. But come the peace, it would be too much to expect Buster to stay put. And he doesn't. Motor racing restarts in 1946, and the season for unmarrying and remarrying starts soon after. The marriage to Esmé has lasted seven or eight years, a record so far, but the circuits and nightclubs are reopening all over Europe, and Buster has to be part of the scene. Quite how much he has to be part of it may not be immediately apparent to his new life partner, Margaret Cawthorn. She is his fourth wife, but the first one to have been married before, twice before in fact. She is the same age as he is, 37, and her father is deceased like poor Reginald but not a bit fictitious (he was a farmer in Leicestershire). For our present purpose, though, the interesting thing about Margaret Cawthorn is the address she gives on the marriage certificate: The Reeds, Angmering-on-Sea.

So she is a neighbour of Unca and Munca. In fact, The Reeds turns out to be no more than five or ten minutes' walk from Blue Waters, up Seaview Avenue and turn right opposite the Angmering-on-Sea lawn tennis club. It is a walk I remember as well as any walk in the world. The Reeds is an overgrown cottage with a thatched roof and leaded windowpanes, a fine example of Angmering Rustic. There are windows like eyes peeping out from under the thatched roof. It even has a separate thatched garage. Buster must have met Margaret during one of his rare visits to see his sister/mother, at a local cocktail party perhaps, or at the Yacht Club at the beach end of Seaview Avenue, where everyone who has nothing better to do in Angmering fetches up. Perhaps I too have met Margaret, without knowing it. These are the years after the war when my sister and I are spending quite a bit of time at Blue Waters. Perhaps, and this is an odder thought still, Buster's visits to Blue Waters are not rare at all. It's just that he only goes there when Francie and I are not there, because Munca wishes her two families, if you can call them that, to meet as little as possible, otherwise the whole edifice of untruth will begin to crumble.

I can imagine the two of them, Margaret and Buster, exchanging wry cracks about their experiences of marriage, and her delight in finding someone so full of fizz in this backwater. There she had been, staring out at the unforgiving sea through the big window, and now all at once life begins again with a dark stranger and another gin and tonic.

Munca cannot be at all pleased that Buster should have picked up his latest on her own home patch. Especially because she approved of his marriage to Esmé, who is also the mother of her first grandchildren. Any breach is likely to mean that she sees less of Lyn and Nicholas. So the new marriage must be bad news for Munca. But it doesn't stay bad news for very long. Within three years, Buster and Margaret are divorced. And in between racing his marvellous HWM on the heels of Stirling Moss, he has embarked on two new projects. He has become a timber merchant and he is marrying again, for the fifth time.

His new wife Philippa Cunliffe-Owen has also been married before, to someone called Denis Macduff Burke, and she has two children, David and Alexandra. Philippa is the daughter of a great industrialist, Sir Hugo Cunliffe-Owen, first baronet. Buster's first four fathers-in-law were a match merchant, a shoe salesman, a furrier and a Midlands farmer. Now, at the fifth time of asking, he marries into the plutocracy. Sir Hugo is President of British American Tobacco, director of the Midland Bank and chairman of Cunliffe-Owen Aircraft Ltd. And it is by virtue of Sir Hugo that Buster graduates to the pages of *Burke's Peerage*. At last he is in there alongside the real Barings, though I doubt whether any of them have noticed.

The Cunliffe-Owens are not only rich, they are liberated from bourgeois constraints. Philippa herself goes on to marry four times, so does her sister Diana; her brother Dudley, a hotel and casino king, a mere three times. Their restlessness as well as their wealth is right up Buster's street. He stays with Philippa for ten years, a personal best, and they have two children together, Adrian and Sarah, bringing Munca's total of grandchildren up to four, not to mention the two children Philippa had by Denis Burke. If Lyn is typical, none of them, it appears, knows Munca as their granny, at least not in her lifetime.

By now, I must confess that I am a little exhausted by keeping up with Buster's domestic life. Perhaps as he comes into his fifties, he might slow down a fraction. Not so. A year after getting divorced from Philippa, he marries again, his sixth wife, Daphne Bateman, the hairdresser 20 years younger than himself. One feels that by now he has only to see a girl in a window anywhere in the Home Counties to find a new bride. He also has a new career. The marriage certificate describes him as a farmer, and gives his address as North Farm, Warfield, Berkshire. What is strange, though, and I have only just noticed it, is that he and Munca are never far apart from each other. Before the war, they were both knocking around central London, in particular Marylebone and Mayfair. Then, during the war and for years after it, both of them alternate between the Berkshire–Surrey borders and Angmering-on-Sea. Their relations may be testy and strained, but it seems that somehow they still need each other, or at any rate need to be close enough to keep an eye on one another. If the mother-son connection is a wounded one, it appears to be a wound that has to be kept open.

Neither the marriage to Daphne nor the farming career lasts any longer than their predecessors. Two years later, Reginald Baring (deceased) is wheeled into action for the seventh and last time as Buster ties the knot with Julia Champion, the daughter of an electrical draughtsman in Dunstable. He is 51, she is 25, the same age as his elder daughter. This marriage has the widest gap between the ages of the bride and groom, 26 years, and the shortest gap between this and the preceding marriage, just under two years. Far from slowing down in middle age, Buster is speeding up into sprint mode. He is changing wives as fast as he once changed cars.

He appears to have sold or given up the farm, and at the time of the marriage he lists himself as residing at Julia's home address, 25 Staveley Road, Dunstable. He now describes himself as 'Author'. I take a fellow interest in his unexpected new profession and I look for his name in the British Library catalogue but can find no trace of him, even after working through the various possible combinations of Archie, Alistair and so on. Perhaps he writes under a pseudonym, but then much later I come upon an item in the Used Books section of Abebooks. The book is called *Know about the Countryside*, by Alistair Baring, published in 1968. I order it up for a mere £3.98, and it turns out to be a handsome big picture book for children, illustrated by the well-known children's book illustrator David Nockels. Here are a couple of sentences taken at random: 'Spring is the mating time for all wild life. Those animals which hibernate in winter, like the squirrel and the badger, wake up to join the general motley which forms the frolic that is spring.' It may seem a bit odd that someone who has just entered on his seventh marriage, leaving behind at least four children from previous marriages, should take to writing books for 8- to 10-year-olds about bunny rabbits and the miracles of Mother Nature. But then we writers are not quite like other people. Of course this could be another Alistair Baring, but the emphasis on trees and timber products suggests that this is Buster. There is a full-page illustration of a tractor dragging some timber through a gloomy fir-wood, which might have been painted from nature in one of Buster's plantations. So he does seem to be, as we say, a published author.

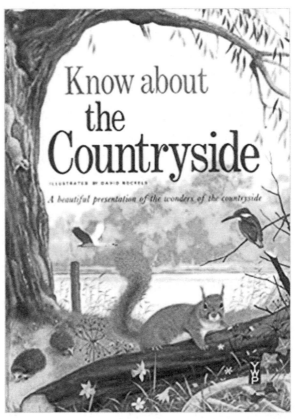

Know about the Countryside – Buster's only published work

That makes his seventh recorded career: electrical engineer, professional dancer, Grand Prix driver, manager of joinery and cabinet works, timber merchant, farmer, author – not to mention the marriage to Esmé, where he described himself as 'of independent means', which may perhaps have been the real truth all along, though I still don't have a clue where the means came from. I like the way, though, that as soon as he takes up a fresh enthusiasm this becomes his profession. I suppose it's rather like how every new girlfriend immediately has to be his wife, which has not turned out so well.

This is the last we hear of Buster in England. Soon after he marries Julia, they move to Switzerland, presumably to avoid tax. Why else does anyone move to Switzerland? So he still has enough money for it to be worth fleeing the Inland Revenue. And then six years later he dies, but not at his Swiss residence on the rue de la Villette in Yverdon-les-Bains, a small spa town at the bottom of Lake Neuchâtel. He dies in the Algarve where he is wintering, at a villa called Colinas Verdes, in Bensafrim, a holiday resort outside Lagos. He has just had his fifty-ninth birthday. His death date is in fact just about the only fact the petrolheads are right about, 21 January 1971. Julia is at his side. She becomes the Katherine Parr of the story. And it is she who provides the British Vice-Consul at Portimão with the necessary information for the death certificate.

He dies with the description 'Writer' on his death certificate, and I think any writer would be quite pleased with the final twist to his story. As a result of residing in Switzerland and dying in Portugal and insisting that he was born in Manila, Buster has to produce proof, presumably for tax purposes, that he is nonetheless a British citizen. And what he does is to claim citizenship through his father under the 1948 British Nationality Act. He does not give his father's name – Reginald is allowed to rest easy for once. He, or rather Julia, enters only 'father born Leeds, Yorkshire, 26 August, 1888'.

This final flourish only deepens the mystery. Who is this new father wheeled on at the very last moment? Certainly not Reginald, who was born at Bideford, Devon, in 1899. And why on earth Leeds? Has Munca, right at the very end, been persuaded to tell him the truth, or at any rate a new version of the truth?

Anyway, that is the end of Buster. He falls asleep in the lemon groves under a pale winter sun with Julia at his side. But for me it is nowhere near the end. I have the facts of his life, or a fair number of them, and I think I also have the feel of him as a person. I can imagine what it would be like to run into him in the clubhouse at Brooklands or the Yacht Club at Angmering or the bar at the Washington Hotel: his urgent, dark eyes, his intense welcome, and then his gnat's attention span, his besetting impatience, his darting from topic to topic, and the way his whole body changes when an attractive woman comes into the bar. But what I still do not know is what he knows. Does he really believe that Munca is his sister, not his mother? Did he ever believe that? Did he ever believe that his father was called Reginald Baring? Does he have any idea where or in what circumstances he was born?

Or does he not bother to ask these questions? Is he perhaps scornful of anyone who is interested in the 'back story', as up-to-the-minute people often are? He would have liked the way people today think of 'moving on' as one of life's most important duties. Perhaps he was just lucky to be born restless and to lack a dwelling nature.

No, I don't really think that is the case. You can almost feel his searchingness, his inability to find anything that really calms his soul, least of all love. There must be a connection between the abrupt and mysterious circumstances of his early life and the way he goes on to live. How strong the need he feels to be married, not just to have an affair. Then, almost as soon as he is married, his inability to accept the strings that go with marriage and his feeling that he has not found what he was looking for. There is an absence that is always with him, and you do not need to be a child psychologist to guess the nature of that absence. But it's no use pursing one's lips. Those of us who have led sedate lives, in the same trade, with the same partner and the same phone number for half a century, must admit a smidgen of unwilling admiration for someone who dashed through life at such breakneck speed, who tried everything and everyone.

Meanwhile, I have to admit that, as far as my own quest goes, I know a great deal more about Buster, too much perhaps, but I still do not know where he came from. I am still stumbling across the shingle, still looking for the little gate in the beach wall. About the basic facts I am as clueless as I was when I started.

4

Charters

Then I had a bit of luck. Not the kind of luck when you have been working on a problem for ages and something makes it all fall into place and you can't think why. Not the kind of reward of which a great golfer once said 'the more I practise, the luckier I get'. This bit of luck was undeserved and unsought. It came from nowhere while I was thinking of other things entirely. In fact I had pretty much given up chasing Munca and Buster. Their tracks seemed so exquisitely covered, not only by their own efforts, which were far from negligible, but by the corrosions and erasures of time. I could waste a lot more time getting nowhere. And out of nowhere was where my luck came.

I was doing some research for what I call 'a tale of history and imagination' and what less pretentious people call a historical novel. It was about Thomas Jefferson and his secretary in Paris around the time of the French Revolution, and I was looking for an article about the Désert de Retz, the garden of follies they visited, and its licentious designer, M. Racine de Monville. The article had in fact been published in the *Architectural Review* in November 1949, but for some weird reason I had got it stuck in my head that it had been published in *Country Life*. And so it was on the *Country Life* shelves in the London Library that I mistakenly went to look it up. The bound volumes are in a particularly murky corner of the basement and I could not locate the light switch, so I had to fossick about in the dark until I managed to pull down the volume for the second half of 1949.

Not surprisingly, there was no sign of the article when I held the volume up to the light at the end of the passage. I rummaged to and fro. Perhaps the article had appeared in October or September or December. I was about to put the volume back on the shelf when my eye chanced on an article that had nothing at all to do with the Désert de Retz. How could it? I was looking at the wrong magazine, and now that I looked at the dateline at the top of the page I saw that I was looking at the issue of 24 November 1944, not 1949 – so I hadn't even got the year right.

The article that caught my eye was headed 'CHARTERS, SUNNINGDALE, BERKSHIRE, the home of Mr Frank Parkinson'. It was written by Christopher Hussey, the doyen of country-house historians. He had been the Architectural Editor of *Country Life* for years, and the magazine was worth buying for his long, superbly illustrated articles describing a single country house and, in the case of the more remarkable houses, stretching over several issues. By the time I met him in the late 1960s he was a sweet old buffer with a white moustache, but his diligence and his scholarship remained formidable. His own country house, Scotney Castle (now in the hands of the National Trust), was famous for its romantic gardens. My mother-in-law-to-be lived a mile or so away over the fields, and the Husseys kindly invited us to hold our wedding reception there. He died a year or so later.

But it was not because of Christopher Hussey or my slight connection with him that I grabbed a chair and settled down to read the article (in fact it turned out to be the first of three articles on Charters). It was because of the house. I went to prep school in Sunningdale at the other end of the road that leads to Charters, and on wet afternoons when the football pitch was too soggy we would be taken on a walk from Dry Arch Road and along Charters Road past the edge of the grounds. Over the fence we could see the house gleaming white in the distance where the ground rose into Windsor Forest.

For architectural historians, Charters was already famous as the last great country house built in England (it was finished in 1938) and one of the very few to be built in a modernist style. For us 10- and 11-year-old schoolboys it was a legend for a different reason.

A couple of years earlier, Charters had been bought by Sir Montague Burton, the 'Tailor of Taste', whose shops dominated the high street in my youth and for many years to come. Burton was born Moshe Osinsky in Lithuania and he was very short, barely five foot tall. What fascinated us schoolboys was the report that he employed on his household staff only men who were shorter than he was. We saw Charters as an enchanted realm of dwarves. We imagined them scampering in and out of the colossal white pillars of the façade or hopping out of pies and from under dish covers at the dining table. It was so piquant, the contrast between this enormous country house and its tiny inhabitants.

Hussey makes the highest claims for the architecture of the house: 'Charters is, in the broad sense, an illustration of how modern science and industrial craftsmanship can help to carry on that tradition of civilisation of which the great English country house has for so long been the highest expression.' Not everyone agreed. The stark white block, outlined against the dark trees of the forest behind, is certainly uncompromisingly modern. But it did not satisfy that stern modernist Nikolaus Pevsner, who in his volume on Berkshire woundingly dismisses Charters as 'a typical case of the C20 style adopted willy-nilly, just in order to be up to date. White and cubic it is, but the great hall in the centre has a front to the S with the giant pillars of the fascist brand and the French windows to its l. and r. are of Georgian proportions.' It sounds just like King's Thursday, the huge modernist country house built for the dashing Margot Beste-Chetwynde by the young Bauhaus architect, Otto Silenus, in Evelyn Waugh's *Decline and Fall*.

Charters – the façade

Otto Silenus would surely have applauded the way the house was designed as a machine for living in. Hidden away from view there was a battery of the latest mod cons. These amazed and baffled Hussey who confessed himself as not mechanically minded and 'as lost in such surroundings as in the engine room of the *Queen Mary*'. The vast underground boiler room contained gigantic gas heating boilers thermostatically controlled, as well as its own central water-softening and air-conditioning plants. The dust and dirt collected from each room was wafted by ducts to a central collecting system. The pride and joy of the house, probably the only one in a private house in England, was an electric plate- and dishwasher providing automatic refuse disposal. The chromium steel and white-tiled kitchen could have been ordered from Poggenpohl today. Charters combined with the refinements of modern life all the hi-tech appliances then found only in factories.

This remarkable house was commissioned by Frank Parkinson, the engineering tycoon, from George Adie, of Adie, Button and Partners, perhaps more famous today as the architects of the Stockwell Bus Depot. Parkinson was as remarkable as his house. He was an innovator of superabundant energy, appetite and imagination. Born in 1887, the son of a quarry owner in Wharfedale, Yorkshire, he was apprenticed at the age of 14 to Rhodes Motors, a firm of electrical engineers. By the age of 19 he had risen to works manager, while studying electrical engineering in evening classes at Guiseley Mechanics' Institute and later at the University of Leeds. At 21, he founded F. Parkinson & Co., Electric Power Engineers, committing to the firm all his Post Office savings, although he had smartly transferred to his mother the money that he had inherited from his father, so that it should not be at risk if the firm failed. Frank and his brother Albert then moved into the manufacture of alternating-current motors. Their factory was among the first to adopt the flow method of production and to lay out their works accordingly. Parkinson then merged with, or in effect took over, the much better-known firm of Crompton of Chelmsford. Crompton Parkinson became a household name, growing at a dazzling pace between 1927 and 1937 as it took over a string of competitors, including the British Electric Transformer Co., Tricity Cookers and Associated Electric Vehicles. Soon the firm had a foothold in all the growth sectors of the age: batteries, cables, domestic cookers and white goods of all sorts. Its electric motors were installed in milk floats, in trolleybuses, in trams and diesel locomotives. From 1932, Crompton Parkinson began marketing the 'one-shilling lamp'. This undercutting threatened the so-called 'Lamp Ring', which had controlled domestic electrical goods from the end of the First World War. Naturally, the only solution was for Parkinson to join the Ring, and so Crompton Parkinson became the name on our light bulbs for years to come. By the end of the 1930s, Frank was the acknowledged leader of the electric orchestra.

He was also an enlightened paternalist. He allotted shares to his employees, set up a superannuation scheme and a central benevolent fund, and offered bursaries to promising trainees. Montague Burton and Frank shared many of the same ideas, being both philanthropic bosses and insatiable rationalizers. The domain of the dwarves had followed the kingdom of the dynamos.

Like all such dynamos, Frank must have been exhausting to live with. Weekends at Charters were a relentless treadmill: two sets of tennis before breakfast, a round of golf at Sunningdale either side of lunch, a rubber or two of bridge before dinner or a trip to a London show. Frank's domain drew to it some of the glitterati of the 1930s, most notably the Prince of Wales and Mrs Simpson. One can see Charters as the modern equivalent of the Désert de Retz. Instead of dressing up as archers or Chinese mandarins and pursuing lubricious liaisons in their towers and pavilions, the pleasure-seekers of Charters put on plus-fours and cocktail frocks and pursued a giddy round from the clubhouse to the Café de Paris and the 400 Club in Leicester Square.

A photograph of Frank at the age of 40 by Howard Coster (the British equivalent of Karsh of Ottawa in the portraiture of Great

Men) shows an embodiment of the unappeased will, looking not unlike the young Marlon Brando. Not surprisingly perhaps, Frank died at Charters of a heart attack when he had not quite reached 60. He was described as charming yet unapproachable, modest but also keen to burnish his reputation, acquisitive but also generous. He left nearly £1.5 million – not far short of £100 million in today's money. There were also considerable bequests to thank the University of Leeds for what he had learnt there – £50,000 for Parkinson Scholarships, £200,000 for the construction of the Parkinson Building. He insisted on marble columns.

Frank Parkinson by Howard Coster

Frank was the very model of a modern tycoon in his impatience, his vim, his insistence on efficiency, his fascination with everything modern. From the outside, Charters looks like the perfect monument to such a man: it is a brute assertion of will, in its size, force and simplicity, plonked there on its gentle Berkshire hill. Other self-made magnates of the period bought famous Georgian mansions, or restored ancient castles, or, like William Randolph Hearst at San Simeon, built gigantic pastiches of the baroque and classical buildings of old Europe. The factories, offices and studios from which they made their millions might be plain concrete blocks, barely adorned if at all, very much in the modern idiom, but their dwelling places exhaled a yearning for the high civilization of the past. Not Frank. He was modern through and through. And Charters is all of a piece with him.

Except that it isn't. For as you walk into the house under those great square pillars (Frank insisted they be faced with Portland stone), you get a shattering surprise. At the beginning of his second article on Charters, Christopher Hussey tries to underplay the shock:

Within, there is more direct reliance on the Georgian style, and the plan is fundamentally akin to that of the typical Georgian country house, with the same regard to spacious symmetrical disposition and to a dignified setting for family and social life. Though it comes as something of a surprise on entering to find oneself in 18th-century surroundings, one cannot deny that country houses of this size are essentially a renaissance conception, which attain perfect development only in that century together with the appropriate furnishings and fittings.

And besides, Hussey adds almost by way of excuse, 'contemporary architects have not so far evolved a form, nor decorators the furnishings, appropriate for a modern counterpart to the Georgian "gentleman's seat"'.

But that last bit is not really true. By 1938, there existed an abundant tradition of modernist décor and furniture. You could see examples in any grand hotel or ocean liner of that date. The Parkinsons could have filled Charters with the stuff from the great modernist designers. But they didn't.

And it really is a surprise. Outside, you might be standing on the grand steps of a fascist party headquarters, or a giant tobacco factory, or the lot of a Hollywood film studio. In fact, very like Waugh's description of King's Thursday: 'the great colonnade of black glass pillars shone in the moonlight; beyond the polished aluminium balustrade the park stretched silent and illimitable'. When the next day dawns, 'the aluminium blinds shot up, and the sun poured in through the vita-glass, filling the room with beneficent rays' – all just as Frank Parkinson ordered.

But inside, you find yourself in a Berkshire Petit Trianon: Chinese Chippendale furniture, chinoiserie hand-painted wallpaper, winged armchairs covered in tasselled brocade, Florentine pietra dura tables, swagged and ruched curtains, landscapes by Joseph Vernet, *trompe-l'œil* paintings of sportive country scenes, scrolled decorative ironwork on the stairs and galleries – everything that disgusted the modernists, coming right out of the traditions they were trying to smash. As soon as he came through the great glass doors, M. Racine de Monville would have felt quite at home.

What is the explanation of this extraordinary contrast? Why so unremittingly up to the minute on the outside, so self-indulgently retro on the inside? I cannot think of another example of such a bizarre disjunction, either way around: those few tycoons who did build modernist houses filled them with modernist fixtures and fittings; those (far more numerous) tycoons who bought old houses filled them with the expensive *objets d'art* they had bought in the salerooms. So far as I know, only Charters is one thing outside and something totally else inside.

But my mind is suddenly distracted from this interesting question, for midway down the second page of Hussey's second instalment a single name leaps off the page at me: *Mrs G. R. Mount*. It is hard to convey what a violent effect this austere, even dull form of address has on me. It brings back a whole strange part of my youth. For Mrs G. R. Mount was how Munca always liked to be addressed, formally anyway. Not Mrs George – Unca did not care for George and was always known as Grig or Greig, 'because he was merry as a grig', my father would say, not without a touch of malice. Her own first name, Elizabeth (actually her second, she was officially Patricia Elizabeth), she seldom if ever used, not even I think on cheques. To her Mount in-laws she was Betty, to some of her older friends Liz, but Mrs G. R. Mount was how we wrote to her on the envelope, and even now when I think of her it runs easier off the tongue than any Christian name, easier even than Aunt Betty.

And what is Mrs G. R. Mount doing in the middle of this article? To my amazement, it turns out that she is responsible for the interior décor, not just the drapes or the wallpaper, but the whole unexpected *mise en scène*. Hussey tells us:

The interior decoration throughout the house, including the selection of all the furniture, has been directed by Mrs G. R. Mount, who, together with the team of artists and craftsmen working to her instructions, collaborated with the architects, Adie, Button and Partners, responsible for the structural works.

So Munca is not just any old interior decorator but one who has landed probably the biggest private commission in England

95

of the decade. And we should remember that the 1930s were a golden age for interior decorators. Think of the famous names Frank Parkinson might have hired: Syrie Maugham, Sybil Colefax, Elsie de Wolfe. These legends of soft furnishings were all working for the Parkinsons' famous friends, such as Mrs Simpson and the Prince of Wales, severally and later together. Yet this commission, huge in its extent, its prestige and not least in the difficulties posed by working in a quite different style from that of the exterior of the house, goes to a decorator who is completely unknown, certainly unknown to her nephew. I knew that Munca liked doing up her own houses, because she did up so many of them, but I had no idea that she was a professional.

Then it comes to me that when we found them in the National Register on the outbreak of war living virtually next door to each other in Bayswater, all three of them – Unca, Munca and Buster – described themselves as being in the furniture business. So it's fair to assume that many of the more routine items – for servants' bedrooms, kitchen fittings and so on – may have come from Buster's workshop. It seems to be a family business, which is amazing for a family that most people would regard as dysfunctional, to say the least.

Even on this mammoth commission, Munca does not have a proper professional name. Mrs G. R. Mount is no sort of moniker for someone who is masterminding the décor of the last great country house in England. Syrie Maugham does not call herself Mrs W. S. Maugham (not least because she divorced Somerset Maugham back in 1928 and hates him); Sybil Colefax does not call herself Lady Colefax, not when she is working, and Elsie does not call herself Lady Mendl. And even if they did, that would not be as determinedly obscure as calling yourself Mrs G. R. Mount.

Now that I have this startling piece of information, I turn the pages of *Country Life* impatiently, staring at each illustration with an intense curiosity. And yes, there is no doubt of it, here on a far larger scale is the décor so familiar to me as it migrates from Blue Waters next door to White Wings, then inland to Castlewood, then Blue Waters again, then back inland to Holthanger, and back to Blue Waters for the third time and finally to White Wings again, now ennobled as Preston House. There are the same Chinese Chippendale chairs and the Chippendale gilt mirrors, the same swags and ruches and marble tables. Nowhere is the similarity more pressing than in the bedrooms. Hussey tells us that 'it is, indeed, in the bedrooms that are found many of the most satisfactory furniture and design *ensembles* organized by Mrs G. R. Mount, who, with Messrs Geoffrey Webster as manufacturer, was in charge of the internal decoration throughout'. Here are those dressing tables with their triptych mirrors and glass tops and pleated valances, the curtains with their scalloped pelmets framing the huge views of most of Surrey, and those padded silk bedheads with their scrolls and curlicues – indistinguishable from the beds at White Wings I bounced on as a child. Hussey loves these bedrooms: 'They are, to my mind, as satisfying as any modern rooms I have seen.' I have less satisfying memories, of tellings-off for making a mess or even, going further back, for wetting the bed. Without knowing it, I found the luxuriousness of those bedrooms a little suffocating. They were so deep-carpeted, so totally insulated that I found them hard to breathe in. I missed the damp and draught of our Wiltshire cottage, just as I found the silent undulations of Munca's Rolls-Royce sick-making and longed for the creaky old Morris Ten. But that these bedrooms come from the same designer's hand there can be no doubt. They have the inimitable stamp of Mrs G. R. Mount.

Then it occurs to me that some of these items may not be merely *like* the stuff she has in her own home. They may be the very same pieces. For most decorators carry a certain amount of stock to fill in gaps in a client's house, either selling them at a good price to the captive customer or lending them until the client finds a permanent replacement, which the decorator probably buys on commission for him, and then retrieving her own piece. Yes, surely there by the fireplace in the hall is that carved figure of a black boy that used to greet you as you came into the hall at Castlewood.

Charters, the morning room

I move on, rather stirred, to Christopher Hussey's third instalment, and there in fig. 6 'The Morning-Room, Paintings by Adrian Daintrey' is a sight that makes my heart thump harder even than the sight of the magic words 'Mrs G. R. Mount'. For there, at the side of the room, hangs a picture that I have known most of my life.

It is a large canvas, five foot by four foot, painted entirely in black and white, the grisaille for which Munca had such a taste. The picture shows three young women, two of them bare-shouldered, sitting at a table outdoors, perhaps in somewhere like the South of France. The atmosphere is languorous, even erotic, somehow all the more so because of the cold grey tones.

I know who the women are too. One is Poppet John, daughter of Augustus. The second is my mother's best friend, Mary Campbell, later Mayall, and the third, leaning forward on the right of the picture and the only fair one of the three, is my mother. The artist, Adrian Daintrey, was one of my parents' best friends. He often came to stay with us. He was a grumpy, charming character and he fascinated my sister and me as he set up his easel to paint our sitting room and dining room and the apple trees in the garden. His work always has an attractive ease about it, but only in this grisaille, I think, does he bring off an effect that is magical. Or perhaps the magic is in my own imagination.

In his autobiography winsomely titled *I Must Say*, Adrian refers rather dismissively to the picture's destination as 'the Parkinsons' concrete mansion in Sunningdale'. He did not care for modernism in almost any form. He would have hated Charters as much as he hated Picasso. But it looks lovely in the morning-room.

The picture must have returned to Munca after Charters was sold to the Tailor of Taste, because you can see it in the background of the photograph my mother took at Holthanger on my day out from school when I was 16: me looking shy-surly in a tail-coat, Uncle Greig next to me and then Munca, Georgie and my sister with arms linked. It is the last photo my mother took of us. She died three months later. In my own memoir, I wrote about my mother taking this photo and how by chance there in the background was the painting of herself when young. I had not expected to be writing about the picture again. After my uncle and aunt died, the picture passed to my sister, who then had it in her farmhouse in Suffolk. Francie had nowhere to hang it properly, and now it hangs in our kitchen.

Holthanger, 4 June 1956, Munca, Francie, Georgie, Unca, FM

But none of this begins to explain why Munca should have got the commission, or why the interior of Charters is so completely different from the exterior. What, I wondered, had happened to Charters after Montague Burton died in 1952? Was it still standing? Who lived there now, if anyone? Idly I tapped in 'Charters, Sunningdale', expecting no more from Google than a resumé of the house's architecture, perhaps a mention in an obit of Frank Parkinson. To my surprise, there were a couple of relatively recent articles, written in the jaunty but informative style of property correspondents, for the news was that Charters was still very much standing and was in fact on the market, or rather the first 10 of the 39 sumptuous apartments into which it had been subdivided were, and being marketed through Savills at prices ranging from £1 million to £3 million. The pioneering developer John Morris had bought the property three years earlier and had painstakingly acquired the planning permissions required to return the estate to residential use.

In the interim, it appeared, Charters had come into the ownership of Vickers-Armstrong Ltd, the division that made aircraft. They had used the house for the very purpose that its detractors had always said it was only fit for: as a factory. Charters became in the later 1950s a huge research lab. Vickers added a large extension, more or less in the original style, plus a long low red-brick shed that housed a linear electron accelerator, cooled with water pumped from Parkinson's carp ponds (there's a stream running down the hill). One side of Frank would have lamented this perversion of his stately pleasure dome. Another part of him would surely have welcomed this cutting-edge, hi-tech activity. Then Vickers left, and the place was taken over by the industrial diamond division of De Beers, which relocated its UK operation from Fetter Lane. The new owners removed the 24 inches of concrete cladding from the accelerator, installed a saw bay and converted the shed into a grinding centre, to manufacture diamond laser sights for self-guided missiles of the sort that, years later, became a legend in the first Gulf War. Those cruise missiles that amazed correspondents in their hotel in Baghdad as they saw them bend round street corners had their beginnings in the long shed at Charters. Frank would have loved that too.

Naturally, in the De Beers time as well as the Vickers era, security had to be the strictest possible. So for ordinary mortals Charters disappeared off the map. Literally so. It was not even marked on the Ordnance Survey. The place became the real-life exemplar of one of those mysterious secret establishments hidden away in the trees that you see in TV thrillers. So it remained until John Morris woke the sleeping beauty and gave the property correspondents their first sight of his amazing refurbishments, and incidentally gave me the key to the mystery of Charters and what Munca was doing there.

James Flint broke the news in the Saturday property section of the *Daily Telegraph* (5 March 2005): 'Parkinson's society wife did not share her husband's passion for extreme modernism, and, to pacify her, he gave her free rein over the interior design. The decision put her into direct conflict with George Adie and led to his eventual retirement from the project.' Possibly even to his retirement from architecture altogether. Adie left his practice and emigrated to Australia where he took up theosophy and became an adherent of the mystic Gurdjieff. But his distinguished practice continues to this day, having later merged with the equally distinguished firm that was founded in an earlier era by the great Alfred Waterhouse. Adie's junior partner H. G. Hammond was, however, still alive at the age of 94, and it must have been he who told Morris the whole story of the bust-up.

So it was Doris Parkinson who had scuppered the original plan for an integrated modernist masterpiece, inside as well as out. And the reason she had the influence to persuade the normally stubborn and self-willed Frank was that they had only just got married, in 1936. For both of them, it was the second marriage, the first having lasted for nearly twenty years in each case. How could they expect to be happy if Doris was condemned to live in a house that she hated? It was the least homage that he could pay to her, the necessary sacrifice to their late-flowering passion – he was 49, she just 40. The décor, with all its flounces and ruches, its watered silk and pink marble, was an offering to Cupid. If Munca's choice of fixtures and fittings harked back to the *galanterie* of the eighteenth century, so did the story of why Doris and Frank were there at all.

But the tale that H. G. Hammond told John Morris was not quite finished. Eager to glean whatever else there might be to find out, I flipped over to the next Google article on Charters. It was an article from *Country Life*, published a month before the *Telegraph* piece on 4 February 2005, and it included one detail that the *Telegraph* had not been told or had not thought worth including: 'Mrs Parkinson, however, was less entranced by the ultra-modern, and insisted on having the interiors designed by her sister in a mix of traditional styles – Queen Anne, early-Georgian, or Louis XVI.'

Her *sister*. So Mrs G. R. Mount was Doris Parkinson's sister. Here at last was the answer to the riddle of why such a completely unknown decorator, who lacked even a proper decorator's name, had been chosen for this enormous commission. From Doris's point of view you can see the logic. Only her sister would stick firmly and unalterably on her side, ready to stand up against Frank and George Adie, and no sister in the world could have had more reserves of willpower than Munca. An outside decorator would surely have bowed to the wishes of the man who was paying the bills – Charters cost £155,000, the 1938 equivalent of about £25 million today. George Adie and his assistants would have dazzled her with their expertise. But Munca and Doris together side by side would be as irresistible as the 'Sisters' in the 1954 Irving Berlin song – a song I can in fact see Munca singing as she cleans out the aviary or plumps up the cushions at Preston House.

And very slowly, from the chaotic back office of the brain, there floated up a recollection, faint but seemingly reliable: that Munca's friend Doris McNicol, who we were taught to call Aunt Doris though she wasn't really an aunt, had once been Doris Parkinson, and that there was something not quite right about her becoming Doris McNicol. Did Munca think that Archie McNicol, a slender *flâneur* of no discernible occupation, was not a patch on Frank? But then, who could be? Now that I have looked up the dates, it also occurs to me that Munca might have thought the interval too short. Frank died in January 1946, just short of his 59th birthday. Doris married Archie in the autumn of 1947. Thoughts of merry widows and fortune-hunting dandies are hard to resist.

I may be wrong about that – I would have been barely into my teens when I picked up that fag-end, though ears are sharp enough at such an age. But there was the unassailable fact: Doris and Munca were sisters. If I still doubted that fact, suspecting, say, that the *Country Life* reporter had misheard or got muddled, further confirmation swam towards me out of the blue a month or two later, when my old paper *The Times Literary Supplement* sent me for review the latest volume in the revised series of The Buildings of England, Pevsner's *Berkshire*. Nikolaus Pevsner himself was long dead, but here it is with all his inherited authority in the updated edition: 'The interiors, however, are or were fully "period", designed for Mrs Parkinson by *Frederick Button* and an interior decorator, *Mrs G. R. Mount* (who was also a sister-in-law).' It seemed that the Fates, those other weird sisters, were now conspiring to force the truth upon me with the same insistence with which they had formerly collaborated in Munca's grand cover-up.

Anyway, there was no denying it. Doris was not a non-aunt masquerading as an aunt. She was a real aunt masquerading as a non-aunt masquerading as an aunt. All at once, it became clear why Munca insisted that Doris was an honorary aunt and must be addressed as one. She did not want Doris to think that she was renouncing her. In an uncertain world – and I was coming to see that few people's worlds were less certain than Munca's – Doris was an ally worth clinging to. Munca must have owed her a good deal, not least the biggest interior decorating job of the decade. It was only decent to aunt her, even if at the same time it had to be made clear (for reasons that were still highly unclear to me) that she was not in fact an aunt by blood.

Which only made their relationship more, not less peculiar. There was Munca living a life full of lies, and there down the road was Doris living a life that was completely open and above board. During Munca's inland years, at Castlewood and later on at Holthanger, only two or three miles down the A30 on the Berkshire side of the Berks–Surrey border, Doris was living first at Charters and then, after she had sold Charters to the Tailor of Taste, at a house called Middleton on Titlarks Hill the other side of Sunningdale golf course, modest only in comparison to Charters and architecturally the opposite in every way, being built of plum-brown brick in the Stockbroker's Tudor style with tall clustered chimneys and leaded windows; thus being able in her widowhood to call the shots externally as well as internally. But in their day the two sisters had owned the two most original modern houses for miles around, in fact two of the most original in southern England.

Yet how peculiar it must have been, them living so close to each other. For both sisters, the village centre of Sunningdale was the port of call for groceries, hairdressing and poodle-clipping. Munca in her Rolls might bump into Doris in her Bentley any day of the week, not as violently perhaps as Archie bumped the Bentley into the window of the estate agents at the crossroads after he had overdone the cocktails one Sunday morning. How did they introduce each other at local cocktail parties, these sisters, one of whom but not the other was pretending to be unrelated?

To the outside observer, the only thing that was clear was that in this relationship, too, Munca was running true to form. An aunt who was not an aunt but really was an aunt simply joined the gallery of people in her life who were not who she said they were: a brother who was in fact a son, a blood-daughter who was adopted, an adopted daughter who was unadopted, a father who did not appear to exist at all. I could not help feeling that the gallery was not yet complete.

All the same, the terms of exchange had suddenly altered. As long as I was reliant on the forms that Munca herself had filled in, she held the upper hand. She could invent whatever she pleased, and the clerks and registrars would obediently enter her fabrications in their scrupulous copperplate.

Doris was not like that. She had not needed to be. Doris told the truth when she filled in a form. The essential facts of her life are recorded in all the usual places, as accurately as you could wish. When she gives you the name of her father and mother, they turn out to be real people whose family histories you can trace back as far as the census returns and the register of births, marriages and deaths go: 1841 for the full national census and 1837 for Births, Marriages and Deaths (although parish records go back centuries further, to 1538 in the case of baptisms). The full census returns are available to the public only up to 1911, to preserve the privacy of people who might still be alive. As for the records of divorce, these are usually available if you visit the National Archives at Kew, though only up to 1937, with a few later exceptions. As it happens, these are the time windows that fit our present needs. As at Brooklands, it is the most dramatic section of the track that is preserved for us to gawp at.

In all these sources, Doris is present and correct from the cradle to the grave. She was born in Sheffield on 15 December 1895, at 53 Thorndon Road. She was the daughter of John William Macduff of Sheffield, a scrap metal merchant. No mysterious Barings, whether bankers or bootleggers, no exotic antecedents in New York or the Philippines. Just Sheffield. And scrap metal.

Her father was born in Sheffield, in 1866. Her mother, Mary Crabb, was born in Sheffield too, in 1870. Her parents were married at All Saints Church, Sheffield, on 2 October 1893. Doris was Sheffield through and through. So, inescapably, was her sister Munca. For the next leg of the journey, therefore, we must travel north.

Before making that pilgrimage, I had to make one last trip to Charters. It seemed wrong to move on to the next stage in the quest without paying my respects to the place where Doris and Munca had had their heyday. It was vital to get inside that amazing palace of modernity, even if I had to pose as a potential buyer for one of those £3 million apartments.

As it turned out, getting inside could not have been simpler. The unsold apartments had only just come back on the market, and there was a superb brochure up on the internet from the new agents, Knight Frank, and a number to ring for Gill Lamprell, the Partner, Residential Development, at their Guildford office. Gill had such a sympathetic voice that I immediately confided my real reason for wanting to visit. She instantly saw the point of my quest without having to have it explained to her.

It was a weird experience, though, to drive down the A30 through the great forest past the turnings to Munca's old haunts. On an impulse, I turned off down Wick Lane to take a look at Castlewood. It proved impossible to catch even the sliver of a glimpse of that stately stucco villa. The high walls all along the road were broken only by even higher wooden gates it would have taken an armour-piercing shell to penetrate. Another high fence continued on around the Virginia Water side. The little gate in the old palings that led out to the woods had long gone. The brambles had obliterated the path. Only the narrow plank bridge over the ditch remained to remind me of the big woolly poodles bounding on past me and my uncle's mild voice calling them back.

The same huge wooden gates shut out any view of Doris's last retreat at Sunningdale, Middleton on Titlarks Hill. Only the titlarks had any chance of a viewing. All I could see were the Jacobean chimneys peeping over the walls. How the rich shrink from our gaze now, sheltering behind their portcullises like medieval barons. Never before, I think, have the super-rich been quite so keen to stay out of sight. Their conspicuous displays of wealth – the villas, the yachts, the balls – are mostly reserved for their fellow plutocrats. The desire for privacy has become the last lust, security the ultimate goal of existence, so hard to attain, harder still to hold on to. Even the old electrically operated iron grilles won't do any more; they are too indecently open to the prying gaze of the underprivileged.

The trees have grown up along Charters Road now and the house is invisible from the road. Its enormous gates would stop a tank, and when they open, they inch apart like the entrance to the lost world in a bad movie. Higher up the hill, there is a second pair of electric gates, as though to say, not so fast.

But there I am at last, walking up the steps into that amazing high hall with Gill and her colleague Emma from Knight Frank and Denzil from Security. 'You won't see much of your aunt's work left, I'm afraid,' Gill murmurs (she is a gentle and graceful person, less like the conventional idea of an estate agent than you could imagine). But we do. There are the white Corinthian pillars at the back of the hall, and the Georgian cornices and the rococo ironwork banisters on the stairs and along the gallery, which Gill says were rescued from an architectural scrapyard where they had finished up in the Vickers years. There are the full Queen Anne *boiseries* lining the walls of the drawing room, the gleaming chestnut panelling with its scrolls and pediments, just as Munca wanted them. There, holy of holies, utterly intact but not on view today because the apartment is one of the sold ones, is Doris's pink marble bathroom, every curve and pedestal of it shimmering a pale raspberry ripple just as it had in 1938.

The apartments have been fully furnished and decorated to give buyers an idea of what they would look like when lived in. Suddenly it comes to me that, for the first time since the house was built, it is done up just as George Adie and Frank himself would have wished. For the chairs and tables, the cutlery and the glasses, are all in the modern minimalist style, all sharp edges and shiny surfaces. The chairs are cup-shaped or L-shaped and upholstered in black and cream leather or bright primary-coloured fabrics. Nowhere a hint of the old brown furniture or the decorative language of the *ancien régime*. After 70 years of ups and downs, the house is decorated according to the original modernist dream. Here at long last has come the architect's revenge.

I ask, 'Who buys the apartments?' 'Mostly people with several other homes around the world,' Gill says. They jet into Heathrow, spend a few days at Charters, take in a show, play a couple of rounds at Sunningdale or watch a match at the Guards Polo Club and then jet out again. Restless people, the sort who came to Charters in the old days, the sort Frank felt at home with.

We encounter a problem with the security system when trying to get into the next apartment. Gill calls Denzil, and while we are waiting for him, she explains that Knight Frank have only become the agents for the property quite recently and are still finding their way about. The original developers went bust, she says, and the new owners wanted a fresh start.

Bust. So John Morris's resurrection of Charters has not gone as smoothly as I had imagined. In fact, that turns out to be an understatement. When I get home, I trawl the internet again and find that in the darkest days of the Great Crash of 2009 the Royal Bank of Scotland put Charters Developments into administration. The company had loans outstanding of £35 million and the bank had lost patience. John Morris was indignant and made scorching criticisms of the bank's failure to stand by what he called 'this world-class development'. But Charters was only one of dozens of ambitious schemes that RBS's open-handed property loans department had flung millions at. Bad property loans were in fact what set off the implosion that engulfed RBS in the worst collapse in British banking history. Charters was engulfed with the rest.

How fragile it all is, how brief anyone's hold on property, or money or life itself. Charters has been standing for over seventy years now. Frank lived in it for only eight years till he died, Doris stayed on another three years, the Tailor of Taste lived in the house for three years until he died, and that's pretty much it. I wonder if a child ever played there.

Before we finally kiss goodbye to that amazing white palace in its gentle rolling park, we must glance at one other souvenir of Doris at Charters, a fragile but I hope imperishable memento. At any rate it is still available on YouTube.

Type in 'The Windsors are Home', and you will find a clip from a British Pathé newsreel shown in May 1947. It lasts only 1 minute 28 seconds, but it confers on Doris an immortality of sorts. The clip opens with the usual excited Pathé music behind the Pathé cockerel and then we have a fine shot of the liner *Queen Elizabeth* coming into Southampton escorted by tugs. Then the Duke and Duchess come down the gangway and pose briefly for the photographers. There is a scant and bemused crowd on the quayside. A couple of hands, no more, are raised in an uncertain wave, and then the royal pair climb into the waiting Rolls-Royce.

The commentator tells us that this is not quite their first visit to Britain since the Abdication. They came on another liner, the *Canterbury*, the preceding October to stay with Lord Dudley at Sunningdale and the Duchess had her jewels stolen. This time, the voice-over assures us, extra security precautions are to be taken. And this time they are staying with 'millionaire widow Mrs Frank Parkinson at Charters, near Sunninghill', and there in the second sequence we see the Duke and Duchess coming down the steps of the vast Third Reich façade to meet the photographers again, with Doris following behind rather clumsily as though she has lost a shoe. Unlike the Windsors she has put on weight, and even more unlike the Windsors, who don't have a hair out of place between them, her hair is blowing about a bit in the wind. They are staying in Doris's house for a week of their three-week stay, if not longer.

The Windsors at Charters, May 1947

It seems appropriate that the only great mansion the exiled couple can find to house them should belong to someone who came from nowhere and who is the widow of the man who built the house from scratch. The friendship between Frank and the Duke seems so revealing of both men, perhaps of Wallis and Doris too. They all share an enthusiasm for what Wallis calls 'pep', an impatient get-up-and-go attitude, a dislike of the old-fashioned and the stuffy and snobbish, at least when it doesn't suit them. Their love of golf is part of being modern. It goes with gin and bridge and Bugattis.

I cannot resist recalling here the famous anecdote of James Braid and the rice pudding, because I am sure that the Parkinsons must have revelled in it at the time.

Told in various versions, the essentials of the story are that the Prince of Wales, as he then was, took James Braid, the leading golf professional of his day, to play a round at the Berkshire Golf Club at Ascot. After the round, the Prince invited his guest in for lunch, only to be told by the Club Secretary that professionals were not allowed in the dining room. At which the Prince flounced out and took Braid off to have lunch at the neighbouring club of Swinley Forest, where they had, among other things, rice pudding, a dish that has remained on the menu at Swinley ever since in honour of the Prince's patronage. The Berkshire never became the Royal Berkshire, or according to another, less plausible version, it was stripped of its royal prefix. Some raconteurs say it wasn't Braid at all but another pro, perhaps the Berkshire's own pro, and that the Prince took him off to lunch at Fort Belvedere, not Swinley. But the essential point of the story is untouched by these variations. It's a story that reminds me of that other pre-war tale – of Bev Lyon taking his fellow amateurs out onto the field together with the pros. Both tales come from a past of now unimaginable class boundaries: Bev and the Duke of Windsor, and Frank too, alike in their raffish dash and their impatience with worn-out conventions.

Seldom have the Windsors seemed more detached and out of it than in this little piece of film, yet seldom more modern.

Watching it, I think of the last line of Betjeman's poem on the death of George V: 'and a young man lands hatless from the air'. Hatless still but not so young now. The Duke is 52 and looks more worn down than that. The only confident thing about him is the Windsor knot in his tie. The Duchess, the voice-over tells us, is wearing a grey two-piece costume with fox fur and blue accessories and her tiny back-of-the-head hat is held in place by a silk turban scarf. In a cubbyhole at the new Charters, there is a photo of the two of them standing on the terrace with her in this outfit. She looks fine.

The Duke is asked whether he is thinking of settling down in Britain. He replies with a tact that he could have used at an earlier stage in his career that 'it's a possibility', which of course it isn't, but adds that 'as for everyone it's a question of finding a home' – or no, I think that it's the commentator saying the last bit, which is perhaps not so tactful in the middle of the great post-war housing shortage. The audience might think that the vast acreage of Charters could shelter quite a few homeless families instead of just Doris.

And now it's The End, and Doris has them on her hands for seven days. From what little one can see of her, she looks decidedly apprehensive. Perhaps she is dreading it but felt she couldn't get out of it. But I do like to imagine the Duchess sitting down in the morning-room and looking over at the grisaille of the young women with the naked shoulders and saying in a bored Baltimore drawl, 'who are those extraordinary fat girls?'

Charters was to hit the headlines one more time. At about 10.30 on the morning of Thursday, 14 August 2014, five unmarked police cars swept up that serpentine drive for a raid on the penthouse apartment belonging to Sir Cliff Richard. It was a joint raid by South Yorkshire and Thames Valley Police because they were investigating claims of sexual abuse by Sir

Cliff at a Billy Graham rally in Sheffield back in 1985. The BBC had been tipped off; it dispatched a helicopter to hover over the grounds and had a camera crew at the gates before the police had even arrived. No evidence was found then or later, Sir Cliff received substantial damages, and both the police and the BBC were fiercely criticized for their appalling witch hunt. Cliff later put his Sunningdale hideaway on the market, and who can blame him? Frank and Doris's concrete palace had been desecrated, and so, too, had Munca's Regency interiors.

5

Brightside

Sheffield could mean a lot of things. It could mean Ranmoor and Endcliffe, where the Master Cutlers built their mansions in the high Italian style. Or it could mean the pleasant garden suburbs of Broomhall and Nether Edge, where the doctors and shopkeepers enjoyed the fresh air and wooded slopes only a tram ride from the city centre. Or it could mean the old bit around the soaring fifteenth-century parish church (later the C of E cathedral), the area between Paradise Square and Surrey Street where the Quaker scissorsmiths like the Broadbents had put up fine brick houses at the end of the eighteenth century.

Or it could mean Brightside.

Brightside does not sound so bad. You picture the sun glancing off a gentle ridge sloping down to the River Don. But then Sheffield doesn't sound so bad either, not as bad anyway as Manchester and Liverpool with their grime and rain, not as bad as the filthy rookeries of the East End of London. When you think of Sheffield, you think of gleaming blades and stainless steel, of the silver-plate fruit dish winking on the stockbroker's table. You imagine, unconsciously perhaps, a great industrial city that was somehow cleaner than the others. But it wasn't. It was, if anything, worse.

Worse even than Wigan. In *The Road to Wigan Pier*, George Orwell wrote:

> But even Wigan is beautiful compared with Sheffield. Sheffield, I suppose, could justly claim to be the ugliest town in the Old World: its inhabitants, who want it to be pre-eminent in everything, very likely do make that claim for it. It has a population of half a million and it contains fewer decent buildings than the average East Anglian village of five hundred. And the stench! If at rare moments you stop smelling sulphur it is because you have begun smelling gas. Even the shallow river that runs through the town is usually bright yellow with some chemical or other. Once I halted in the street and counted the factory chimneys I could see; there were thirty-three of them, but there would have been more if the air had not been obscured by smoke.

One scene especially lingered in Orwell's mind:

> A frightful patch of waste ground (somehow, up there, a patch of waste ground attains a squalor that would be impossible even in London) trampled bare of grass and littered with newspapers and old saucepans. To the right an isolated row of gaunt four-roomed houses, dark red, blackened by smoke. To the left an interminable vista of factory chimneys, chimney beyond chimney, fading away into a dim blackish haze. Behind me a railway embankment made of the slag from furnaces.

He was looking at Brightside.

Orwell went to Sheffield in the mid-1930s. But the industrial north of the city was just as ghastly at the end of the nineteenth century. J. S. Fletcher was looking at Brightside too when he wrote in 1899, when Doris was 4 years old, in his rather misleadingly entitled *Picturesque History of Yorkshire*:

> Under smoke and rain, Sheffield is suggestive of nothing so much as of the popular conception of the infernal regions. From the chimneys, great volumes of smoke pour their listless way towards a forbidding sky; out of the furnaces shoot forth great tongues of flame which relieve the sombreness of the scene and illuminate it at the same time; in the streets there is a substratum of dust and mud; in the atmosphere a choking something that appears to take a firm grip of one's throat. The aspect of the northern fringe of Sheffield on such a day is terrifying, the black heaps of refuse, the rows of cheerless-looking houses, the thousand and one signs of grinding industrial life, the inky waters of river and canal, the general darkness and dirt of the whole scene serves but to create feelings of repugnance and even horror.

This was where Doris was born and, I am presuming, Munca too.

It is an old town, Sheffield, and its industry is old too. You have to revise your ideas about the Industrial Revolution only starting at the end of the eighteenth century and being driven by new men from the middle classes and bright lads watching kettles boil. Sheffield had been famous for its blades since the Middle Ages. Chaucer in *The Reeve's Tale* tells us that the Reeve went fully armed:

> There was no man for peril durst him touch,
> A Sheffield thwitel bore he in his hose.

(A thwitel was a short knife, what we would call a dagger.)

The area had everything: fast-flowing streams from the Pennines to turn the mill wheels, plentiful deposits of coal and iron ore, millstone grit for grindstones and acres of woodland for charcoal to smelt the iron. Later on, they switched effortlessly to coking coal, of which the local pits had plenty too. It was the great landowners of the region who took the initiative in squeezing every penny out of its natural wealth. The aristocratic exploitation of mineral resources is one of the under-sung stories of British history. We are so attuned by Marx and his followers to thinking of the Industrial Revolution as driven by the new class, the bourgeois capitalists, that we do not notice the ruthless part played by the old feudal barons. It is hard to think of a really wealthy noble family that did not owe a great part of its fortune to the stuff that lay beneath their rolling moors and pastures: the Cavendishes to the copper mines of Derbyshire, the Godolphins and Osbornes to the tin and copper mines of Cornwall, the Crichton-Stuarts, Marquesses of Bute, to the coal mines of South Wales, the Londonderrys and the Lambtons to the coal mines of Durham. You can still see the disused mineworkings in the park of Lambton Castle. Wentworth Woodhouse, the mega-palace of the Fitzwilliams, has been collapsing for decades from the coal workings beneath its interminable façade.

Similarly, the Dukes of Norfolk, hereditary Earl Marshals of England, derived much of their splendour not from their antique lineage but from the subterranean deposits they inherited by marrying well. You can see in Sheffield Cathedral the lovely alabaster tomb of George Talbot, sixth Earl of Shrewsbury. He reposes in knight's armour on a tasselled cushion with his virtues inscribed on the large panel above his head. You might imagine that he is resting after some chivalric tourney. In reality, he was more likely to be having a siesta after grinding the faces of the poor and of anyone else who got in his way. Shrewsbury was the most restless and grasping entrepreneur of the Elizabethan age. He brought in Frenchmen from the Sussex Weald (then the centre of the iron industry) to build charcoal blast furnaces and forges at Attercliffe on the north-eastern edge of the city. He ruthlessly exploited the coal reserves under his Sheffield Park estate, so much so that the manor house had ultimately to be abandoned because of the mineworkings. He made strenuous efforts to monopolize the export of lead from Derbyshire. His days were spent not so much in hunting and hawking as in vicious litigation to raise his tenants' rents or to secure exclusive rights on the local wharves.

George Talbot, sixth Earl of Shrewsbury, Sheffield Cathedral

If posterity remembers Shrewsbury at all, though, it is because for 15 years he was the roving jailer of Mary, Queen of Scots. He had been selected for this task by Queen Elizabeth because only someone of his vast wealth could accommodate Mary and her extravagant entourage, because he was a sound Protestant and because his numerous castles and manors all lay in the North Midlands, well away from the intrigues of the court in London. Mary spent much of her stretch under Shrewsbury's eye at Sheffield Castle and the adjacent Sheffield Manor. Oddly enough, for such a skinflint he was rather nice to her when he wasn't moaning about the cost ('the Queen of Scots coming to my charge will soone make me greyhaired'), much nicer than he was to his horrible second wife, the legendary Bess of Hardwick, with whom he had a running dogfight until they finally separated.

Why have we mostly forgotten Mary's years in Sheffield? After all, it makes a piquant picture; the Queen languishing up above, playing billiards and sitting for her portrait by Nicholas Hilliard, while in their tunnels down below the naked wretches are literally undermining the manor. The answer, I think, is that the Manor had to be abandoned because of the subsidence, and the castle overlooking the River Don was demolished after the Civil War as a punishment for Sheffield having been a Parliamentarian redoubt. Later, the town's market was built over the ruins. So there was nowhere left to make a pilgrimage to.

Shrewsbury's estates in Yorkshire and Derbyshire passed to his granddaughter Alathea, the wife of Thomas Howard, Earl of Arundel and Surrey. Alathea's grandson was created, or re-created, Duke of Norfolk, the title that earlier Howards had forfeited on their way to the scaffold. For three centuries, the Talbots and the Howards were the lords of Sheffield. The street names in the old city are all Arundel or Surrey, Howard or Norfolk. As late as 1900, it is reckoned that half the Duke of Norfolk's income of £100,000 a year came from Sheffield. The wealth that funded those enormous Howard houses all over the country – Worksop Manor in Nottinghamshire, Carlton Towers in Yorkshire, Norfolk House in St James's Square, London, and above all that extraordinary half-medieval, half-Victorian pile, Arundel Castle, Sussex's answer to Carcassonne – came ultimately, as Orwell would have put it, from those poor devils in aprons grinding and scraping and coughing their lungs out up in Sheffield.

The year that Doris was born, the fifteenth Duke had just become the last Mayor of Sheffield, and he then became the first Lord Mayor when the town became a city. During the great coal strike of 1912, His Grace was pleased to 'give limited encouragement' to desperate outcroppers to scavenge for coal on his land, provided the coal was distributed to the poor at sixpence a bag. No wonder that Munca was so keen that Georgie should shine at the Arundel Ball. As in Shakespeare's Scottish play, the Macduffs deserved their revenge.

Already by the middle years of the nineteenth century, the human cost was terrible. In *The Condition of the Working Class in England*, the young Friedrich Engels, only 24 years old, records that:

by far the most unwholesome work is the grinding of knife-blades and forks, which, especially when done with a dry stone, entails certain early death. The unwholesomeness of this work lies in part in the bent posture, in which chest and stomach are cramped; but especially in the quantity of sharp-edged metal dust particles freed in the cutting, which fill the atmosphere, and are necessarily inhaled. The dry grinders' average life is hardly thirty-five years, the wet grinders' rarely exceeds forty-five.

Engels records too the despairing report of Dr Knight of Sheffield:

> Spitting blood, inability to lie down, night sweat, colliquative diarrhoea, unusual loss of flesh, and all the usual symptoms of consumption of the lungs finally carry them off, after they have lingered months, or even years, unfit to support themselves or those dependent upon them. I must add that all attempts which have hitherto been made to prevent grinders' asthma, or to cure it, have wholly failed.

Engels tells us that 'Dr Knight has often told grinders who came to him with the first symptoms of asthma that a return to grinding means certain death, but with no avail. He who is once a grinder falls into despair, as though he had sold himself to the devil.'

View of Sheffield suburbs circa 1912

All this was before Brightside came into its prime. In Engels' day, that strip of land to the north of the sharp bend in the River Don had barely been developed at all. Only a few cottages straggled along the high roads out to Barnsley, Wakefield and Leeds. The grinding of knives and forks and files and rasps and saws, the forging of anvils and hammers, took places in premises scattered all around the city and the nearby hill villages. The forges and workshops were often one-man bands, operated by the fiercely independent 'little meesters'. The age of mass production did not take off until the mid-1840s. In the second half of the century, the population of Sheffield's eastern and northern districts rose dramatically, especially around the new mega steel works, the greatest in the world. The city centre south of the river was full up, and where better than Brightside to build the new factories on a scale to make the rest of the planet gawp in wonder? There were the railways now coming in along the riverside to bring up the coal and iron ore and take away the heavy product, the rails and strip steel and boilers; the same purposes were served by the new canal dug down to Tinsley where the Don became navigable.

Up they rose, some of them as big as a small town and proudly named after the more spectacular volcanoes and the giants of classical legend: Charles Cammell's Cyclops Works, Spear and Jackson's Aetna Works, the Hecla Works (Hecla is a volcano in Iceland known locally as 'the gateway to hell' – the great Victorian steelmakers positively relished the infernal reverberations of their trade), John Brown's Atlas Works, the Vickers River Don Works, which had the largest crucible capacity in the world and provided much of the armour-plating for the shells and tanks of the First World War. If ever that overused phrase 'the cutting edge' fitted, it fitted Sheffield then. For it was here that steel was first hardened with tungsten and manganese, here that Robert

Hadfield invented stainless steel, and Bessemer and Siemens first tried out their new techniques.

Right close up against the countless chimneys belching noxious fumes into the broody Pennine sky (which soon hurled them back down again in sooty rain), then stretching on up the steep hills behind, were the dwellings for the workers, thousands of them, row upon identical row, built back to back according to the regulations. The population of Brightside rose from 12,042 in 1851 to 73,088 in 1901.

Among the 60,000 new arrivals are John Willie Macduff and his family. John Willie was not born in Sheffield, although he is to spend all but three years of his life there. His parents, Thomas and Matilda, move to 131 Main Road, Attercliffe-cum-Darnall, to the east of Brightside proper, in 1869, the year after John Willie's younger sister Susannah was born. In all, they are to have nine children, six daughters and three sons. Thomas describes himself as an 'iron dealer'. And the three boys follow him into the trade: John Willie starts at the age of 15 as an iron merchant's clerk; Joseph, four years younger, becomes a turner engineer, and George, six years younger, becomes a mechanical draughtsman. George is the only Macduff to rise noticeably. By 1911, he is manager of a steel rolling mill, though he still lives a hundred yards from his by then widowed mother in Page Hall Road. As for the girls, Eleanor becomes a milliner, so does her younger sister Alice. Lillie or Lily becomes a domestic servant, then the default occupation for millions of unmarried girls.

The Macduffs resemble thousands of other families in Brightside in two respects: they have a great number of children, and they come from somewhere else. That is how urban populations explode. Thomas and Matilda both come from the other great iron and steel region of England, the Black Country: Thomas from West Bromwich, Matilda Tingle from nearby Tipton. Why on earth would you want to move from one infernal region to another, even more notoriously hellish one? Quite simply, because the wages in Brightside were better, much better. Again, like thousands of other new arrivals in Sheffield, the Macduffs are fleeing poverty. The word 'grinding' is all too appropriate.

The entry in the 1841 census tells its own miserable story. Thomas Macduff, then aged five, is living with his family in the West Bromwich Union, Lambeth's End. That is, the entire family is living in the workhouse: Joseph and Eleanor Macduff, their son Thomas and his three brothers and two sisters. Joseph is a coal miner. So are his two elder sons, William, aged twelve, and Joseph junior, aged ten. They are the children who push the trolleys along the pit floor and pick up the spillings. The law has not yet forbidden child labour, and the employers are still claiming that the lads enjoy the comradely atmosphere down below. Even so, the three wages between them are not enough to support a family in independence. Thomas's father dies at the age of 35, and Thomas becomes a butcher's boy living over the shop with the butcher's family, and when he gets married to Matilda and they have their first children, they move to Sheffield and he becomes an iron merchant, because iron is where the money is.

Like other Brightside families, the Macduffs move house quite a bit, either because the family is expanding or contracting or because the landlord has turned sour. But they do not move out of Brightside. Of the dozen addresses I can trace for various branches of the family, not one is more than ten minutes' walk from 39 Catherine Street, where Matilda lives most of the years she is widowed, before she makes her final move to Page Hall

Road. When they marry, they marry people like them, local boys and girls whose parents have come from somewhere else and who all their days have breathed the smoke from Atlas and Cyclops and Hecla and Aetna, because the chimneys are at the end of the street or over the back wall.

At the age of 25, John Willie is courting Mary Crabb, who is three or four years younger. Mary has been away in Manchester, working as housemaid in the household of an East India merchant, Sydney Hudson. The Hudsons live in the suburb of Chorlton-upon-Medlock and they live in some style. They employ a governess and two nursemaids for their three children, three more maids (Mary being one of them), a cook, a kitchen maid and a footman – nine indoor servants. Quite a Downstairs. How strange it must be for someone who has never been out of Brightside and has known nothing but back-to-back houses all her life. How strange, and how seductive. It must be a comedown when she goes back to Sheffield. But it is a miserable homecoming for another, unspeakably worse reason.

Mary's parents, Samuel Crabb and Mahala Vail, both come from somewhere else too. They were brought up in Ely, where Samuel learnt to be a tailor. When he came to Sheffield, he tried being a grocer for a while but then went back to being a tailor again. Presumably the grocery business had not worked out. Certainly their addresses in the 1870s, 80s and 90s suggest a poverty even more wretched than the Macduffs: they lived first in a hovel at the back of 14 Savile Street between the foul waters of the river and the Norfolk Sheet Steel Works, with the Atlas and the other infernal works further along the road. Then they moved a few yards around the corner to successive addresses in Greystock Street, No. 57 and No. 60, which cannot have been much of an improvement. Walking from Catherine Street to call on Mary, John Willie would have followed one of the nastiest lovers' lanes anywhere in the world.

The rest of the Vails came north with Mahala. Her father Joseph had been a builders' labourer in Ely. He became a brickie in Sheffield too, and he had the usual quiverful of children: four girls and two boys. His wife Thirza died of peritonitis in 1872 (what lovely Old Testament names the Vail women had), and the three youngest children went to live with their sister Mahala in 57 Greystock Street. So she now had five to look after, her own two daughters plus her brothers Joseph junior, who was a navvy on the roads, and Robert, who was a labourer in the steel works, and her youngest surviving sister Betsey-Ann, who was still only eleven but was soon out earning her living as a domestic servant. Labourer, servant, labourer, servant: none of them except the upwardly mobile George Macduff escaped.

Well, Joseph Vail the younger did. When he was 30, he drowned himself in the new canal, just behind the Bacon Lane Bridge, no more than 400 yards from his home in Greystock Street. There was a full report of his death in the *Sheffield Daily Telegraph* for 11 October 1886, under the headline STRANGE SUICIDE AT ATTERCLIFFE, and then another report the next day from the inquest, under the headline THE STRANGE SUICIDE AT ATTERCLIFFE, the definite article now underlining the 'somewhat peculiar circumstances' of the case. Joseph's father, Joe senior, identified the body and testified that during the past week, his son had been drinking hard and that when he came to borrow a shilling on Thursday he was 'very wild in his manner'. Several weeks earlier he had been accidentally struck on the head while at work and from then 'had raved very much' when under the influence of drink. He had threatened to drown himself about eighteen months before.

The Bacon Lane bridge

James Holmshaw, a hammer man in the steel works, said that he had been acquainted with the deceased for four or five years and saw him alive last on Friday night about twenty minutes past ten o'clock in Bacon Lane, near the Canal Bridge. The deceased was not sober and on the witness wishing him 'Good Night' and asking him where he was going, he replied, 'I am going to drown my bloody self' (the *Telegraph* naturally puts a dash for 'bloody', so it could have been 'fucking', I suppose). Holmshaw did not believe this and proceeded to the Woodbourne Hotel, about 100 yards further on. He then mentioned the circumstance to the landlord's daughter, who replied that Vail had told her the same thing. The witness immediately decided to go and see what was the matter with him (Vail) and went to the canal bridge. Seeing no one, he whistled and called out Vail's name, on which the deceased replied, 'I'm here' and immediately jumped in the water. He then shouted to the witness to fetch him out, but Holmshaw replied, 'Joe, I can't; I have a wife and six children and I can't swim.' He then ran to the hotel for assistance but the people would not believe him, so he went to the police station for drags to get the body out. When he got back, however, the body was lying on the bridge. It had been retrieved by another passer-by with a boat-hook.

The Woodbourne Hotel, where Joe Vail had his last drink

After evidence had been given by the daughter of the landlord of the Woodbourne Hotel as to the deceased telling her he would drown himself, the jury returned a verdict of 'committed suicide during a state of temporary insanity'. There is something terrible about the slow drunken tempo of the night's events, as though nobody was much bothered about poor Joe. The verdict was the standard one in such cases, allowing the deceased to be buried in the churchyard. Only an insane person, after all, would wish to abbreviate his life in Brightside.

Soon, the sibling lodgers were all gone. Joe was dead, Robert was married and living in Salford, and Betsey-Ann had gone off to live with another of her married sisters, Eliza, who lived in Salford too, to be joined there by Robert's three children, because his wife Sarah had just died of a thrombosis at the age of 27. How sad and short the lives of the Vail women, and how sad too the early lives of their children, cooped up in the house of a sister or an aunt that was wretchedly overcrowded even before they came.

Samuel Crabb now had the little house in Greystock Street to himself and his wife and their two daughters. And then, quite suddenly, he didn't have Mahala any more. She was 45 and she died 'from injuries sustained by jumping from a cart she was driving'. That is all the death certificate tells us. Not how most grandmothers leave us. It's the sort of adventurous conduct that Munca would have approved of. What a pity she couldn't tell us the story. We would surely have asked, 'Why was your granny driving a cart? Why did she jump? Where did she die? Was there blood on the road?' – cobbles, I suppose, at that date.

The true story of her death. The inquest was held at Sheffield General Infirmary in Shalesmoor just across the river, where she died. What had happened was that Mahala was mounting a cart laden with vegetables in order to go to market. At this point her husband was still a greengrocer and had not gone back to tailoring. The road, which was Sutherland Street, just around the corner from Thorndon Road, was very wet at the time, and the pony slipped down and rolled over. Mahala jumped from the cart to save herself and fell on the causeway. The *Sheffield Daily Telegraph* as usual had all the details: 'Her foot got wedged in between one of the wheels and the kerbstone and was very much crushed. The ankle was dislocated, and a piece of bone protruded through the skin. She was removed to the Infirmary where she was detained. Blood poisoning and mortification set in, and she died as stated.' Is this why Samuel goes back to tailoring, because he no longer has Mahala to drive the cart, or because he no longer has the heart? These days, I suppose, antibiotics would have saved her.

At all events, this is when the little household in Greystock Street breaks up for good. Within six months of Mahala's bizarre death Charlotte gets married and goes to live around the corner at 102 Lyons Street, and Samuel goes to live with them. Another six months and Mary marries John Willie. Did she only meet him after she had come back from the high life? Or had they been childhood sweethearts and had some kind of understanding before she went away? No, it seems more likely that she came back because Mahala had been killed, and she got married because that was the natural next stage in her life and Brightside was where her real life was.

They were married on 2 October 1893 in the magnificent All Saints Church on Ellesmere Road. Its 190-foot spire soared above the dismal rows of back-to-backs. The church was built at the expense of Sir John Brown, who began in the old file and cutlery trades but made his serious fortune out of the steel and rolling stock he turned out at the Atlas works a few hundred yards away beyond the low houses of his workers, his chimneys competing on the skyline with his glorious spire. Like his brothers, John Willie, or Johnnie as he appears in the school register, attended the big church school behind All Saints. The school took in 200 pupils from ironworks families every year and seven years later spewed them out again into the ironworks if they were boys or into domestic service or silver burnishing or the retail trades if they were girls.

All Saints, Ellesmere Road, where Mary and John Willie were married

The one thing the workers never went short of was churches. Everywhere in Sheffield the welfare of every denomination was catered for. The Duke of Norfolk built Catholic churches and chapels. The middle classes built nonconformist chapels and temples of every variety. In the worst parts of Brightside, you could find a great hulk of a Methodist or Congregationalist place of worship on every street corner.

The groom's brother and sister Joseph and Susanna are there as witnesses. They could have walked the half-mile from 39 Catherine Street with their mother Matilda and their sisters Sarah, Alice, Lillie and their youngest brother George, the one who becomes a manager. Matilda has all seven of them living with her at Catherine Street, which may be a squeeze, but at least the boys are all bringing in good money. Mary is given away by her widowed father with her now married sister in attendance.

Nothing could be more intimate, more respectable than this wedding day. It is a day of which the newlyweds will be daily reminded, because they go to live at 53 Thorndon Road, no more than 250 yards from the back of the church. From their back window they can see the spire. From their front window, they can see the chimneys of the Atlas works 200 yards away, and the Harleston Iron Works, which are closer still, the places where John Willie collects his scrap and carts it off to his yard. The tops of the belching chimneys must be more or less on the same level as their windows. Nobody was ever more securely or more unhealthily lodged between God and Mammon than Mr and Mrs J. W. Macduff.

Thorndon Road, where Munca was born

It is at 53 Thorndon Road that Doris first sees the smoky light of Brightside two years later on 15 December 1895. A home birth, like virtually every birth then and not just among the working classes either. The idea that the increased dangers of a first child require a delivery in hospital had not yet taken root. For the poor the expense would have been unthinkable anyway.

I had assumed that Doris was the younger of the two sisters. For one thing, the only fact about Buster's birth that we do seem to have established is that he was born in 1912 and probably in January. That is what he said when he got married to Lyn's mother; that is what the crazy motor sport bloggers seem to agree on. So if Munca was born a year after Doris, she would have been only 15 when she gave birth. Not impossible but it seemed more likely that she was 17 and so born a year earlier than her sister, some time in 1894.

Either way, it should not be too difficult to establish the truth. But it is. There is no sign of an Elizabeth Macduff born anywhere in Sheffield in the entire decade. Nor a Patricia Macduff, or a Patricia Elizabeth Macduff, or an Eliza, or a Liz, or a Betty. There is a Nellie Elizabeth Macduff, but she is born in April 1893 and in south London, Norwood to be exact, and her parents are called Gilbert and Alice. No good at all.

It seems hardly credible that even as a newborn baby Munca manages to cover her tracks so effortlessly. I try every permutation of her name that I can think of, but nothing comes up.

Then I realize that Buster's birth must have been recorded under the name of Macduff if he was born illegitimate. So I tap Archie Alistair Macduff, 1912, Yorkshire, into the births section of the BMD site. The index says that there was an

Archie Alfred Macduff born in Leeds in January 1912, which sounds promising. No Alistair, no Sheffield, but at least we have the Archie and the right date. But his mother doesn't fit at all. She is down as 'Eileen Constance Sylvia, now the wife of Harold Cecil Drury Ridge', who is also named as the father of the child. There is something peculiar about this entry, because the index has a handwritten addendum directing me to the index for March 1916, and when I order that up I get the same certificate as the one for 1912, except with a different date for the registration. The earlier certificate has been replaced, it says, 'on the authority of the Registrar-General', which I don't quite understand, except that Eileen Constance Sylvia, whoever she may be, was not married to Harold Cecil Drury Ridge when she had the baby and now she is. But this is all of academic interest because these are not the people we are looking for.

Once again, for what must be the third or fourth time, I abandon the chase, baffled and not a little annoyed by my failure to clear it all up. Life must have more to offer, I console myself, than poring over census records and combing the General Register of Births, Marriages and Deaths. I turn to more wholesome pursuits, such as lawn tennis. Unfortunately, late in this soggy summer the courts on Highbury Fields are more than usually slippery. Lumbering to retrieve a lob, I take a spectacular fall and I twist both my knee and my ankle with a noise that sounds like the rasp of a ship's hawser. In the irksome convalescence that follows, my thoughts turn to Munca as easily as an unreformed junkie reaches for the white powder.

She must be there somewhere. Nobody slips into this world unrecorded, not in England anyway. Mary and John Willie have behaved with such decorum so far. It seems grossly improbable that they would have failed to register the birth of one of their children, even if they were not married at that time, which I doubt. But there is absolutely no sign of Munca. More bizarre still, when I look forward to the 1901 census, I can find no trace of any of them, no John Willie, no Mary, no girls. Did they perhaps emigrate to the Philippines after all? Were there unsuspected opportunities in the scrap metal line out there, after the Spanish-American War of 1898 – perhaps half-sunk ships waiting to be broken up in Manila Bay? Were Munca's memories of riding her horse into the sitting-room based on something that had really happened to her?

Is there any potential lead that I have not already followed up, often several times over? The only possibility that occurs to me – and it really isn't much of one – is that Archie Alfred Macduff, son of Eileen Constance Sylvia, may be Buster after all. At least that outside chance needs to be properly ruled out, even if it doesn't sound very plausible. I start by looking up Eileen Constance Sylvia Macduff to see if I can find any trace of her birth certificate. Not the least joy there. There have been only three persons called Eileen Macduff born in England in the past 250 years, and all of them were born after 1940. So apart from the fact that I do not think she is the person I am looking for, she doesn't appear to have been born at all.

There is one last possibility, worth pursuing only in the interests of an insane pedantry – I am becoming as deranged as the historians of motor sport. I could order up the marriage certificate of Eileen and Harold, so that I can officially shoo them off the stage.

A week later, as regular and reliable as ever, the certificate arrives from the GRO. E. C. S. Macduff and H. C. D. Ridge were married on 12 December 1913, at Leeds Register Office.

He is described as a chartered accountant, and they are already living together at 42 Claypit Lane, Leeds, which is not surprising since they have had a baby together 18 months earlier. And then, at first I cannot believe it, perhaps groggy with fatigue I have dreamed the words into copperplate on that pale green form, but no, there it really is. In the column for bride's father it says 'John William Macduff'. And in the space for rank or profession of father, it says 'Iron and Steel Merchant'.

Eileen Constance Sylvia Macduff is Munca. Not Patricia Elizabeth, or Elizabeth, or Patricia, or Liz or Betty, but Eileen. How dumb and slow and stuck-witted I have been. Munca had reinvented every other detail about herself. Why should she not have reinvented her Christian names too? How pathetically bourgeois to imagine that you always cling to the first names you were born with, the names you were called as a child, because you have an ineradicable fondness for them.

She says on the form that she is 21, which would make her born in 1892, too old to be the legitimate child of John Willie and Mary, which I am convinced she must be. What seems more likely is that for the first, perhaps the only time in her life she is pretending to be older than she really is, because in those days you cannot get married without your parents' permission until you are 21. So my guess still is that she was born a year before Doris, in 1894.

I start on the final lap and try the bare surname and date in the births section, 'Macduff 1894' – first names have tantalized and frustrated me too long – and here at last comes the jackpot. The GRO Index says there was an Ellen Constance Macduff born in Sheffield in the third quarter of 1894. Ellen, Eileen – in this morass of confused and obscured identities, who's noticing the difference? Not, for once, the indefatigable indexers of the GRO. Because when I order Ellen's birth certificate, it turns out to be in the name of Ileen Constance. Ileen has been misread as Ellen and then later altered by Munca herself to the more usual spelling of Eileen. And there finally we are.

She was born on 19 June 1894 and, like Doris, at 53 Thorndon Road. So she was still 16 when she conceived Buster and 17 when she gave birth to him. She was 42 when she married my uncle, claiming to be 30. By the time she claimed to have given birth to Georgie, she was 47. And she had to lie about her age on her marriage certificate because her mother had not yet forgiven her and refused to approve her getting married.

Slightly to my surprise, I feel no sense of triumph at having tracked her down. I feel more, what can I call it, a sort of odd comradeship, like when you finally come upon the place where your best friend has hidden in a game of hide-and-seek.

Now that Ellen/Ileen/Eileen has finally been officially born, she unleashes a further blast of reality. Armed with her real name, I try the 1901 census again, and there they are, the little family of four: Mary, John Willie, Ileen and Doris. They haven't emigrated to New York or Manila or anywhere else. They have simply moved around the corner to 111 Grimesthorpe Road, not to be confused with the Grimethorpe Colliery and its famous brass band. They have travelled a distance of perhaps 200 yards, 300 at most. They are still in Sheffield, still in Brightside, still in that same small patch where they have always lived. And I feel unaccountably happy.

For the time being, their life doesn't seem so bad, certainly not by comparison with how John Willie's father started life, in the workhouse at West Brom. The Macduffs have their own house, they don't need to take in lodgers, and Sheffield, grimy and polluted as ever, is still the boom town of the age. Eileen and Doris have their Aunt Charlotte's children around the corner in Lyons Street to play with, only a year younger, Elsie and Albert Edward. They have grandfather Samuel Crabb in Lyons Street too and grandmother Matilda Macduff over in Catherine Street and a flock of other uncles, aunts and cousins within scooting distance.

Like many other children at that date, Albert Edward is named after the pleasure-loving Prince of Wales, who is about to become King Edward VII. He and Alexandra had paid one of their several visits to Sheffield in 1897, the year of Victoria's Diamond Jubilee and the year that Albert Edward junior was born. For royal visits to the city, they erected arches and turrets of painted canvas at the bridge over the Don with bunting strung from the battlements, and the royal party trotted under them on their way out of the city centre to receive an ecstatic welcome in Brightside. This was the heyday of working-class patriotism. There were street parties to celebrate jubilees and coronations and royal weddings and, after 1902, for Empire Day too. After all, Sheffield was the forge and furnace of the Empire. The steel that subdued the natives by shell and bayonet was also the steel that went into the rails and locomotives that enabled a handful of British soldiers and civil servants to administer a far-flung empire.

But it was the churches like All Saints that were the singing heart of industrial Sheffield. Every Whit Monday, thousands from every church and chapel paraded in their best behind the banners of their Sunday schools and walked, often quite long distances, across the city to meet other congregations in Norfolk Park and sing hymns and listen to sermons. Picturesque as these Whit Walks and Whit Sings may seem to us, the sermons were probably much too long for one of Munca's impatient temper.

I wondered what if anything in the way of secondary education Munca had managed to scrape in the wastes of Brightside. It seemed both laborious, and a little vindictive too, to plough through the records of every school in the city of Sheffield to track her down. It was more in a general unfocused sweep that I tapped in 'Eileen Macduff Sheffield' on the British Newspaper Archive. To my surprise, and pleasure too, I came up with a cutting from the *Sheffield Independent* for 23 July 1908 that gave a list of the candidates from the Sisters of Mercy Convent School of Music, Burngreave, who had scored in that term's piano tests. There it was, among the lower passes: 'Eileen Macduff'. I felt like cheering. For once Munca had told the truth about something. She *had* been educated by nuns, and so had had a more intense experience of religious education than the C of E would have inflicted on her. The Sisters of Mercy had set up schools in the poorest districts of half a dozen big industrial cities, and the one established at 'Underwood', a handsome Regency villa at 152 Burngreave Road, just around the corner from the Macduffs, had chosen to specialize in music. The regime at Underwood was certainly not a soft one. Those who left the Sisters of Mercy school decades later, after it had moved to different premises, recalled how harsh the Sisters could be. The actress Judy Parfitt, who plays Sister Monica Joan, the nun with dementia in *Call the Midwife*, went to the Notre Dame convent high school in the city centre during the Second World War, and recalls how the nuns walked about carrying leather straps to punish girls who misbehaved. Is it possible that Munca derived from her years at Underwood not merely her loathing of organized religion but a taste for the corporal punishment she inflicted on Georgie?

Underwood, formerly the Sisters of Mercy Convent School, Burngreave Road

The thought of Munca struggling with her scales — did they even have a piano at home? — made me think of her differently. I began to sketch out an alternative future for her. Two or three years after passing the piano exam, she must have left school and gone off to get a job in Leeds. If only she had not got pregnant, she and Harold might have led a respectable middle-class existence in Claypit Lane, Munca sending the children off to the grammar school at nearby Woodhouse Moor, perhaps making sandwiches for Harold to take to the Test Match up the road at Headingley. But somehow I don't think so. Whatever fate chucked at her, she could never have knuckled down.

All the same, the lives that Munca and Doris led in their childhood were beginning to seem a little less bleak. Too much to say that things were going swimmingly for the Macduffs, but they seemed to have their heads above water. At least the scrap metal business was paying enough for the modest fees at the Sisters of Mercy. I moved on to the 1911 census with some interest to see how they were getting on, with John Willie and Mary now in their forties, and Ileen and Doris in their mid-teens, 16 and 15 to be exact.

And here came out of nowhere a nasty shock, something I hadn't catered for at all and that shattered my growing sentimental expectations of their lives. For here was John Willie Macduff, metal broker dealer, aged 45, and he was living with his widowed mother Matilda, at 117 Page Hall Road, up at the top end of Brightside. Also in the household were his younger brother Joseph and Joseph's wife, another Mary Macduff (Mary Elizabeth, seven years younger than her sister-in-law), and John Willie's younger sisters, Alice the milliner and Lillie the domestic servant. No sign of Mary née Crabb, or of Ileen/Eileen or Doris at Page Hall Road, or as far as I could see anywhere else in Sheffield, or in England for that matter.

The family had split up, and the three female members of it had disappeared off the map. Once again, the old Philippines idea reared its romantic head. Had Mary decided that life as a scrap merchant's wife was too grim to be tolerated a moment longer, and whisked her two daughters off to a new life in the Pacific, leaving her disconsolate husband to crawl back to his mother? Such a catastrophic break might begin to explain Munca's impatience with her own past and her eagerness to bury it.

Yet somehow I could not quite swallow this theory. I was not convinced that Mary would be capable of such wilfulness. So I went on rummaging about in the 1911 census. Then, rather late in the day, I noticed that I had been hunting for Macduff in that exact spelling and had failed to tick the 'or variant' box, which I now did. And immediately up popped Doris, in the guise of Doris McDuff. She was living in Sheffield and, as usual, only a few hundred yards from where she had always lived. She was now a boarder at 31 Nottingham Street, and she was described as 'Assistant, Mantle Trade', the girl who held the pins and brought up different gloves and scarves for the customer to try on with her new outfit. No. 31 Nottingham Street was the home of Sidney Brooks, a grocer's assistant, and his wife. It would have been full up already with Doris and the Brooks's uncle lodging there too, without the addition of one other person who was spending the census night of Sunday 2 April there: Doris's mother Mary. When first filling in the form, Sidney Brooks describes Mary too as a boarder. Then, seeing that he has made a category mistake, he crosses out 'boarder' and writes 'visitor' instead. Doris is a resident, but Mary is only visiting and not expected to stay long.

How terribly broken the little family is: John Willie lodging with his mother in Page Hall Road (not much room in that house either), Doris occupying the attic at Nottingham Street, with Mary, I imagine, dossing down on a mattress beside her. And Ileen/Eileen? Who knows where she is? Once again, I cannot find her anywhere. Munca is as elusive at the age of 16 going on 17 as she is at any of the other ages she lies about.

What is peculiar about this break-up is that, unlike other break-ups I have come across in my own life, there seems to be no family home any more, no home still occupied by the deserted wife or husband or by whichever of them has thrown out the other. They are all scattered. Then I realize that this can only be because there is no money coming in. Nobody is earning enough to pay the rent. They are destitute.

This then is the ultimate secret. Not Buster being born out of wedlock. That happens in the best regulated families. No, the worst, the bitter worst is that they are out on the street. The abyss has opened and swallowed them up, the abyss that is always there, always waiting at the end of every nightmare.

Why has this terrible thing happened? I don't imagine that the scrap metal trade has suddenly taken a downturn, not with every foundry in Sheffield going full blast to feed the biggest arms race in history. No, the only explanation is that John Willie must be ill. And it occurs to me in the same moment that I know exactly when he was born, in the spring of 1866, but I have no idea when he died. I have until now allowed this forgotten father of Munca's to slip away into the shades unmourned and unrecorded.

This turns out to be the easiest thing in the world to put right, and one of the saddest. John William Macduff dies on 17 May 1911 at 117 Page Hall Road, at the age of 45. The cause of death is cardiac failure brought on by phthisis, which is what doctors then termed what ordinary people called consumption. As with half the adult men in Sheffield, it was his lungs that finished him off. The rates of infant and child mortality were terrible in the city, as they were everywhere among the poor, but what was so striking about Sheffield was the number of men who died in early middle age from diseases of the lung. That 'grinder's lung' identified by Dr Bell and Fred Engels half a century earlier was still the sharpest of the reaper's scythes, Sheffield's peculiar blade. It killed John Willie six weeks after census night.

So this is the simple and awful explanation of why the family broke up. John Willie was dying and there was no longer anyone to pay the rent. But how sad it is that Mary cannot be with him at the last and has to bed down at Doris's side instead. Perhaps she and her mother-in-law never really got on, and even at this terrible moment Matilda has made it clear that Mary is not welcome at Page Hall Road. And so it is Matilda who has to mop the night sweats and clear away the diarrhoea and listen to the groans and watch her son's flesh waste away.

Except that, at the very last, Mary *is* there. Because when I read the death certificate more closely, I see that under 'Signature, description and residence of informant' it says 'Mary Macduff, widow of deceased, in attendance, 15 Ranmoor Park Road'.

John Willie's long illness and the destitution that follows from it have driven them apart, but death itself has brought them back together again.

This entry makes it clearer why she is a temporary visitor at Doris's lodgings. This hasty arrangement has come about because Ranmoor Park Road is right out on the western edge of the city, too far distant for Mary to rush round when her husband takes a turn for the final worst. She needs a temporary perch close to the deathbed.

But now another puzzle looms out of these chaotic last days. What is Mary doing out at Ranmoor Park Road? For Ranmoor is not just any old commuter village. It is Millionaire's Row. The splendid Italianate villas strung out up the steep hill past St John's Church, the finest Victorian church in Sheffield, are lived in by the cream of the city. At No. 5 is Colonel Sir John Bingham Bart, a former Master Cutler like his father before him and chairman of Walker and Hall, the great manufacturers of electroplate. At No. 7 lives Bryant Turner, steel file and cutlery manufacturer, at No. 9 is the Rector, the Rev James George Williams from Carmarthen. Further along there are three more householders who describe themselves as cutlery or steel manufacturers. A little further along still lives Alfred Denny, the first Professor of Biology at Sheffield University, where the museum of zoology still bears his name. There could be no more respectable, even distinguished address in the whole city than Ranmoor Park Road, and no finer view from anywhere than the panorama of the smoky glistening city stretching out across the valley of the Don and on beyond to the bare distant hills. And No. 15, still standing today, is one of the finest houses in the road. It is the work of the first-rate local architect John Dodsley Webster (1840–1913), who could run up classical mansions like this one as fluently as he designed churches and chapels, these usually in the Early English style.

Ranfall, 15 Ranmoor Park Road

But who lived there? On the amalgamated census lists for 1911, there is no entry for No. 15. Perhaps, I thought, the owners were away on 2 April, taking their Easter holiday at another handsome residence somewhere else, Scarborough perhaps or Harrogate. But then Clea Carroll at Sheffield Archives found another route for me, which revealed that the inhabitants of No. 15 were not absent but simply too numerous to fit on the same sheet of paper as their neighbours.

There were 16 of them, even for those teeming days quite a crowd. Walter John Walsh and his wife Edith Winifred had four boys and two girls (another child had already died), and Edith was to bear three more children. To look after them, she employed a governess, two nursemaids, a cook, a kitchen maid, a parlour maid, a housemaid and a laundry maid. But oddly, no housekeeper to run the show.

Walter Walsh

Walter Walsh, then aged 38, describes himself as 'Draper and House Finisher'. What he was in fact was Chairman and Managing Director of the largest department store in the city, John Walsh and Co., at 39 High Street, opposite Castle Square. His father John, an Irish Catholic who must have come to England soon after the Great Famine, had opened a small baby-linen and ladies' outfitters on the site in June 1875. Walsh's grew rapidly and retained its pre-eminence until its premises were destroyed in the Blitz in 1940. But the business survived to be rebuilt and reopened after the war, when it was taken over by Harrods, still under the name of Walsh's. The famous Harrods green vans would make the journey north once or twice a week carrying special choice items, and the ladies of Sheffield's high-class suburbs (like Ranmoor Park) would insist that their orders should be delivered directly by the Harrods van. Those who still remember the store in its last days in the 1950s and 1960s describe it as just like Grace Brothers from *Are You Being Served?*, a survival from a more punctilious age.

John Walsh and Co., 39 High Street, Sheffield

Walter Walsh himself seems to have been a model proprietor, as concerned for the welfare of his employees as for the satisfaction of his customers. He left £20,000 in his will for the establishment of a staff pension fund. During the Great War, he and some other benevolent local businessmen clubbed together to buy Shirle Hall, Sharrow, outside Ripon, as a home for Belgian refugees.

The inescapable conclusion is that Mary Macduff was in the Walshes' service. She had had experience in domestic service twenty years earlier with the Hudsons in Chorlton-upon-Medlock. The Hudsons might well know the Walshes, both being significant figures in different ends of the textile trade. They could have supplied Mary with a reference. Now as a respectable married woman in her early forties with two grown-up daughters, Mary would be ideally qualified to act as housekeeper over the young household (most of the maids were in their twenties), the equivalent of Mrs Hughes at Downton Abbey. Edith Walsh herself would be too exhausted having babies to run such an elaborate show. Nothing is more likely too than that the benevolent Walter would readily give permission for Mary to take the tram across town to Brightside to help tend her dying husband. And now, just as I am putting all this together, it comes back to me – I don't know why it has never occurred to me before – that the one thing, the only thing that Munca did say about her mother was that she had once been a lady's maid. I don't know why she said it and perhaps she wished she hadn't, because she never said it again. But her saying it at all suggests that it was a fact of some importance in Mary's life, perhaps even one that had changed her life.

So now we know where three of the four Macduffs were on 2 April. But where is the fourth? Where is Ileen/Eileen? I shuffle through my pile of BMD certificates, quite a sheaf of them now as my halting quest has taken me deeper into the heart and lungs of Brightside. And I take another look at the nearest evidence I have of Munca's whereabouts when her father is dying, namely the birth certificate of Archibald Alfred Macduff. And what comes to me at this moment is what would have come to any half-awake woman several months earlier: that we know exactly where Eileen was at the time. Because John Willie dies just eight months before Archie Alfred is born on 10 January 1912. So as he is dying, what Eileen is doing is going to bed with Harold Ridge somewhere in Leeds. In fact, she might well have conceived Buster on the night when the census was taken. And that, no doubt, is why she is reluctant to record her exact location for the benefit of the authorities. She has fled the poverty and disgrace of Brightside and the long slow grind of her father's illness, and she has taken a job in Leeds, as a domestic servant or a shop assistant, and she has fallen for Harold Ridge. She has escaped from one sad mess and landed straight in another.

Eileen may not be present in the census, but Harold is. He is living with his parents, Alfred and Rachel, and like Eileen he is 16 years old. Alfred is a school inspector, and Harold is described as a clerk in an accountant's office. Harold is an afterthought, twelve years younger than any of his elder siblings, two boys and two girls who are long grown up and who are respectively a bank cashier, a bank clerk, a cookery teacher and a pupil teacher. So Harold is the junior member of an unbelievably respectable white-collar family. And because he is so much younger, he must also be the darling of the family. The last thing any of them can have in mind for him is that at the age of 16 he should impregnate the daughter of a destitute and dying scrap metal dealer, a girl who is herself only 16. The whole thing is a disaster.

I don't imagine that Harold's elderly parents are much better disposed towards the alliance when, 18 months later, in December 1913, Harold and Eileen decide to get married. Certainly none of the family signs the register. Now it seems even more likely that the reason they both lie about their ages is that they do not have parental permission to marry. This is the first lie that Munca puts on an official form. This lack of permission, I discover, invalidates the marriage and would have gone on invalidating it until the Family Law Reform Act of 1969 lowered the age of majority to 18. In any case, a false statement would have been an offence punishable by law, though it was a law that plenty of other under-age couples had broken too. I also wonder how they managed to persuade the Registrar to go ahead without producing their birth certificates. But this too is not the last thing Munca gets away with when dealing with officialdom.

Eileen is the first of the two sisters to have a baby. But she is not the first to get married. Doris, only just 17 herself, has nipped ahead of her and married Alfred Burke in February that year. Alfred lives around the corner like everyone else, in Roe Lane. He is a lot older, 29, and he is a clerk in the steel works, the only one in his family to have a white-collar job. Perhaps this is partly why Doris has picked him out. His father, Thomas Harrington Burke, is a furnace man in the Vickers armour-plate works. His brother John is a die grinder, his brother Tom an engine minder, his sister Edith a silver burnisher. Iron and steel through and through, like the Macduffs, and, like the Macduffs, the Burkes come from the Black Country, from Tipton, Staffs, where Matilda was born, so the two families may well know each other from way back. The Burkes were originally Irish. The Macduffs came to Sheffield to escape the workhouse, the Burkes came to England to escape the Famine. They are Catholics, and Alfred and Doris are married in St Catherine's RC Church in Andover Street, one of the churches built at the expense of the Duke of Norfolk. They are better off here than in the west of Ireland in money terms, much better, but not much better in their expectation of life. When I was trying to find when Thomas Harrington Burke died, I noted down the ages at death of the ten Thomas Burkes who died in Sheffield between 1880 and 1900. They were: 3, 63, 0, 39, 0, 5, 24, 61, 17 and 57 (the latter being THB himself) – an average life expectancy of 27 years. For the sake of comparison, I looked to see if the women had fared any better. They did even worse. Over the same period, the ten Mary Burkes who died in Sheffield died at the following ages: 2, 37, 0, 63, 2, 0, 0, 0, 2, 3 – an average life of just eleven years.

If you were born in Sheffield then, the best way to improve your life expectancy was to leave. Never was this truer than in the steaming hot summer of 1911, the year that George V was crowned but also a year of bitter political crisis and industrial turmoil spreading from the coal mines to the docks and then back to the mines again. In Sheffield, the carters came out in sympathy with the railwaymen, who were already out. Blacklegs were brought in to distribute everything from vegetables to domestic coal. There were 600 Gordon Highlanders on duty at the railway stations to protect the strike-breakers from the strikers. When the national coal strike in pursuit of a minimum wage got under way the following March, Sheffield endured daily cuts in electricity and gas supplies, and 15,000 steelworkers were laid off. It was the worst of times.

Doris had stayed in Sheffield, in the little patch of Brightside where she was born and where she was to live all her married life with Alfred. She had a son in Sheffield, in the spring of 1914. She proudly christened him Denis Macduff Burke. No concealing her origins there. As I digest this, I suddenly remember both the name and the man. For Denis now and then appeared at Preston House, at other Munca residences too, I think. He was a quiet slight figure, rather amiable, and treated in a questionable way by both Unca and Munca. They were both a little patronizing, almost contemptuous towards him. He seemed to have some connection with Lennards, but not a prominent one, something like an assistant company secretary. He was certainly a notch down from Unca. Georgie told me she danced with him at the office dance once, again with a faint note of contempt. I remember thinking that he was a rather nice person and being puzzled why they thought so little of him. So he was Munca's nephew. Then, almost in the same instant, I remember where I have come across his name quite recently but failed to click. Denis was also Philippa Cunliffe-Owen's first husband.

Philippa was only 19 when they got married at St Margaret's, Westminster, in September 1945. It was an unimaginably grand wedding for a lad born and bred in the back streets of Brightside. Princess Marie Louise, Queen Victoria's granddaughter, was there. The wedding snaps of the reception at the Dorchester, by the ever-present society photographer Barry Swaebe (always greeted by Munca as an old friend), fill a whole page of the *Tatler* a fortnight later.

The wedding of Denis Burke and Philippa Cunliffe-Owen

There are the bride and groom, Denis with a beatific smile on his face, not in uniform like so many of the *Tatler* grooms at this date (several of them also leaning on sticks as they come out of the church). Philippa looks a little nervous, I think, compared to her younger sister Diana. Below them on the page are the groom's mother, Doris, and the bride's father, Sir Hugo, with their present spouses. On paper, it was a perfect match. Hugo Cunliffe-Owen was a buccaneering tycoon not unlike Frank Parkinson, though without the scientific expertise. He too had built himself a huge mansion at Sunningdale, only a few fields away from Charters. Sunningdale Park, as it was called, later became the Civil Service College, and in that role entered the language as the site of the Northern Ireland talks that produced the Sunningdale Agreement in 1973. The Cunliffe-Owen mansion equals Charters in size and opulence, but it is in the classical style, all pediments and ionic pillars.

Sunningdale Park

In a Jane Austen novel, such a marriage between children of the two grandest neighbours for miles around would be an occasion for rejoicing. But even Barry Swaebe with his twinkling specs and his gnome's smile seems to have found it hard to conjure up much joy from the photo session. Sir Hugo looks implacable, Mauricia, his second or third wife, looks frantic, while Doris seems to be trying to put on a cheerful face. Frank Parkinson has a genial but distant smile as if the whole thing isn't much to do with him, which it isn't (Denis was grown up before he met Doris). In fact, Frank is ill and dies of a heart attack only three months later, after which Doris loses little time in finding her third husband.

For their part, the Cunliffe-Owens have been quarrelling for years over Hugo's love affairs, and only a few months later they get a judicial separation, after which he takes up with a well-known dancer from New Zealand with the delicious stage name of Marjorie Daw. Then Hugo dies too, but not before Marjorie takes his name and he makes a new will, leaving her nearly half his vast fortune – upon which Mauricia sues Marjorie for enticement.

The proceedings are as colourful as they are brief. Hugo and Mauricia had been married in 1935, a year after the mother of his children had died. He was 65, she about 39. She had been his investment adviser and, in view of the difference in their ages, continued to take a keen interest in his portfolio and her prospects as a widow. About five years before Philippa's wedding, she had fended off one of Hugo's mistresses, but the marriage went from bad to worse, especially after Hugo's elder son, also called Hugo, a sub-lieutenant in the Fleet Air Arm, was killed on board HMS *Indomitable* during the siege of Malta. Like many other bereaved parents during both world wars, Sir Hugo took up spiritualism to contact his dead son, but had no luck with the Ouija board.

More recently, Mauricia had developed a phobia that Philippa's sister Diana was trying to engineer a final break-up of the marriage. Diana was a skittish teenager whose boarding school had already asked for her to be removed. She was said to be in trouble with the bookmakers, and she annoyed her stepmother so much that Mauricia gave her several smart slaps. On a business trip to the States, Mauricia noticed Sir Hugo receiving several letters that he took into the bathroom to read.

Suspecting the letters to be from Diana making trouble, she got her maid to filch them from her husband's briefcase. They turned out to be love letters from the previously unsuspected Marjorie Daw.

Worse still, Marjorie wrote that she had hired several mediums who had succeeded in contacting Hugo Jr in the Beyond. The sub-lieutenant, looking just as he had in life, had apparently insisted that his father must marry Marjorie if he wished to stay in contact. The defunct Hugo, as transcribed in pencil by Mrs Luke the medium and reported in the *Dundee Courier* of 30 November and 1 December 1949, predicted a bright future for Marjorie: 'You will be made clean of gossip and scandal – big ship will sail and land in port bringing a man whose eyes have been opened – he will unlock to you his full desire – watch the big day – I see you making a new start in life – the light is yours and will give you much satisfaction – he is giving you what he has secretly wished for three years.'

Just as the courtroom was warming to this bulletin from the Other Side, the parties settled at the lunch interval on the second day of the hearing. There were to be apologies all round, but no damages.

Not surprising then that they all look somewhat frazzled in Philippa's wedding photograph four years earlier when the above events were reaching a climax. Coming from a background like this, it is not so surprising either that Philippa's first marriage was not destined to last. Only six years and two children later, Denis divorced her, and the same year she married Buster. In other words, Munca and Doris each had an only son, and Philippa married both of them. I remember Munca mentioning the Cunliffe-Owens, but only as rather grand people she seemed to know vaguely, perhaps in an earlier period of her life. It would have been difficult to guess that they were near neighbours and that one of them had married her only nephew, before going on to marry her only son. But it is not hard to imagine the *froideur* between the two sisters. It was less than three years since Buster had married his fourth wife, Margaret from Angmering-on-Sea, and now here he was snatching his first cousin's well-heeled wife to become number five. Even in Buster's erratic career, he can seldom have behaved worse.

After about 1937, the full accounts of divorce proceedings are no longer kept on public record, at any rate nowhere that I know how to track them down. All that can be obtained from the Principal Registry of the Family Division in High Holborn is the certificate that a decree nisi has become a decree absolute. In view of the bother and expense, I had not applied for any of these certificates so far. But to make sure I had got the facts right, I now put in for the one certifying the divorce of Denis and Philippa.

My diligence was rewarded. There in the slot for co-respondent is the toast of the divorce lawyers, Archibald Alistair Baring. So it wasn't just a case of him comforting Philippa, as the gossip columns like to say, after her marriage to Denis had broken up. He was the one who had broken it up. For a delicious moment I wondered if his nickname had been awarded because he was a habitual marriage buster. But then I remembered that he had the nickname years earlier, before the war, appearing as Buster Baring in the photograph taken at my parents' wedding, for example. The origins of Buster probably lay way back in his childhood, taken from some film or comic in the 1920s. As a little boy, Archie could well have looked like Buster Keaton. In fact, now I come to think about it, when he was grown up, he still looked rather like the film star. And why was Joseph Frank Keaton nicknamed Buster? Keaton came from a vaudeville family, and according to the tale he himself told, when he was only about 18 months old, the escape artist Harry Houdini had seen him fall down a long flight of stairs and emerge uninjured and unruffled, and had remarked in some awe: 'that was a real buster!' Perhaps our Buster too was like that as a toddler. He certainly seems to have been like that in later life. Tumbles down, picks himself up, proceeds as before. That's Buster.

But then it occurred to me that the decree absolute certificate, laconic though it would be, might also offer some clue to the truth about how Buster's own marriage to Philippa broke up ten years later. Did their divorce have anything to do with the break-up of Buster's old racing crony Charles Mortimer and his beautiful wife Jean, which happened at much the same time? What the certificate would show in both cases was the identity of the co-respondent, if there was one, a fact as glaring and unmissable as the shoes associated at that era with the suave and creepy figure of the interloper. 'Co-respondent shoes' were buckskin brogues in two ill-suited shades of cream and dark tan. It was beginning to look as if they might fit Buster.

Not for the first time, my darkest guess turned out to be correct. I was beginning to understand that if I thought the worst of Buster in any situation, there was a reasonable chance that I might be close to the truth. The co-respondent cited by Charles Mortimer in his petition against the delicious Jean was none other than 'Alistair Baring'. He was, as I had suspected, the Somebody Else who came between them. Their 17 years of marriage had been wiped out, and their three children left without a mother, at least temporarily, because of Buster's charms, still irresistible apparently though he was over 50 now. The decree was made on 26 June 1963. Three weeks earlier, Buster had married his sixth wife, the hairdresser Daphne Bateman. Not merely had he betrayed his old friend and business partner; he had ditched the lover who had left her family for him. Worse still for Jean, if she ever got to hear of it, Buster's marriage to Daphne lasted not much more than a year. It is almost as though he married the first girl he happened to see in order not to have to marry Jean. Both the Mortimers were wounded so grievously that their remarriage failed too, and it was another decade or more before they learnt to live together again.

Buster's divorce from Daphne is the second occasion on which he is, in the eyes of the law at least, the innocent party. As in the case of his second wife Josephine, it is he who is the petitioner on the grounds that she has committed adultery with the co-respondent Stanley James Hurley. In other circumstances, one might assume that the age gap of 21 years between groom and bride had something to do with the lightning break-up. Could it be that Buster was no longer able to keep up with a woman so much younger than himself? Well, no, it couldn't. Because only a fortnight after the decree absolute comes through, he gets married again for the seventh and last time, to Julia Champion, who is even younger than Daphne. Again, as after Josephine, he has the next Mrs Baring already lined up. I think we can assume that his innocence is somewhat relative. He has now been married seven times and divorced six times, not to mention being cited as co-respondent three times in the divorces of other couples.

So he continued the trail of marital destruction. He had already cuckolded – I cannot avoid the old-fashioned word – his cousin Denis, the nearest relative of his own generation. Now I began to understand the awkwardness in the air when Denis and Munca met. It was her son who had done him wrong, and I imagine Denis had strong if perhaps well-hidden views about the way Buster had been brought up, an upbringing that had made him such a danger to traffic. For her part, Munca, who believed in the survival of the fittest, would probably have felt a tinge of contempt for Denis's failure to hang on to his wife. I cannot imagine that Doris thought very kindly of Buster either.

But all this mayhem was a long way in the future. We left Doris in Sheffield in March 1914 waiting for Denis to be born.

During the great strike of 1912, she could have walked down from her mother's house at 171 Shirecliffe Lane, and watched the outcroppers scrabbling for coal at the top of Burngreave Bank by kind permission of the Duke of Norfolk: the men with their shovels all respectably dressed in white shirts and ties, the women with their baskets still wearing their white aprons. How strange to be short of coal when you are living on top of a mountain of the stuff. But how weirdly gay they look, those pinafores fluttering in the wind off the moors. Perhaps Doris clambered up the steep bank to join them. Perhaps not. She did not seem very athletic.

No.1200. Coal Strike.1912.Poor digging for coal. Sheffield.

Outcroppers scavenging for coal on Burngreave Bank during the 1912 strike

Doris stayed in Sheffield for another 20 years, which is why she kept a little of her Yorkshire accent. But Eileen Constance Sylvia was gone.

6

Crawford Mansions

It must have been hard. Eileen was still only 17. She was on her own, in a strange city, and her father had just died. Perhaps her mother came to help her. After all, Mary had managed to get away from Ranmoor Park Road to be at John Willie's deathbed the other side of Sheffield. She could have made it across to Leeds, only a short train ride away. But Mary did not sign the register when Eileen and Harold got married 18 months later. She may not have been on speaking terms with her daughter. She may not even have known for months that Eileen was pregnant.

What the birth certificates tell us, in duplicate, is that Archibald Alfred Macduff was born at 66 Lofthouse Place, Leeds, on 10 January 1912. On his death certificate, as we have seen, Buster asserts his claim to British citizenship through his father having been born in Leeds. But it was not his father who was born in Leeds – Harold Ridge was born in Sandal Magna, a suburb of Wakefield. It was Buster himself. How did he stumble upon this fragment of near-truth? Was this a final figment of Munca's quick wit? Had she let slip some hint of a Yorkshire connection and recovered herself by saying airily, 'Oh yes, your father [or our father] was born in Leeds', much as she had told Georgie that she had been born in the High Wycombe in Cornwall?

Buster's birthplace, 66 Lofthouse Place, Leeds

Lofthouse Place is not a bad part of town. It's at the bottom end of Headingley, not far from the Yorkshire County cricket ground and the University. But it is not palatial either. No. 66 is a plain little terraced house, two up and two down, and it had a lot of people in it. The householder was Alexander Charles Husbands, a 42-year-old cabinet-maker who had come up from Hackney five years earlier. He and his wife Alice had five children now, ranging from the 15-year-old Alexander Ernest, who was a pawnbroker's assistant, to the 5-year-old Cyril Leslie. The ménage also included a lodger, Reuben Rayner, who was a hotel carver by trade, and two full boarders, Mary Wallace who was a dressmaker and single and Mary Allborne who was married, though with no sign of a husband. There was also Arthur William Holden who had an 'Appartment' in the house. He was a 'tourist agent' and also describes himself as married, though with no sign of a wife. Altogether 11 persons. Seven Husbands in the house and no husband for Eileen.

So No. 66 was what people call a common lodging house, though I have never heard of an uncommon one. Eileen Constance is not on the list of those who spent the night of Sunday 2 April 1911 there. She is not on anyone's list for that night. But any of the floating tenantry might well have moved on in time for Eileen to have her lying-in there nine months later. It is hard to think that Alice Husbands can have welcomed a tenant in that condition. But that is an uncharitable thought and perhaps a mistaken one. Alice had five children of her own, and must have known some hard times during the traipse from Hackney to Leeds. She might have taken pity on Eileen. Someone had to.

I am quite pleased to have got Buster born at last, even this far on in my quest. It is about the same stage in *Tristram Shandy*, Book Three to be exact, that Tristram finally manages to be born, so by the standards of classic literature we are not doing too badly, even if it has taken two birth certificates to do the trick. It is a whimsicality that the author of *Tristram Shandy* himself would have been proud of that the two birth certificates *should say exactly the same thing*, apart from the differing dates, 1912 and 1916. In fact, I realize now that Buster must have had a total of *three* birth certificates, the first one being issued in 1912 at the time of his birth and then replaced by the new 1912 one issued in 1916. I hope that's absolutely clear. A peculiar start to a peculiar life.

After a renewed enquiry to the long-suffering General Register Office, they type me up a copy of the original 1912 certificate. It is an altogether bleaker affair. There are long blanks drawn in the spaces for the father's name and surname and occupation, and it is therefore the mother, E. C. Macduff, who is the sole informant of Buster's birth. But what this certificate does record after her name, which the other two don't, is the mother's profession: 'Eileen Constance Macduff formerly a typist'. It seems almost an afterthought. The form does not require the mother to put in what she does, motherhood being enough of a profession to be going on with, and none of the other birth certificates I have collected has this information. I can only imagine that Eileen puts the fact in to rescue a small portion of respectability from her dismal situation, for being a typist was then, and for many years later, as good a way as any other (except marriage) for an unmarried girl to get on in the world. What is clear, though, is that we now have the answer to how Eileen and Harold met. She was the new typist, he was the fresh young clerk, both just 16 in an office full of stern middle-aged men in stiff collars and middle-aged lady typists wearing cameo brooches. It was the most natural thing in the world that they should get together.

What the surviving certificates also tell us, in duplicate, is that it was quite a performance for Harold to get himself officially recognized as Buster's father. Then as now, if the parents are married, either parent can go down to the town hall and do the registering. If they are not married, then the mother must fill in the form, and if the father wishes to be included on it, he has to go along and sign for himself. The matter was and is further complicated if the child was properly registered at birth and the father wishes to add his name later, in this case much later. Buster has, after all, had his fourth birthday before he becomes officially the son of Harold Cecil Drury Ridge, and the grandson of Alfred Ridge, from whom he takes his second name, though the Alfred is soon dropped and never appears again anywhere that I have come across.

But these efforts do not make Buster legitimate. To achieve that, he would have had to be born after the Legitimacy Act of 1926 enabled the subsequent legitimizing of a child whose parents were married after his or her birth. There had been much lobbying for this new law from women's organizations, which argued, quite rightly, that the law as it stood offered no encouragement for unmarried parents to get married, or indeed for the father of an illegitimate child to register himself as such. I only mention these details to indicate that Harold and Eileen must have had a special reason for going through the whole rigmarole four years later. Surely the natural time to have put Harold on the certificate was when he showed his commitment by marrying Eileen two years earlier at the end of 1913.

At first I thought that perhaps it was the pretty sight of the toddling Buster that had stirred an irresistible paternal throbbing in Harold's breast, not to mention the strong persuasive powers of his wife. No doubt both these factors played their part. But there was another thing. Idiotically, barely conceivably in fact, I had forgotten the war.

The first two battles of Ypres and the slaughter at Loos had taken an awful toll. If the war was to be carried on at this intensity, more men would have to be found. On 31 December 1915, the Cabinet finally approved the Military Service Bill. All unmarried men were to be called up by March 1916, married men by May. If Harold Ridge went to war and never came back, Buster would not have a father to remember. As it turned out, he was not to have a father to remember anyway, or rather he was taught to remember a father who never was.

The introduction of universal conscription in the spring of 1916 was a watershed event in British history. To previous generations it would have been unthinkable. Not since the feudal era had every serf and villein laboured under a legal duty to put his life on the line for his country. Conscription marked the beginning of a new sort of national life. From now on, the State would take it as read that it could call on its citizens to do pretty much anything it fancied.

Harold and Eileen had to rearrange their lives to a timetable not of their own devising. Like thousands of other couples, they moved to London. I think Eileen would have moved to London anyway, war or no war. She had the bright lights in her eyes all the 30-odd years I knew her and I am sure they were there from the start.

And Buster? No, I don't think Buster came to London too. He was 4 years old now. If ever there was going to be a break with his mother, this was the time. The sensible thing was to leave him with his grandmother Mary in Sheffield, widowed now and with time on her hands. It was, after all, the standard thing to do. A girl in her teens fell – that awful expressive verb – and her mother, if she was plausibly young enough, took over and brought up the child as her own. Mary was only 41 when Archibald Alfred was born. Easy enough to present him as a cherished afterthought, the last souvenir of John Willie.

What was to happen further on down the line might for the moment be left vague. Perhaps Harold and Eileen would send for him. Or they might come back up north when the war was over. Or Mary and Buster might come down to London, and they would all live together or close by. Who knew? There had never been a world war before. You had to live from day to day. Long-term planning was a waste of time.

And so Harold and Eileen Ridge came down and took a flat a few hundred yards from Marylebone station where the Sheffield trains came in, at 3A Oxford and Cambridge Mansions, a great cliff of red-brick apartments lowering over the Old Marylebone Road where it comes into the Marylebone Road proper. This, it turns out, is the area in which Eileen is destined to spend large parts of her twenties and thirties: red-brick mansion flats just south of the Marylebone Road and well north of Oxford Street and scattered along an east–west axis from the Tottenham Court Road to Edgware Road, a terrain inhabited by newcomers, transients, widows and widowers, adulterers and spies. All erected within a few years of each other at the end of the nineteenth century and the beginning of the twentieth, these beetling ziggurats still stand today and still serve much the same clientele.

I do not know exactly what Harold is doing in London. Perhaps he is training to be a soldier, waiting to go to France; perhaps he is actually away at the front. Or perhaps he is in some sort of reserved occupation, something where his qualifications as a chartered accountant will come in handy, something to do with the wholesale commandeering of financial and logistical resources that a world war involves. I haven't got a clue. There are dozens of Harold Ridges in the military records but not one of them that fits H. C. D. Ridge. He has, for the moment, but only for the moment, vanished without trace, as people do in the shadow of Armageddon.

But I know where Eileen is, a good deal of the time anyway, and what she is doing, also a good deal of the time. She is having an affair.

This is happening around the corner, no more than 100 yards away in fact, down the little lane opposite that is called Homer Row, at No. 1 Crawford Mansions, in another of these frowning red-brick redoubts. Her lover is called Donald George Pilcher Clark. He was a lieutenant in the Cheshire Regiment earlier on in the war, but he transferred to the Royal Flying Corps, later to be enlarged into the RAF. And he is now a Flying Officer, which sounds a good deal more glamorous than being a chartered accountant. He is also a painter and later on in life becomes a full-time artist. His origins, too, are rather more likely to appeal to Eileen than Harold's. His father, George Clark, is a banker with connections in Bombay. While he is away in India, his family live in a nice street in Fulham. Not at all like Brightside.

Crawford Mansions

So how do Eileen and Donald get together? Their backgrounds seem so far apart. Well, it is surely more than a coincidence that the flats they live in should be so close together. You can see Crawford Mansions from the front windows of 3A Oxford and Cambridge Mansions. My bet is that they bumped into each other at one of the pubs in these back streets where Marylebone goes shabby and begins to turn into Paddington: the Olive Branch, which is just across the road from Crawford Mansions, or the Windsor Castle, which is a couple of doors beyond the Olive Branch, or the Beehive or the Duke of Wellington, both further along Crawford Street. Who picked up whom? They probably fell into each other's arms. It was wartime, after all, and things moved quickly.

Quite soon too, only two years after he has made such efforts to get his name entered on Buster's birth certificate, Harold is suing Eileen for divorce. How grim and unassuageable is the language of these petitions:

> that after the said marriage your Petitioner lived and cohabited with his said Wife at 42 Claypit Lane and 15 Winstone Gardens Leeds, and at 3a Oxford and Cambridge Mansions, Paddington, in the County of London and that there has been no issue of said marriage …
>
> … that on the sixteenth day of November 1918 at a house situate at 1 Crawford Mansions, Marylebone, the said Eileen Constance Sylvia committed adultery with David Clark …
>
> … and from the month of November 1917 to the month of March 1918 at a flat situate at 26 Ridgemount Gardens and from March 1918 to November 1918 at a flat at 1 Crawford Mansions, the said Eileen Constance Sylvia …

And so on, and so forth. I am struck, not for the first time, by the redundancy and pomposity of legal language – 'lived and cohabited', 'situate at' – and also by the inability of lawyers to get the simplest fact right; for example, the Christian name of the co-respondent. There is about this particular petition, I think, an air of rage and hurry. Although the affair has been going on for a year, the whole thing has suddenly exploded and Harold wants to be rid of Eileen as soon as possible. The petition is dated 5 December 1918, only a month after we presume that the private detective has last seen Eileen leaving No. 1 Crawford Mansions at a compromising hour.

Another thing the petition tells us is that 'Harold Cecil Drury Ridge is living at the George Hotel, Victoria, and he is an Accountant's Clerk now serving in His Majesty's Army'. So Eileen has gone off with Donald while Harold is away doing his bit. But where is he serving and in what capacity? Undeterred by my earlier failure to track him down in the military records, I return to the site. This time I turn to the War Pensions records, which are said to be fuller than the records of enlistment and service, and there I do find him. What I find is not what I expected. In fact it is an unpleasant discovery.

Harold Ridge enlisted for a Short Service with the colours the moment that war was declared. His enlistment is dated 27 August 1914, and his service was for a period of three years. He was passed fit into the King's Own Yorkshire Light Infantry with the regimental number of 11590. His next of kin was given as Eileen Constance Sylvia Ridge, formerly Macduff. They had been married only eight months.

Harold is described as 5 ft 11⅝ ins, weighing 153 lbs with blue eyes and medium brown hair and a member of the Church of England. By joining up so early, he qualified as one of the Old Contemptibles, who proudly assumed the nickname after the Kaiser's sneer at 'Kitchener's contemptible little army'. How splendid he sounds.

So it is a let-down when the next thing we find on his record is that, only four weeks later, he has been admitted to Connaught Hospital, Aldershot, to be treated for gonorrhoea. In those days before antibiotics, the standard treatment for gonorrhoea was as nasty as the disease. 'Irrigation', as it was called, involved pumping water up the penis via a catheter. It seems, however, to have done the trick for Harold, and he was discharged as cured on 12 October, to be further discharged nine days later, alas, not merely from the Connaught Hospital but also from His Majesty's Army. In those early days of the war, the military could afford to be choosy about the health and morals of their fighting men. Later on, they were to need every man on two legs. Harold must have re-enlisted when conscription came in at the beginning of 1916, if not before, only to be rewarded by Eileen's defection. On the other hand, the fact that he had contracted the clap less than a year after their marriage might have suggested to her that he was not a reliable long-term bet. She may have felt entitled to look around.

But even more striking than Harold's unhappy debut in the Forces, in fact the real shocker in the petition is the statement that 'there has been no issue of said marriage'. At a stroke, Buster has been un-created again. Technically, it may be true that he was not born *of* the marriage as legally defined, but lawyers are capable of devising a formula that makes it plain that the warring couple have between them produced a child. That, after all, was the purpose of the double birth certificate that they went to such trouble to acquire not three years earlier.

This seems to me adequate proof, if we needed proof, that the plan to restyle Buster as Eileen's little brother has already been agreed, and now they are stuck with it. From here on in, Buster is to disappear from Harold's life, and Harold is to disappear from ours.

Or not quite. I would not wish to leave Harold eternally typecast as a provincial bean-counter who hadn't a hope of satisfying someone as sparky as Eileen. He had an after-life and a surprising one.

Three years after obtaining his divorce from Eileen, he marries again, in January 1922, in Sunderland, to Gladys May Brown, and they go on to have two children, John (born 1923), and Cordelia (born 1925). So Buster has a half-brother and a half-sister. Does he even know they exist?

But what catches my eye about the marriage certificate is that Harold here describes his occupation as 'professional musician' – the opposite end of the interestingness scale from 'chartered accountant'. This new guise is every bit as surprising as when Buster suddenly comes on calling himself a professional dancer. I imagine Harold as playing in a dance band, and sure enough there he is in the invaluable online *Dance Band*

Encyclopedia compiled by M. G. Thomas. Harold is playing piano in the John Birmingham Band. He probably took over from John Birmingham's brother Cyril, who used to play piano when the band was a regular fixture at the Hotel Cecil in the early 1920s. Later, the JB Band, known as the Big Twelve, toured the country and made quite a few recordings for Edison Bell Winner and Duophone. Perhaps Harold met Gladys when the band was playing in Sunderland.

The *Encyclopedia* has a photo of the band at work, with John Birmingham in his trademark white tie and monocle keeping time, while Harold, half-turned towards the camera, is seated at a white grand piano raised up above the brass section. Harold has slicked-down black hair and a generally alert and dapper look. He looks not unlike Buster Keaton, as a matter of fact, and not unlike Buster Baring. You would not be surprised to hear that his son inherited rhythm in his feet.

The John Birmingham Band, Harold Ridge on piano

The JB Band has been described in *Melody Maker* as 'a pioneer of syncopation', and they apparently kept a lively beat in such 1920s favourites as 'Oh Boy What a Girl', 'Carolina Sweetheart', 'Dinah', 'That Night in Araby', 'Isn't She the Sweetest Thing' and (a personal favourite of mine) 'When the

Red, Red Robin Comes Bob, Bob, Bobbin' Along' – all of them recorded on one or other of the two labels. After several hiccups the band was still going in 1928, but shortly afterwards John Birmingham began to suffer bouts of giddiness and fainting. On 5 May 1928, while waiting for some friends to arrive, he went to the balcony of his flat in the Earls Court Road to get some air and fell to his death. The inquest blamed vertigo.

A sad end, and a pity too that Harold and Eileen split up before he got his musical break, because that was the sort of music she loved and danced to all through the 1930s to the baton of Harry 'Tiger' Roy and of his brother Syd and of Ambrose and the rest of the pre-war big bands. Perhaps if she had heard Harold's piano solo in 'Isn't She the Sweetest Thing?' it might all have turned out differently. Or possibly not. Perhaps Harold was already being eclipsed by the great Lou Preager, who joined the JB Band in its last years. A hot pianist who was no longer hot might have been worse than a chartered accountant.

Anyway there Eileen was, unmarried again and living with Donald Clark in No. 1 Crawford Mansions. Later on, they took another flat in the block as well, No. 15, so that when they got married at Marylebone Registry Office in January 1920, he was registered at No. 15 and she at No. 1, for all the world as though this was a chaste romance struck up in the hallway.

It so happens that we have a lively account of life in Crawford Mansions from another couple who lived in the block at this period. A floor up from No. 15 and next door to the entrance to No. 1 were living none other than Mr and Mrs T. S. Eliot. They moved into 18 Crawford Mansions in the spring of 1916. Vivienne Eliot, who had been in poor health all winter, loved the new flat. She wrote to her husband's brother Henry:

> We are very proud of this flat. It is the tiniest place imaginable – just a dining room – a drawing room – a large bedroom – a kitchen and a nice bathroom. We have constant hot water, which is a *luxury* in England, and as this building is quite new, we have 'every modern convenience'. I chose all the papers, and we have some rather original effects. We have an *orange* paper in our dining room (which is also Tom's dressing room and study!) and black and white stripes in the hall.

To Tom's mother, she described Crawford Mansions as 'in a little noisy corner, with slums and low streets and poor shops close around us (and yet within a stone's throw of great squares with big houses and one of the most expensive residential districts) – it is like being in a wilderness, we are just two waifs who live perched up in our little flat – no one around us knows us, or sees us, or bothers to care how we live, or what we do, or whether we live or not'. Viv thinks of this flat as 'a remote tower, somehow it seems so secret and shut off from all the street noises'.

The other waif was not so enamoured of the remote tower. 'Crawford Mansions we have come to loathe on account of the noise and the sordidness', Tom wrote to his mother in 1920. They had found a new flat 'very much more respectable, very much less noisy, and in a better neighbourhood in which not so many people are arrested. In any case, we shall be free from the neighbourhood of prostitution.'

Their windows at Crawford Mansions looked down upon the Olive Branch, Homer Row, a poetic-sounding hostelry but one that could be raucous at closing time. There was noise pollution inside the block as well as across the street. According to Osbert

Sitwell, there were two sisters who lived above the Eliots and had a habit of shouting down from their window to friends in the street, as well as playing the phonograph very loudly. The sisters were actresses, and when Eliot complained to the landlord about the commotion they made, the landlord replied, 'Well you see sir, it's the artistic temperament; we ordinary folk must learn to make allowances for artists. They're not the same as us.' I wonder if the Eliots complained about Eileen and Donald too. Some of their RAF friends probably made quite a racket in the last days of the war and during the celebrations for the Armistice. Yet it was in this rackety environ that Eliot wrote the first pieces that were to come together in *The Waste Land*. That wonderful pub dialogue in Part II, 'A Game of Chess', was probably taken straight from the backchat at the Olive Branch as the landlady was calling time:

> Well if Albert won't leave you alone, there it is, I said,
> What you get married for if you don't want children?
> HURRY UP PLEASE ITS TIME

Those snatches of conversation floating up through the window on hot summer nights all went into the poem. And so quite possibly did the flitting of Eileen and Donald between No. 1 and No. 15, the rows, the making up and the dancing. Viv loved dancing too – Bertrand Russell paid for her to have dancing lessons. Perhaps they all went dancing together, the Eliots and the Clarks, or out to a show – Tom loved the music hall. Or perhaps they never got to know each other, and Eliot just glimpsed Eileen in the passage and imagined her love life quite wrongly: a typist seduced by a spotty young house agent's clerk, rather than an aspiring interior decorator who had run off with an RAF pilot, although of course she had actually been a typist. What is certain is that the greatest English poem of the twentieth century was being written on the floor above where Eileen was having her greatest romance. If Munca knew this, she never spoke of it, which was not surprising. She didn't approve of people who always had their head in a book. Anyway, Eileen was someone else entirely.

The Eliots were still living in Crawford Mansions on that January day in 1920 when Eileen and Donald set off from their separate flats to the register office in the Old Marylebone Town Hall, only five minutes' walk away. Perhaps the two couples bumped into each other in the hallway or on the corner of the street. I can imagine Mr Eliot noticing their wedding finery and raising his dark Homburg hat and wishing them good luck in his courteous New England way. The entrance to Nos 15 and 18 is actually in Homer Row, which surely ought to have been the address for the Homer of the 1920s.

Eileen's wedding day was not, as it happens, the first occasion on which she made a public appearance as Mrs Donald Clark. Nearly two years earlier, on 1 April 1918, the Royal Flying Corps and the Royal Naval Air Service were amalgamated to form the Royal Air Force, which thus became the first independent air force in the world. Throughout the month of April, the new combined force was mustering its personnel and sending them all a form to fill in, which as usual in military forms included the ominous space labelled 'Name of Person to be informed of Casualties'. And the person whom Donald George Pilcher Clark had nominated was Mrs Ellen Clark, at his own home address of 1 Crawford Mansions, Crawford Street, London NW1. And in the space for Relationship he had put 'Wife'.

Which of course she wasn't, yet. Eileen/Ellen — the old confusion on her birth certificate surfaces again — could not be Mrs Clark, because she was still Mrs Ridge and had a few more months to endure in that now uncongenial state. But an RAF wife she was, at least in the eyes of the RAF, which now was added to the list of public institutions whose files contained untruths about her. Anyway, wife or not, there she was waiting and fretting in Crawford Mansions while Donald underwent his training. He had joined the Cheshire Regiment straight from St Paul's School and then transferred to the RFC in September 1916 when he was just 19. To begin with, like many of the first RFC pilots, he trained on the Shorthorn 'pusher' biplane designed by the dashing racing cyclist and pioneer Grand Prix driver, Maurice Farman. 'Pusher' meant not that someone had to push the plane to get it airborne but that the propellers were mounted behind rather than ahead of the engine and faced backwards like the screw of a boat, unlike the later front-mounted or 'tractor' propellers. Then Donald trained on Avros and Curtisses and the range of B.E.2s – for 'Blériot Expérimental' – designed by Geoffrey de Havilland. He was now a qualified pilot and one who had also graduated in aerial gunnery by the time he went to France.

The Shorthorn pusher biplane

The B.E.2cs were generally regarded as vulnerable to fighter attack, especially from the new Fokker Eindecker. They were nicknamed 'Fokker Fodder'. The British ace Albert Ball VC called it 'a bloody awful aeroplane'. The men were magnificent; the flying machines as yet, on the whole, were not. But then it is amazing that they were already flying on combat missions at all. When Donald started his training, it was only seven years since Louis Blériot had first limped across the Channel. Donald spent only two months at the No. 1 School of Aeronautics at Reading, where he was just ahead of the future creator of Biggles, Captain W. E. Johns, who also began his training on a Shorthorn.

In November 1916, Donald was moved to No. 24 Reserve Squadron, the main body of which had already been in action over the Western Front (the Somme is among the Squadron's battle honours), but after only a month there he went on to the famous 55 Squadron, which had just received a consignment of Geoffrey de Havilland's DH.4 bombers. The DH.4s were known as 'flaming coffins', because the petrol tank was situated between the pilot and his rear observer and presented a plump target for enemy aircraft. At one period, the life expectancy of a DH.4 pilot was 11 days. Even the subalterns in the trenches below them could expect to live a little longer. W. E. Johns also flew DH.4s when he joined 55 Squadron, and his misadventures in them form the basis of the first Biggles stories.

The last part of Donald's war was no less adventurous. In February 1917, he was promoted to Flying Officer and moved to No. 17 Squadron, which flew B.E.2cs all over the Near East, from the Western Desert and Arabia up to Macedonia and Bulgaria, employed in tactical reconnaissance and artillery spotting. As Lawrence of Arabia swept the skies with his binoculars, he would have been looking for one of 17 Squadron's B.E.2cs coughing its way over the barren sands.

After all that, Donald came safe home to Crawford Mansions – just in time to be cited as co-respondent in Harold Ridge's divorce petition against Eileen Constance Sylvia. Only now does it strike me that their entire affair has been conducted during Donald's leaves from the RFC. Their meetings were not only clandestine, they were painfully brief, with long months in between, and both of them left wondering whether there would be another meeting and whether anything would come of it.

Donald was lucky. Like Biggles, he was miraculously unscathed. His comrade Reginald Baring was not. He had joined the RFC straight from Haileybury College and did his training first at the No. 5 School of Aeronautics at Denham, and then in April 1918 followed in the wake of Donald and Captain Johns to the No. 1 School at Reading. He was gazetted a full lieutenant after he had learnt to fly the DH.6, the Avro, the Sopwith Pup, the Sopwith Camel and one of the Sopwith bombers, either the Cuckoo, which carried torpedoes, or the Strutter, which carried four 25 lb bombs under its wings.

It was to be the Sopwith Camel that Reginald flew when he was transferred to No. 73 Squadron on 8 May 1918. The Squadron had been flying fighter patrols and bomber escort missions over the Western Front since it had moved to France in January. From March onwards, it was pressed into action to repel the last great German offensive, launching repeated sorties against ground forces. Then, as the Allies counter-attacked, the Camels flew at low level in support of the Allied armour. No more perilous activity on this planet can be imagined.

The service record of someone killed in action ends abruptly. Under the Movements column, usually filled with the incessant traffic from one unit or course or school to the next, Reginald's record says simply: 'Reported Missing 9/6/18', in a more elegant hand than the usual clerk's scrawl, as though for this ultimate Movement some finer scribe was drafted in. Then, a little lower down the page, in another, rougher hand, the confirmation '9/6/18 Missing'. That's all.

So the commanding officer turns to the 'Name of Person to be Informed of Casualties', in this case, 'Mrs Baring, Verne House, Newton Road, Sudbury, Suffolk. Mother', and begins his letter of condolence. And for the fourth time in less than two years, the telegram boy cycles down Newton Road. That is the last we hear of Reginald, except for his name beside the names of his three brothers on Sudbury War Memorial – and on his would-be son Buster's seven marriage certificates.

But Eileen and Donald are married, not an event that either of them could have been sure of during their first nights together at Ridgmount Gardens and then at Crawford Mansions. They have come through. Those words spoken so often, 'when the war is over', spoken so speculatively, so vacantly almost, as of a theoretical but hard-to-imagine thing, are now a reality. At any rate, Donald is in one piece, and Eileen is free of Harold. She is free of Buster, too, I think. No room for a boisterous 6-year-old in Crawford Mansions. In any case, by now she may have persuaded herself that he will have a better life with her mother in Sheffield than she could have given him herself, certainly over the past few frantic years. She can always catch the train up north from the station across the road and see how he is getting on. No, I don't think it is really like that. I don't believe that she goes through a single night without bitterly wishing she hadn't done it. I have received enough of her love myself to know that much. Perhaps I am the son she never properly had. That is an obvious thought, I suppose, but I have never thought it before and I find the idea unsettling.

What neither Eileen nor Donald can be expected to know, because there has never been a world war before, is that wartime romances are different. Perhaps there are in truth no more mismatches in wartime than at any other time, but the disillusion may be sharper and the failure easier to explain away as a wartime thing. All I know is that in 1924 Donald George Pilcher Clark sues Eileen Constance Clark (formerly Ridge, formerly Macduff) for divorce. Six years on, Eileen is back in the courts. This time the co-respondent is named as William M. A. Anderson. And here begins the strangest chapter in her life.

7

Eileen and Elizabeth

As soon as my search in the National Archives yielded the news of this second, quite unsuspected divorce (not that I had ever had a previous inkling of the marriage), I turned to the GRO Index to see if this William Anderson had, like Donald, progressed from co-respondent to husband at some later date. But there was no sign of any such marriage in the ten years after 1924. Perhaps William is just a passing fancy, attractive enough to break up the marriage but not much more than that. So I turned instead to Donald's petition to see what I could glean. It is a fatter folder than the others in the box, and unlike the others gives the appearance of having been handled a good deal.

The petition starts off as if it is going to read pretty much like Harold's petition six years earlier. There is a recital of the bare facts of the marriage, then the bare facts of the adulteries, strung out in all their grim particulars:

> after the said marriage, your Petitioner lived and cohabited with his said wife at 1 Crawford Mansions, Crawford Street, Marylebone, 8 Cardinal Mansions, Carlisle Place, Westminster, 222 Finchley Road and at 35 Craigton Road, Eltham in the County of London and there is no issue of said marriage ...

A glum procession from one flat to the next and nothing coming of it all. A suggestion too of money running short, and serial downshifting, which is supported by the bleak statement in the next para that 'your Petitioner is of no occupation'. But the next para also offers the first hint that something unusual is afoot.

'The said Eileen Constance Clark formerly resided at 26 Welbeck Street in the County of London (but whose present address is unknown to your Petitioner) ...'

So Eileen has scarpered, done a runner, and done it so effectively that Donald has no idea where she is; at least he doesn't on 22 March 1924, which is the date of the petition.

'That the said Eileen Constance Clark has committed adultery with one William M. A. Anderson ...' There then follow the dates when and addresses where Eileen and her new beau have coupled: in October 1922 at 12D Hyde Park Mansions; in January 1922 at Manor House, Marylebone; in February, March, April, May and June 1922 at Albemarle Chambers, Albemarle Street; from July 1922 to January 1923 at 26 Welbeck Street. How exhausting the petition makes it all sound. The two of them have been traipsing around central London between Piccadilly and the Marylebone Road for months on end, and in the course of these traipses adultery is what they commit and according to the petition commit it with gruelling frequency.

And then Donald or his private detectives lose the scent. Some time in the early months of 1923 the trail of adulteries runs out. There is no sign of Eileen or William at 26 Welbeck Street, or anywhere else. But if Donald wants a divorce, he needs to track them down. In the next para comes an intimation, typed on a different typewriter and with a couple of inked-in insertions, suggesting that something close to panic has gripped the offices of Donald's solicitors, Messrs Appleton and Co. of 2 Lancaster Place, Wellington Street: 'petition to be delivered to Eileen Constance Clark and to William M. A. Anderson both late of 26 Welbeck Street whose present addresses are unknown but who are believed to be residing at California in the United States of America'.

So Eileen and William have lit out for the furthest reach of the New World. At any rate, that is what 'at California' sounds like. You feel that the people in Appletons wonder whether either of them will be heard of again and whether there is a hope in hell of ever serving the petition on them.

But the next sheet in the grubby plump folder tells a quite different story. It is an affidavit from a clerk in Appletons, who confusingly is also called Clark. He, Joseph Clark, testifies that, on the contrary, the petition dated 22 March 1924 'was duly served by me on the said Respondent, Eileen Constance Clark, at "the Samovar Tea-Rooms", 94 St Martin's Lane, on the 26th day of March, 1924, by delivering to the said Eileen Constance Clark personally a sealed copy thereof'.

Far from sunning herself on the beach at Malibu or sipping a cocktail in the Polo Lounge at the Beverly Hills Hotel, Eileen is watching the Russian tea-urn hiss in St Martin's Lane, with or possibly without William M. A. Anderson at her side. In the event, it took only four days to track her down.

It must have been a scene of high melodrama. For Joseph Clark adds: 'At the time of such service I was accompanied by the Petitioner Donald George Pilcher Clark who pointed out the said Respondent Eileen Constance Clark to me, and she admitted on being served with the Petition that she was the said Eileen Constance Clark.'

No. 94 St Martin's Lane still stands, towards the Trafalgar Square end of the street, a sturdy gabled Victorian block. The premises are now occupied by Freed, the world-famous ballet shop. I shall never be able to pass the satin pumps and tutus in the window without thinking of Donald pointing his finger at the startled Eileen while Joseph Clark thrusts the envelope with its red seal into her hands. In the background

I imagine impassive Russians behind the hissing urns, White Russians perhaps, aristos even, who have fled the Revolution and for whom this scene of denunciation is everyday stuff. The Samovar Tea Rooms is popular with the chorus boys and girls from the Coliseum and the students from the St Martins School of Art, then nearby in the Charing Cross Road. Edward Burra and his friends spend quite a bit of time there. There must be a shaggy bohemian crowd looking on as the two Clarks bear down on Eileen, the clerk no doubt dressed in a pinstriped suit and stiff collar.

So, anyway, the petition has been served after all, and only four days after it was signed. Yet Eileen still refuses to respond to it. For it is nine months later, on 20 January 1925, that Joseph swears his affidavit, and the point of the affidavit is to enable the High Court to summons Eileen to come and answer. She is accordingly summonsed to the Court on 23 January, then summonsed again on 23 February and given one final summons on 23 March.

Still no show. Now she is in contempt of court and is liable to be arrested. But things turn out to be much worse than that.

Attached to the affidavit by a rusted paper-clip there is a small piece of white paper with a few lines scrawled on it in pencil. It looks like a memo hastily jotted while holding a telephone.

Re Eileen Constance Clark, now in custody.
   This woman is believed to be bigamously married to William Anderson and the lawful husband is suing for a divorce.
   Particulars required of lawful husband

… and then in ink in a different hand: 'supply particulars given in Petition/ WJ 19.xi.24'.

In custody. Bigamously married. Suddenly we have moved from a light tale of cocktails and adultery into the pages of a dark and criminal thriller, the sort of thing that a few years later would be starring Joan Crawford or Barbara Stanwyck, the latter not unlike Eileen as a physical type. So while this little note is being scribbled by someone in Appletons, Eileen is shivering in a police cell somewhere.

But can it all be true? Might it not rather be a case of pardonable confusion and misunderstanding, of legal loose ends not dealt with, or alternatively the story of a betrayed husband launching a baseless slander against his faithless wife? Perhaps the private detectives who have been following Eileen and William up and down the West End have got the wrong end of the stick.

This latest discovery puts my normally sluggish pulse rate into overdrive. I find it hard to maintain any sort of inner cool as I think out the next step. What I need to do first is to find out if any such bigamous marriage is on the books. No marriage certificate, no crime. At worst a haze of rumours about an unlawful marriage conducted by some dodgy judge in California, something virtually impossible to check out.

So far I have, quite logically, consulted the GRO Index only for the years *after* 1924, when Eileen would have been free to marry again if her second divorce had gone through. Now I need to look back through the years 1920 to 1924, the years of her marriage to Donald.

And there it is, bold as the brassiest brass. A week later, on my desk I have enough evidence to send her down for the maximum sentence of seven years, as prescribed under Section 57 of the Offences Against the Person Act of 1861.

What the certificate before me states is that on 18 April 1922, William Maurice Alistair Anderson was married in the Register Office of the parish of St George's Hanover Square to Eileen Constance Baring. This is indubitably Munca, because she gives as her father John William Macduff (deceased), steel merchant. She is at the chrysalis stage of her mutation into Patricia Elizabeth Baring, half in and half out. How come she is called Baring and not Macduff? Because, outrageously, barefacedly, she puts her condition as 'Widow'.

Munca's bigamous marriage certificate

William is a bachelor of independent means, a mere 22 years old. And he is marrying this tragic young widow two years older than himself — in fact six years older, but that's a detail. In fact it turns out on further investigation that William is only 20 years old, so he's really eight years younger than she is. Once again, in order to qualify for the dubious privilege of marrying Eileen, the groom has to add on a couple of years to avoid the embarrassing question of parental consent, which is unlikely to be forthcoming.

It also turns out that William was born in the Philippines, in Manila, where his father William Robert Anderson was a shipping merchant. His mother, Beatrice Mauricia Earnshaw, was the youngest daughter in one of the leading industrial families in the Pacific, founders of the Earnshaw Docks Company, which later merged with the Honolulu Ironworks Company. Her father Daniel Earnshaw had come out from England in 1861 to build ships for the Spanish authorities. He had married two Filipino ladies and fathered eight children. Beatrice's elder half-brothers, Manuel and Tomas, became leading figures in the new Americanized Philippines: Tomas was Mayor of Manila for six years and Manuel was the country's Resident Commissioner in Washington DC. The Earnshaws had a finger in most things: shipping, sugar-drying machinery, urban and harbour construction, sugar plantations, gold mines. William Robert could look forward to a great future with his in-laws.

Unfortunately, he died in 1908, at the age of only 35, and only eight months later, Beatrice Mauricia married again, at the British Consulate in Yokohama, to another expat British merchant, Walter George Stevenson, who like Beatrice had been born in Manila.

Little William, still only seven years old, must have been surplus to the requirements of the newlyweds. Like many another colonial child, he was shipped to the England he had never seen, to be made a proper Englishman at the Grange prep school, which like all self-respecting prep schools lay in a desolate belt of heather and pine, in this case at Crowborough, Sussex. Two dozen of the 100 pupils in the school came from as far away as he did, from Hong Kong and Johannesburg and Montevideo. The only day-boy in the school, nearly four years younger than William, was Tom Driberg, later the sinister eminence of the Labour Party and gossip writer for Lord Beaverbrook. Tom's father, John Driberg, had retired to Crowborough after a lifetime in India, ending up as Chief of Police in Assam. The head master of the Grange was a former county cricketer called Frank Gresson. Driberg describes him as 'a practising sadist' who thrashed the boys on the hands and wrists rather than their bottoms because it hurt more.

A far cry from the sleepy, scented verandas of Manila. William must have cried himself to sleep more bitterly than most, his father gone, his mother remarried the other side of the world. And now it comes to me that this is not only where Munca plucked the idea of Buster being born in Manila from, but probably also where she picked up the story of riding a horse into the dining room, only it was little William riding the horse or pony and not herself. She is like a bird building a nest of any materials that come to hand: sticks, bottle tops, moss, fag-ends, particularly fag-ends.

Eileen's real husband has been erased and replaced by the shadowy and dead Mr Baring. No doubt if she were challenged, she would say that her first husband's Christian name had been Reginald and that he had been killed in the war, over France. Which for Reginald's RFC comrade, Donald Clark, would have been the last straw if he ever got to hear of it.

It is as flagrant and mendacious a case of bigamy as can ever have come before the courts. But did it ever come before the courts? Does William Anderson ever get to know that, far from being a widow, his new 'wife' had contracted another marriage only two years earlier and only half a mile the other side of Oxford Street to a husband who is very much alive and consumed with rage against her? Or has William been in on this reckless caper from the beginning? Is he as wild as she is?

I do not know what becomes of this blighted 'marriage'. Do the scales fall from William's fresh young eyes when he realizes what he has got himself into and the sort of person he has got himself into it with? Or is he so besotted that he plunges deeper into the *folie à deux*, perhaps even recognizing what a folly it is and glorying in it all the more?

But perhaps he is not worrying too much about the state of his marriage or what the world thinks of it. Because he has something else to think about, something altogether more pressing.

Like millions of other young men all over Europe at that time, William has contracted pulmonary tuberculosis. There is as yet no cure for TB, only palliatives and sanatoriums. Some patients do recover because their infection is a relatively mild one. Many more do not.

William does not. He dies at a private sanatorium, St Katharine's, Hook Heath, near Woking on 23 January 1926. He is 24 years old. I do not know if Eileen is with him. The death certificate is signed by the superintendent of the nursing home, Dr Alan Snowdon.

If Eileen is in attendance, I doubt whether she pauses to consider the irony that, by her own lights anyway, she now really is a widow. It is a bleak end to what started as a madcap caper.

Or perhaps there was something more to the marriage than I have so far realized. It is quite possible that William's TB had already been diagnosed in 1922 and that he knew how slim his chances of long-term survival were. He might well have wished to get married as soon as possible in whatever time remained to him, perhaps even to leave a child behind him. It could have been he who insisted on the marriage. Eileen would not have disclosed to him that she was already married. There was no impediment that she could admit to. And every instinct of pity would have told her to go ahead.

What a brief and sad life William's was, though. A tropical childhood, of ponies and palm trees and splashing in the Pacific surf with dark-eyed cousins, all cut cruelly short by his father's death, then not being wanted on his mother's new voyage, and the years of grim British private schools, bullied no doubt for being a half-caste and a Catholic; then his grimmer diagnosis from the specialist, momentarily forgotten in the excitement of his madcap marriage and the humiliating end to that marriage, and then the last months in the sanatorium at Woking.

All the time I have been finding out about William's life and its wretched conclusion, I am still in the dark about what happened to Eileen and the bigamy charge. It seems oddly difficult to track down court proceedings that far back, especially if you do not know which court you are looking for. At first I tried the Central Criminal Court, better known as the Old Bailey, but could find nothing in their records. Then the ever-helpful website of the National Archives suggested that the best place to begin a criminal search was in the indexes of the Director of Public Prosecutions, because serious cases from all over the country have to pass through his office.

Almost immediately in DPP 3/60, I found her under 'Clark, Eileen'. Turning to the actual charge sheet, I read that on 4 December 1924 the DPP received an application from the Commissioner of Police at Scotland Yard and Police C Division, Vine Street, for permission to prosecute Eileen Clark for bigamy.

The application was granted. And Eileen Constance Clark went on trial on 13 December at Marlborough Street Police Court. It is a strange thing to see her name on the same list as those of two men who are being prosecuted for murder and who both have 'Sentenced to death' scrawled against their names. Bigamy crops up quite a lot. There are 28 cases of it in this DPP volume, which covers offences between December 1924 and June 1925. One or two stiffish sentences are imposed: three years' prison in one case, four months' hard labour in another.

But opposite Eileen Clark, the DPP's record says simply:

No evidence offered
— Discharged.

She gets off. I cannot resist an inward cheer, but at the same time I cannot help wondering. It is an open-and-shut case after all, its gravity compounded by her perjurious statements to the

Registrar of Marriages. The doziest CID team could not have failed to track down the false name she gave at the wedding, because William gave his real name in full, 'William Maurice Alistair Anderson'. The Marlborough Street Police Station is virtually next door to the Register Office, for heaven's sake. What the Police Court actually is next door to is the London Palladium. When Munca steps out of the Rolls dripping with jewels to see Danny Kaye or the Crazy Gang 30 years later, I wonder whether she ever thinks of her earlier unwanted visit around the corner. By a pretty quirk, the Marlborough Street Police Court has now been converted into a five-star hotel of the sort that was second home to Munca. We too can catch a faint remembrance of her experiences in 1924, because the No. 1 Court has been preserved with bench and dock as the Court House Hotel's Thai restaurant, and several of the cells have been converted into guest bedrooms. The former dock and magistrate's bench are now adorned with oriental brassware.

The Silk Restaurant, formerly the Marlborough Street Police Court

So why do the police ease off? Why do they not even produce the documentary evidence, which they must possess, or the DPP would not have given the go-ahead? Could it be because Eileen has already spent four weeks in custody, perhaps more, and they think she has been punished enough? Or because they now know that Donald is divorcing her and she will soon be free to marry William legally? Or is it because they have been told that William is now very ill – he is to die only just over a year later – and he needs her care? Does her lawyer enter a defence stating that she only went through the marriage ceremony because William pleaded with her and he was so ill that she gave in, although she knew she shouldn't? Perhaps it is all these things, but especially the last, which together tip the balance and persuade the police to drop the charge. Yes, I think she gets off because he is dying.

But I cannot help feeling that there must be more to come out about the case. It is months later, though, that it occurs to me that, so far, I have been combing the criminal records. Might there not somewhere be a snippet in the press? And I google Eileen Constance Clark, and straight away up comes this little paragraph from the *Gloucester Citizen* for 5 December 1924:

UNSUSTAINED FALSE PRETENCES CHARGE
Eileen Constance Clark (28) of The Long Platt, Great Missenden, Buckinghamshire, was acquitted at Marlborough-Street Police Court on Thursday on a charge of obtaining £110 by false pretences with intent to defraud in 1922; but was remanded on a self-confessed charge of bigamy.

Bigamy *and* obtaining money by false pretences, and not such a small sum either: £110 in 1924 is the equivalent of £6,000 today. So she comes up for trial at Great Marlborough Street twice in ten days and gets off both times. It is perhaps easier to understand the police not pressing the bigamy charge if she has already confessed to it. I note that the alleged fraud took place when she and William were on the run from Donald, moving house every few weeks. They were probably desperate for cash, and false pretences were, after all, Munca's forte. It may well be Donald who is the instigator of both charges. That would probably explain why she gets off on the false pretences at least. The Court would reasonably see it as a quarrel about money between a furious couple and would conclude that it was probably six of one and half a dozen of the other. She has retreated from her usual haunts, up the Marylebone line to the pretty village of Great Missenden, to get away from the implacable Donald and prevent a repeat of the scene in the Samovar Tea Rooms. Presumably William is with her there, in a rural idyll that is overshadowed by his illness and her impending prosecution.

At first sight, in a cruel sort of way, William's death might seem to simplify things. But it doesn't. For Donald's divorce petition is still sitting there, and Eileen's business with him is still a long way from being concluded. For one thing, she dares not appear in the divorce court to answer his petition, for fear that her earlier court appearances and the facts of her bigamy will come up and be splashed all over the popular prints, which must be why she fails to respond to the three summonses issued in January, February, March 1925.

That is the bigamist's bind. She can cease to be in a bigamous state only by divorcing her legal husband, but the process of the divorce will inevitably expose her bigamy. So she has every incentive to lie low and refuse to answer any and every summons. This is Munca's Catch-1922.

In fact, her legal marriage to Donald has many more years to run yet. There are two more sheets of paper at the back of the grubby folder that contains Donald's petition (I see now why it is so much fatter than any of the others in the box). The first is a positively final summons to the respondent to 'attend at the Divorce Registry of the High Court of Justice on the third day of June 1954 at 10.45 of the clock in the forenoon to show cause why an order should not be made dismissing the Petition dated the 22nd day of March 1924 herein'. And behind that sheet of paper there is another, which turns out to be an order dated 3 June 1954 dismissing the petition.

Nineteen fifty-four! Donald's petition has been lying there unanswered *for 30 years*. And as I slide the whole folder back across the returns counter at the National Archives, I notice for the first time that it has 'Dismissed' written in a fine Dickensian flourish across its cover.

All those years Donald and Eileen have remained legally married. They could have celebrated their silver wedding if they had been on speaking terms. And the consequence of that extraordinary fact is that it is not just the sadly fleeting William Anderson with whom she committed bigamy. She did it with my uncle too.

All this comes to light so many years later only because Donald has at last recovered from the ghastly experience of his first marriage and now wants to get married again. His bride-to-be is Alexandra Barishnikov, a schoolteacher of Russian descent who is 20 years younger than he is (Donald is now 57). But first he must clear up the unfinished business. Having got the original doomed petition out of the way, he now launches another petition against his long-vanished wife. This time he seeks to have his marriage to Eileen Constance Clark dissolved, 'by reason that the respondent had deserted the petitioner'. So she had, and then some. In fact, she had deserted her old self too. Eileen Constance Clark had been dissolved long ago, back in the 1920s, and this really is the last whisper of her anywhere. So it is not before time that on 12 October 1954 the High Court grants Donald his decree nisi, which, the respondent not dreaming of responding, for that would mean acknowledging her former existence, becomes absolute on 20 November, just in time for him to marry Alexandra at the Chelsea Register Office in December that same year, 1954.

Jarndyce v Jarndyce was a quickie compared to *Clark v Clark and Anderson*. How weird it is to think that while Munca was pruning her roses on the lawn at Blue Waters and I was playing French cricket with my sister and Georgie, this interminable case still had years to run, and I was being looked after by a double bigamist.

Now that William is gone, what is left for Eileen? She is adrift. Just turned 30, no husband, or none that she can stand to live with, and no child with her. And she has just escaped a jail sentence by the skin of her teeth. If she is not a fugitive from the law, she is certainly a fugitive from respectable society. Where does she live? What does she live on? Or if she has a partner, who does she live off? Somewhere in those red-brick cliffs between the Marylebone Road and Oxford Street she is bivouacked as remote from our gaze as if she had been lost in the Empty Quarter of Arabia, waving in vain to a passing Sopwith Camel.

As with any lost person, we have rumoured sightings, stray reports, but nothing very reliable, no names, no addresses. Munca herself speaks in later life of the 'sugar daddy who bought me a hunting box in Gloucestershire'. My bitchy old cousin John Saleby remembers seeing her on the arm of (in fact he says married to) the captain of the Gloucestershire Cricket team. So Gloucestershire seems to be our next destination. Somewhere in the rain-sodden Cotswolds is where she begins to remake her life. That must be where she is reborn, becomes a new person. Not as ordinary people do these days, by taking up yoga or running or a new religion, but by calling herself something entirely different.

But not by calling herself Mrs Bev Lyon. There my cousin John's recollection seems to have been ruinously muddled. For I look it all up and it is true that Beverley Hamilton Lyon is married three times, but each of his brides – Edith Huxtable (1926), Iris Gow (1932) and Grace Collins (1948) has a provable independent existence, and none of them was Munca even under a hitherto undiscovered alias. On the other hand, in her divorce proceedings against Bev in 1931, Edith alleges, and is not contradicted, that 'during the years 1928, 1929 and 1930, the said Beverley Hamilton Lyon frequently committed adultery'. So Eileen could well have been one of the 'frequentlies'.

But as we come into the 1930s, another line of enquiry opens up. By March 1931 Buster is well launched on his new life as Alistair Archie Baring. He has come south and is putting up in style at the Washington Hotel, Curzon Street, before getting married down the road at Christ Church, Mayfair, to Kathleen Dorothy Lennard. The source of his funds is as elusive as ever. But at least we can identify the source of his new surname.

'Baring' can only have been, well, fathered on him by his mother. She first appeared on the scene with that surname nine years earlier in front of the registrar at St George's Hanover Square. Whether she plucked the name hastily because she was in a tight spot or whether she gave it a lot of thought, the choice is not a mysterious one, if we look attentively at the time she chose it in. Barings Bank had never quite recovered its commercial pre-eminence after it had been rescued from the great crash of 1890. But between the wars the family was at its social zenith. Its various branches had spawned four peerages and a baronetcy, and every branch had numerous descendants (only

Reginald's branch was sadly truncated). There was safety in numbers. Among the swarm of Barings in the ballroom and the boardroom, who would notice one more? What other surname could inspire greater confidence or respect?

But now Eileen Constance Baring was no longer a safe half-alias to go about under. She needed a new set of first names to match it. What would sound suitably distinguished? What would sound least like Eileen or, for that matter, Doris? It never does to underestimate Munca's ambition in such matters. What is the date range we are considering? I would say 1925 to 1929 at the latest. So what names spring out of the *Tatler* and the *Sketch* in those years? If we are looking in the right place, the answer is not so hard. In 1926, Elizabeth, Duchess of York, gave birth to her first child and called her Elizabeth. The year before, Edwina Mountbatten gave birth to her first child and called her Patricia.

So there I think we have it: Patricia Elizabeth Baring. She has finally kissed her old self goodbye. Her new wings are fitted. She is ready to fly again.

What a dazzling confection, what a *nom de guerre* in the class war. There isn't anything so original about borrowing names from the Royal Family. We have already seen how up in Sheffield before the Great War parents often christened their sons Albert Edward after the fat king. But somehow doing it in your early thirties as part of an assumed identity gives a unique sparkle to the trick.

More daring still is her response when she realizes that Buster needs a new father. Or perhaps I have things back to front and it is this need that is the motor for the whole Baring project. The new father must be irreproachably well born, but he must also be irreproachably dead. So she calls to mind that poor boy who was killed in his Sopwith Camel only a month after he went to France, and who was trained at the same flying school as her just discarded husband. Possibly she had actually met Reginald at some RAF hop. Or perhaps she had only heard the terrible story of his being the last of his four brothers to be killed in the closing stages of the war. Anyway, Reginald would do. No boy could start adult life with a finer father.

Buster's first wedding begins a new life for both of them. It also occurs to me to find out whether Munca herself had tried out her new identity before she married my uncle in December 1936. That was more than a decade after her last 'marriage', which is a long time for someone who has been married before, two or three times, to stay single. So I try the GRO Index for the years 1924 to 1930 to see if any Patricia Elizabeth Barings have got married. Nothing at all, not a speck of confetti. But I have learnt one lesson from tracking Buster's marital career, viz, that even within the shortest time frame there is always one more marriage to be winkled out of the records. So I try the same enquiry for the years 1930 to 1935. And there I find a single entry. On 20 January 1933, Patricia Elizabeth Baring marries Dallas Alexander Chancellor Page. He gives his age as 21 and his occupation as 'lieutenant, Gloucester Regiment (retired)'. At last a registered Gloucestershire connection, though it seems a tenuous one, if he has already left the Regiment. She describes herself as a spinster and gives her age as 30. She is in fact about to be 39, and she isn't exactly a spinster either. But no matter.

This must surely be her most daring effort yet. This is the fourth time she has taken her vows, her second bigamous marriage under an assumed name, and to a man who is 18 years younger than she is, in fact only a couple of months older than her son. How much does Dallas Page know about all this?

And 1933, days before Hitler comes to power and, more to the point, only three years before she marries my uncle. How does it all come about? She meets this young man at who knows where – a hunt ball, perhaps, this is Gloucestershire – takes a fancy to him and in no time they run off to the register office at St Marylebone, which she knows pretty well by now. She got married there last time under her old name. You might think that she would be worried about the registrars recognizing her, but she doesn't worry about things like that. As it turns out, the registrars have all changed in the intervening 13 years. She probably feels at home too, because she is back in her old territory. Both she and Dallas give their address as 12 Newcastle House, Northumberland Street, St Marylebone. The street is called Luxborough Street today, but Newcastle House still stands, another of those grim blood-red blocks to which Munca seems so drawn.

She too needs a father for the marriage certificate, but for some reason that I'm not absolutely clear about, she shies away from putting Reginald Baring. The fact of the real-life Reginald being five years younger than her may trigger some vestigial scruple or anxiety. Instead, she gives her father's name as John Drury Baring, of independent means. The 'Drury' has a ring to it. It must be borrowed from the third name of her first husband. Once again, this doesn't exactly square with her little brother Buster being the son of Reginald B. But who's counting?

At least she has come back onto the radar, and in circumstances if possible even more vexed than before. Who exactly is Dallas Page? Why does the marriage go wrong? How does she get rid of him in such short order? What happens to him afterwards? Does he die, and if so when and why? With an unusual Christian name like that, this should not be too hard to establish, and indeed it is not. The GRO has one and only one Dallas Page in the Deaths between 1933 and 2000, and it is our Dallas A. C. Page, and he is unmistakably dead.

His death is registered at Cirencester, Glos, in the third quarter of 1936. His age is given as 25. He and Patricia Elizabeth Baring have been married just over three years. Two bigamous marriages, and both the 'husbands' dead in their mid-twenties, in both cases less than four years after she married them.

What has she done to him? My first thoughts scurry into the darkest regions imaginable. Has he discovered her past, not to mention her true age, and has she somehow got rid of him to shut him up? Or has his disillusionment with the marriage driven him mad, or provoked him to some fatal act of recklessness? Murder, or suicide, or what?

The truth, when it comes to hand a week later on the pale green copy of the death certificate, is less lurid than my imaginings. Just the same, it is tragic, an all too common tragedy in the mid-1930s, but a tragedy none the less.

Dallas Page died on 2 September 1936, at the Cirencester Memorial Hospital. He had been injured in a motor accident the day before. His car had collided with a motorcyclist on the main Gloucester–Cirencester road in the parish of Duntisbourne Abbots. The motorcyclist had been 'guilty of an error of judgment amounting to negligence in entering the main road from a minor road but such negligence was not gross and minimal. No p.m.' The Coroner's verdict is almost soothing in its cool precision. Dallas's address is given as The Old Barn, Stratton, Cirencester, and his means as independent. At last in these sad circumstances we have a certified Glos connection. And we have an address for that 'little hunting box in Gloucestershire' of Munca's, which for half a century I had regarded as one more spin-off from her unquenchable fancy. The Old Barn still stands, an ancient thatched barn on the corner of School Hill at the edge of the village. Dallas was only a couple of miles from home when he crashed.

The Old Barn, Stratton

My researches in Sheffield have shown that any fatal accident is likely to receive decent coverage in the local paper, even when the victim is working-class like poor Joe Vail or Mahala Crabb. So I traipse up to the old Newspaper Library at Colindale again to see if there's a story in the *Gloucestershire Echo*, which is the paper that covers the immediate area.

It was a shock to learn of Dallas's sudden death, but that is nothing to the shock I get when I turn up the *Echo* for 2 September 1936. Right across the front page it says in a four-decker splash head:

COUNTY CRICKET CAPTAIN'S FATAL CAR ACCIDENT

MR D. A. C. PAGE DIES IN CIRENCESTER HOSPITAL

CAR OVERTURNED IN EFFORT TO AVOID MOTOR CYCLIST

TRAGEDY ON CLOSING DAY OF SUCCESSFUL SEASON

The death of Dallas Page, as reported in the *Gloucestershire Echo*,
2 September 1936

Next to the headlines there is a photo of Dallas in cricket whites smiling a big smile as he shakes hands with Charlie Barnett, the team's opening bat, to congratulate him on being selected for the forthcoming MCC tour of Australia. At the bottom of the page, there are two pictures of 'The scene of the fatal accident': above, the long straight Roman road with the side turning coming in on the right and the signpost to Duntisbourne Abbots; and then below, the spot where Dallas crashed into the drystone wall, reducing it to a heap of rubble after charging through and over a twelve-foot-high hazel bush.

It seems particularly tragic to the *Echo* that the accident should have happened as he was driving home after leading his team to a brilliant victory over Nottinghamshire that had pushed Gloucestershire up to finish fourth in the County Championship. The year before, Dallas's first season in charge, they had finished a dismal fifteenth.

He did not die immediately. Courteous to the last, he was able to crawl out of the overturned car and enquire after the condition of the motorcyclist and his pillion passenger. Neither of them was seriously hurt. There was no external mark on Dallas's own slender body. At first, the bystanders thought that his passenger, Mr Herbert, a commission agent who also lived in Stratton and who was thrown out of the car and pinned against the wall, was the worse hurt, but he was not seriously injured either. The motorbike was nosing out into the main road so slowly, at about 5 mph, that the pillion passenger was able to jump clear as he saw Dallas bombing along towards them at an estimated 65 mph. It only took a touch of the motorbike's rear wheel to send the car careering into the wall. It sounds to me as if Dallas was the only one driving without due care and attention. He was certainly the only one to suffer. He died of unstoppable internal haemorrhaging.

Dallas at the crease

The *Echo* is full of tributes to him from his team mates. The most illustrious of them, Walter Hammond, said, 'It is a very great shock to me. He will be greatly missed, probably more by me than most people.' And Wally Hammond was generally accounted a hard man.

The match that had just finished had featured one of the most splendid of all Hammond's innings. Notts were not a negligible team. That final weekend of the season, they fielded at least three immortals: Joe Hardstaff, George Gunn and Bill Voce. The most famous Notts man of all, Voce's fast-bowling partner Harold Larwood, the hero or villain of the Bodyline controversy three years earlier, was out injured with fluid on the knee. D. A. C.

Page's predecessor as captain, B. H. Lyon, was also off, with a sprained wrist.

It was a glorious occasion, with summer frocks and straw hats seen round the boundary for the first time that damp summer. For the first time at Gloucester, there was a BBC van broadcasting a live commentary on Hammond's tremendous knock of 317, which was the deciding factor in Gloucestershire's victory by an innings and 70 runs. It was his highest innings in England and fell only one run short of W. G. Grace's record for the county.

Dallas's own performance was more modest. He made only eight runs before falling lbw to G. F. Heane. But he did take the winning catch and he had made 1,000 runs that season for the first time, including his first century. From being merely the useful amateur who came in at No. 7 and could be expected to knock up a quick 20 or 30, he was developing into a serious player. Of course he had been made captain only because, except for Bev Lyon, he was the single amateur who played regularly for the team. Professionals were not yet thought to have leadership qualities. Bev was up to his eyes in business that year, nursing his fledgling career as a director of Wireless Music Ltd, and had to give up the captaincy for that reason.

At 5 p.m., after the match had ended, by popular demand Dallas made a little speech to close off the season, thanking all concerned. These were, I suppose, his proper last words, apart from the odd aside to his passenger on the way home. What he said was: 'We started rather badly this season but we have finished in brilliant form. I want to thank all the players who have supported me, and especially the two members of the team who are going to Australia, and Tom Goddard. We have had a very enjoyable game today, and I am looking forward to next season with confidence.'

A captain's farewell. He was cheered with genuine affection by the large crowd that had gathered round the pavilion. As he drove back to the Old Barn over the tops of the Cotswolds, it was a triumphant homecoming. You can see from the photo of him with Charlie Barnett what a delightful, easy fellow he was. He looks as if nothing had ever bothered him except whether he was taking his bat up straight.

The next day, the *Echo* splashes the story again in reporting the funeral: PATHETIC STORY OF COUNTY CAPTAIN'S DEATH. How quickly they held inquests and funerals then. At the funeral, the vicar of St Catherine's, Gloucester, the Rev H. J. Hensman, an old friend of the family, spoke as follows:

> So to you, my brothers, who will in future take the field without his earthly presence, let me say this. Your old 'skipper' will rejoice in knowing that you are carrying on the traditions he helped build up and playing the game as he played it and inspired you to play it. I fancy that he will rejoice in your victories; but what will interest him more than these will be the knowledge that you are playing the game as Christian gentlemen.

At the side of the coffin was a magnificent floral emblem sent by the Gloucestershire team, representing a cricket pitch with bat and ball and one of the stumps knocked back. A Gloucestershire county tie lay folded on the emblem. I should love to have seen it.

And Mrs D. A. C. Page? Where is Patricia Elizabeth? She is not among the summer frocks and straw hats strolling round the county ground. In fact, she has missed the last match of the season and she misses its awful aftermath too. The *Echo* tells us that 'Mrs Page at the time was travelling home from France but did not arrive in time to see her husband before he died.' In one of its later reports, the paper amplifies: 'Mrs Page had been on holiday in the South of France.' She was not there to see either his triumph or his tragedy.

This does not really surprise me. Munca had as little interest in ball games as any woman I have ever met. I cannot imagine her sitting through a whole day of a county cricket match, let alone three. The wonder is that she should go out with not one but two captains of the Gloucestershire County Cricket Club. For now, in a sad and blinding flash, everything has become as clear to me as it is ever likely to.

Old Cousin John Saleby was not muddled at all. He had a sharp brain and I should never have doubted him. It was I who, startled by the fresh light he was casting on Munca, had failed to take in exactly what he was telling me. The point is that he was giving me two separate pieces of information: that she had an affair with Bev, and that she then married the county captain, the next one, not Bev himself. When he moved on to another of his 'frequentlies', she hooked up with the cheerful young batsman whom she had already seen a bit of in Bev's company. It may be that she only married Dallas on the rebound when Bev told her that his next wife was going to be Iris and not her. She would be eager to show him how much a younger man could desire her. I had remembered Cousin John as saying that she had had pretty much everyone in the hunt, but perhaps what he had really said was 'everyone in the team'. Hunting never sounded like Munca's style, unless the quarry ran on two legs and wore gleaming white flannels.

Bev came to the funeral. So did the Duke of Beaufort, who was the club's president, and G. O. 'Gubby' Allen, who was leading the MCC team in Australia, and Walter Hammond and the much loved veteran slow bowler Tom Goddard and Charlie Barnett, who had travelled back from the MCC match at Folkestone where the flags were flying at half-mast for Dallas. Let us leave him, though, in his glory. In the autographed Gloucestershire team photograph for 1934, his first year as Captain, there he is in the middle next to Goddard and Hammond, fresh and brylcreemed, without a scratch on him.

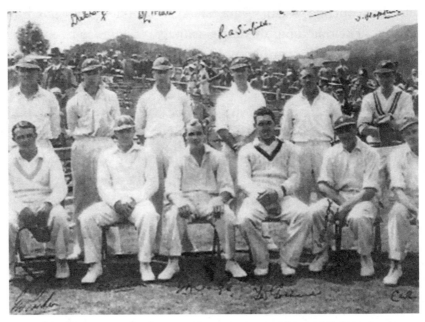

Dallas as captain, Gloucestershire CCC team photograph for 1934

By now Patricia Elizabeth was back from Antibes or Cannes. This time she really was a widow, or would have been if she had been legally married to Dallas. Other family mourners recorded in the *Echo* included Mrs H. V. Page (mother), Mr and Mrs A. A. Baring (nephew and niece) and Mr D. Burke. Even in the pages of the otherwise scrupulously accurate *Echo*, Munca cannot help spreading confusion. Denis Burke, who is a perfectly genuine nephew by marriage, is left untagged, whereas Buster appears, again for the first and only time, quite erroneously, as a nephew. The Mrs A. A. Baring who is at his side is the second holder of the title, Josephine the professional dancer, Buster himself also being a hoofer at this period. Josephine has only a year or so before she ceases to be his second wife.

And who thinks up the nephew story? Munca, I suppose, as ever thinking on her feet in response to the man from the *Echo* who is hovering, pencil in hand: 'Oh yes, that's my nephew Archie.' The one thing this fully grown married man cannot be allowed to be is her son. I don't imagine that Buster went home from the funeral in the best of tempers.

And I don't imagine either that he is much better pleased when exactly three months later, his widowed mother stops being a widow and marries George Richard Mount. For my own part, I cannot help feeling a bit like Hamlet:

But two months dead: nay not so much, not two
… O God! A beast, that wants discourse of reason,
Would have mourned longer – married with mine uncle.

Three months, true, not two, and the circumstances are slightly different, me not being the Prince of Denmark for one thing, but the comparison seems to have some purchase, all the same.

I cannot help surmising that among her companions in the South of France was the man who was to be her fourth or fifth husband, depending on how you're counting. Unca was not a great one for foreign holidays, though he enjoyed his business trips to Italy and Africa for Lennards. But he did like being in the South of France. The stylishness and the *bronzage* suited him. He was happy sitting in dark glasses at a good table on the quay at St Tropez or strolling along the Croisette at Cannes. In later life, he and Munca sometimes took a holiday villa in the hills behind Antibes. So I wouldn't mind betting that the two of them were out there together, while Dallas was sitting in the pavilion applauding Hammond as he moved majestically on from his second century to his third.

Afterwards, Munca packs up the Old Barn and heads back up to Mayfair, which is where she sets out from for her final appearance on a marriage register. It is her most spectacular public appearance yet. If we assume that she really is residing in Mayfair at the time, this is just about the only true statement she makes on the certificate. She marries as Patricia Elizabeth Baring, aged 28, Spinster, the daughter of Anthony John Baring, Gentleman. In fact she is 42 years old, this is her third bigamous marriage, and as for her parentage, we have been through all that. It is ironic, too, that this is the second marriage certificate on which she could, if she liked, call herself a widow, and she doesn't, having only adopted that style in 1922 when both her previous husbands were still living, as incidentally they still are. 'Every word she writes is a lie including "and" and "the"', as the novelist Mary McCarthy famously said of the playwright Lillian Hellman.

Most outrageous of all, Munca is married in the little church at Wasing according to the rites and ceremonies of the Church of England, which at this epoch and for many years after is extremely strict about not marrying people who have been divorced once, let alone twice, and both times the guilty party with both her exes still very much alive, and that's before we even start on the bigamy. She is married by my great-uncle the Reverend Harvey Thursby, a rich and saintly old boy very fond of horses. Uncle Harvey's Christian charity extended to bailing out my father when he was in deep with the bookies. I doubt whether it would have extended to marrying Munca if he had known the true facts. Also on hand as witnesses are my Uncle Bill and my grandmother Hilda, both of them among the most upright citizens in Berkshire. My father also signs the register, lowering the prevailing moral tone a little but not much, for he too could be surprisingly strict on such matters.

Does Patricia Elizabeth tremble, if only for a moment, during the little silence after Uncle Harvey does the bit about 'I request and charge you both, as ye will answer at the dreadful day of judgment when the secrets of all hearts shall be disclosed, that if either of you know any impediment ...'? Does she hell. She has answered, or rather not answered, quite enough dreadful judges already not to be fazed by such empty threats.

You could hardly describe this marriage as made in heaven then, but by a pretty trick of fate it is to last 45 years and is broken only in the prescribed manner, by death parting them. For the one thing I am sure of, the one genuine thing, is that they were devoted to one another. If the refuge they shared was built upon a multi-storey building of lies, it was a happy refuge all the same.

How much does Unca know? Does he know about Sheffield and the Macduffs, for example, or about the true relationship between Eileen and Doris and hence between Buster and Denis? Does he know about Harold Ridge or Donald Clark or William Anderson? Or about the Marlborough Street Police Court? Does he know about Dallas, even? That he surely must know, because she goes straight from the South of France to the funeral.

Perhaps he knows all of these things, or suspects some of them anyway, but doesn't care. It may be that he likes being in on secrets and likes keeping them. My father's family tend to be secretive. But it may also be that he is preoccupied with his own affairs. It may be that Munca is not the only one with a secret.

Before the war, Greig became friends with a young dress designer called Michael Sherard. I imagine that Munca knew him too, possibly even knew him first. When they adopted Georgie in 1942, they chose Michael Sherard to be her godfather. After the war, he had a famous couture house on Parisian lines and lived in style with his business manager in an apartment in Albany. In the 1950s, he ran a yellow-and-white salon in Curzon Street where he dressed stars like Margaret Lockwood and Margot Fonteyn and also dressed quite a few stage productions. Much later on, towards the end of his long life, after Unca and Munca were both dead, he confided to Georgie that Greig was caught up in some sort of gay scandal and had to marry Betty — we are on to Liz or Betty now — in order to fend off trouble with the police.

At first sight, the story does not quite hang together. How would his getting married avoid trouble with the police? What is conceivable, I suppose, is that Greig might have thought that trouble was on the way and that taking cover in marriage might make him less conspicuous. He could still think this and get married for this reason, although the looming trouble might be largely imaginary. At the very least, whatever it was would be preying on his mind, so that he would not be thinking much about his wife's background. If he did know about Dallas and his tragic death, he could also be thinking in a kindly way — because he was on the whole a kindly person — that he would be rescuing her from grief and solitude, just as she would be bolstering him in what had so far been a faltering life. And that she certainly did.

I know what Munca would say about all this. In fact, I can hear her saying it with a toss of her tawny curls and a sniff from her high-bridged nose: 'What you don't know can't hurt you.'

But this is not true. At least it isn't always true. If Greig was ignorant about half of the things in her past, it might have done him no great harm. It could even have been a blessing. But what Georgie didn't know did hurt her, very badly. In fact it ruined her life. And what Buster didn't know, or only half-knew, or was lied to about or himself had to tell lies about, all that certainly hurt him, maddened him, I suspect, more and more as the years and the wives went by. And hurt the wives too, as one by one they woke up to the reality that they were only bit-players in someone else's family drama.

What you don't know can sting the heart worse than the worst thing you do know. And go on stinging, because while knowledge brings some sort of ending, not knowing never ends.

8

W. F.

I must have been about eighteen when Doris's third and last husband started giving me his cast-off clothes. By then I had grown to my full height, just over six foot, and I was still thin, 11 st 7 lbs when I was weighed for the College football team. Archie McNicol was my sort of height and skinny too, though not as skinny as he had once been. Hence the cast-offs. As far as I could gather, much of his life had been spent in the pursuit of pleasure, properly attired – though I may be doing him an injustice because I never knew him that well. He would occasionally come over from Sunningdale with Doris. At this period, Munca was at Holthanger on the Wentworth Estate, only separated by a couple of golf courses from her sister at Titlarks Hill.

I took to Archie. He was a dark and melancholy figure with a touch of irony and self-deprecation. I was intrigued too that Unca and Munca seemed to disapprove of him. Because he was idle? Or because they thought he was after the fortune that Doris had inherited from Frank Parkinson? I could not quite make it out. I thought perhaps that he might have views about them too, especially about Munca, views that he had perhaps once expressed or intimated and so caused a coolness. Perhaps it was simply that Doris and Archie had got married so soon after Frank's death, and not in such a quiet manner either. The *Yorkshire Post* reported that 'the bride wore a full-length dress of white silk jersey, with a bolero effect, white tassel embroidery and paillettes – a copy of the model worn by Lady Mountbatten at the Royal Wedding [the wedding of Princess Elizabeth and Prince Philip a month earlier] – a hat of brown velvet with Bird of Paradise plumes and a mink coat'. The reception was of course at Claridge's. The bride had arrived with her son and daughter-in-law, Denis and Philippa (shortly to be snatched away by the unstoppable Buster). There is no mention of Munca. Perhaps she was too furious to attend her sister's wedding.

What I did not know then was that Munca and Doris were sisters. In that light, Archie could reasonably regard me as almost part of the family. More likely, though, there was nobody else around of the right height and build to inherit the glad rags he could no longer fit into.

There was quite a wardrobe of them: first, a morning tail-coat with striped trousers and black waistcoat, perhaps the tails that he had worn at his wedding to Doris; then, a set of evening tails and two white evening waistcoats made of that dimpled material that I have never learnt the name of. Both sets of tails came from Anderson and Sheppard of Savile Row and looked almost new. To accompany these, there were three stiff white shirts, 'dickey' I think is the technical term for them, and two boxes of stiff collars, ordinary for daytime and winged for evening, plus a box of white bow ties in the same dimpled material. For more casual wear, Archie threw in two pale lemon-yellow silk shirts from A. Sulka & Co. of Old Bond Street. I didn't wear the silk shirts much, if at all. They had a slithery feel I was uncomfortable with, and I left them in the tissue paper they came in. But I did wear the evening clothes on the rare occasions that called for them, until I too could no longer fit into them and anyway had stopped going to anything that called for such formal gear.

It was a generous haul, and I have always thought kindly of Archie because of it, and I salute his memory whenever I drive past the estate agent's window in Sunningdale, on the right just before the level crossing, the window he smashed the Bentley into after overdoing the cocktails one Sunday morning.

The problem, though, was what to take my new acquisitions home in. Not that the suitcase I always took to stay with Munca was a mere overnight bag. On the contrary, it was a substantial if cheap piece of luggage, but three-quarters of it was taken up by the large rubber asthma pillow that I still carried everywhere with me, by this date more as a psychological prop than because it actually helped to ward off an attack.

Munca said I must borrow an old suitcase of theirs, and Unca was sent up to the attic to dredge out one that I would not have the bother of returning because they didn't need it back. He came down with a fair-sized leather case in a rusty brown colour. Its sides went in and out as if breathing, like the flanks of an old dog fox. The case was a bit battered at the corners but otherwise serviceable, though it was covered with dust and clearly had not been used for years.

I took it from him and was startled by how heavy it was, almost as heavy when empty as my own case was when fully packed, including the asthma pillow. Through the dust I could see some initials stamped on the side of the case, and I rubbed the dust off them with the palm of my hand.

'W. F. … Who's W. F.?'

'Oh.' Munca had not bargained for this, not having vetted the choice of suitcase in advance. Perhaps she had forgotten about the initials. But as always she was quick on her feet.

'Oh,' she said. 'That was my foster-father. He was the one who put Greig into Lennards.'

I did not enquire further. The word 'foster' warned of territory too tricky for me to venture into. Why had she needed a foster-father? What had happened to her real father? It would surely be painful to ask. The answer would be embarrassing, bringing a revelation that we would rather not have had revealed, assuming we got any sort of answer out of her, which we probably wouldn't. There is a limit to children's curiosity, a self-protective boundary, and children who know what is good for them do not stray beyond it.

Now and then we used the W. F. case for other trips, but not for preference, because it was so heavy. But the question of where it originally came from slid to the back of my mind. I did not seriously expect to find out who W. F. was or whether Munca was telling us anything resembling the truth.

It was only now, half a century later, that W. F. turned up in my head again. I began to speculate about him with a growing frustration. There was, after all, one gaping hole left in the jigsaw, a hole that gaped all the more as the other bits were filled in.

Where did the money come from? That was the outstanding question. The more I discovered the dreadful destitution the Macduffs had suffered in Sheffield, along with the equally wretched Burkes and Vails, the more fragments I picked up of Munca's hand-to-mouth existence, first in Leeds then in the cramped hutches of Marylebone, the more mysterious became her sudden translation to Mayfair and Claridge's. The same was true of Buster. There he was, an illegitimate child abandoned by his mother and his father, buffeted between Leeds and Sheffield, then suddenly at the age of 19 we find him set up in the Washington Hotel in Curzon Street and about to embark on a life in which he will be buying the most expensive racing cars and supporting half a dozen wives and four children, admittedly not all at the same time.

Somewhere there must be a fairy godfather who does the transformation scene. And this shadowy figure, referred to casually or not so casually as 'my foster-father' or 'my sugar daddy', must be it. He is the missing link, the one who makes the whole chain hold. Unfortunately, I don't have the first idea where to start looking for him.

Then it occurs to me that what fairy godparents do is turn up at rites of passage. They come, famously or infamously, to christenings in particular, but they also bring their fairy wands to cast stardust over the wedding scene that brings the whole panto to a happy end.

The presence of witnesses is not expected or required for birth certificates, but it is *de rigueur* for weddings, to prove in case of later dispute that the marriage actually took place and that the vows were exchanged between the parties who were supposed to have exchanged them. Was it not possible that Sugar Daddy had attended at least one of Munca's weddings? Well, no it wasn't, as it turned out. Nobody with the initials W. F. stood as a witness at any of the five known ceremonies she went through. On second thoughts, this should not have surprised me. Each wedding had in its own way a furtive or clandestine quality. At her wedding to Harold Ridge, both bride and groom had lied about their ages, obviously because they did not have their parents' consent to marry before they were 21. Her second wedding, to Donald Clark, was the union of a divorced woman with her co-respondent. Not an occasion for fairy godfathers, something that was even truer of her bigamous union with William Anderson. Nor was the third/fourth, in which she made her debut under her assumed name and was pretending to be a spinster 14 years younger than she was. Ditto with the fourth/ fifth wedding, which was held in a tiny church and swamped with members of her new family. Any guest who might stir up suspicions about her track record would not be welcome.

So no sugar daddy there then, not anywhere. I turned, without much greater expectation, to Doris's three weddings. True,

Doris at least was not in the concealment business. On the other hand, I had no strong reason to think that she too had benefited from the largesse of Sugar Daddy, for I suspected that he might well have been a sexual partner of Munca's rather than a stand-in parent and so have no reason to be interested in Doris at all.

There was no sign of W. F. at Doris's first marriage, to Alfred Burke, which wasn't much of a surprise. After all, they were getting married in the smoke and stench of Brightside in 1913. Whatever Sugar Daddy might do in the future, there was no sign that he had as yet commenced operations.

So I turned to her second marriage, to Frank Parkinson at the Westminster Register Office, on 21 January 1936. And there I see it.

The first of their two witnesses is Walter Forrest. W. F. at last. Once again it is Doris whose life-record has broken the cipher. It has been the same all the way through. If you want to find out the truth about Munca, look up Doris. And once the cipher is broken, the truth tumbles out in a rush, as they say it does from a secret agent whose resistance has finally cracked.

Walter Forrest is the daddy of all sugar daddies. He is, for a start, Sir Walter Forrest, and he is a zillionaire from Yorkshire. When T. S. Eliot, sitting upstairs in Crawford Mansions, wrote that bit for *The Waste Land* about the small house agent's clerk 'on whom assurance sits / As a silk hat on a Bradford millionaire', he might have been thinking about Walter Forrest, except for Bradford read Leeds. Walter and his father William Croft Forrest belonged to the last generation of West Riding wool magnates. The firm of W. C. Forrest and Sons was long established at the Prospect Mill in Pudsey, which is almost but not quite part of Leeds, to the west of the city. Walter lived in a fine mansion, Meadowhurst, on Tofts Road, Pudsey, within a bobbin's throw of the Prospect Mill. He was three times Mayor of Pudsey, outdone only by his father who was Mayor seven times. They are the uncrowned kings of the town. When George V is proclaimed King in 1910, it is Walter who does the proclaiming in Market Square to the assembled citizens of Pudsey in their flat caps.

Father and son are the largest employers in Pudsey, and the largest benefactors. It is William Croft who donated the bowling green and the handsome pavilion that sits behind it. It is Walter who presides at 'the substantial meat tea' reported in the *Pudsey and Stanningley News* (prop. and ed.: Walter's brother-in-law Thomas Stillings) after the charity cricket match for the Red Cross at the St Lawrence ground. During the match, the great Jack Hobbs, imported at some expense for the occasion, hits Wilfred Rhodes for three sixes into William Croft's back garden. What a match it is: Rhodes and George Hirst on one side, and Hobbs and the young local lad

Meadowhurst, Pudsey

Herbert Sutcliffe on the other. On the same ground years later, the young Len Hutton learns his trade. The Forrests are the fairy godfathers of Yorkshire cricket as well as Munca's. How strange it is that Munca, who never showed the slightest interest in cricket, should have had all these family connections with the giants of the game. The Forrest estate next to the ground, Meadowhurst, occupies six and a half acres with views over the hills as far as Ilkley Moor. Shortly before Walter's death in 1939, with typical munificence he offers the whole estate to the town, but the war comes and I don't think the offer is ever taken up, because Meadowhurst is sold in 1946 for the bargain price of £2,000.

Father and son were both knighted, but it was only Walter who sat in Parliament, as a pillar of the true Liberal faith, from 1919 to 1922 for Pontefract, and again, from 1924 to 1929, for Batley. In 1931, he defected to the Conservatives, explaining in his letter to Stanley Baldwin that he had lost faith in Free Trade because he thought it was 'largely responsible for the consistent and deplorable increase of unemployment', or to put it another way, because it was killing the wool trade in the West Riding. But by then he and his father were out of the trade. They had sold W. C. Forrest in 1917, in time to avoid the British textile industry's long years of decline.

Walter was a dynamic figure, as dynamic in his way as Frank Parkinson. He had been a pioneer motorist, though not perhaps a skilful one. Driving on holiday in Scarborough in 1911, he attempted to avoid a horse and trap coming out of a side street and swerved into 'a feeble old man', Sergeant-Major Garnett, who was lifted off his feet and fell on his head, fatally. The Sergeant-Major was a veteran of the Crimea and had been decorated by the Emperor of the French for his gallantry. He had survived the horrors of Sebastopol only to meet his end on Victoria Road, Scarborough. Walter escaped unharmed, and unprosecuted, although 'reckless driving' was already an offence under the Motor Car Act of 1903.

After his father's death, Walter became a different sort of pioneer. In the modern style of tycoon, he diversified. Through the 1920s and 1930s he built up stakes in a great variety of companies, ranging from investment trusts and insurance companies to heavy industry and consumer goods. By branching out, he weathered the Depression and became a very rich man, far richer than his father could have hoped to be. He had a magnificent London house, No. 1 Great Cumberland Place, large enough to accommodate a butler and a lady's maid. He had a country place, another Old Barn, this one at Churt in Surrey, next door to the lair of his old chief Lloyd George. In his last years he sold both these properties and took an equally splendid flat at No. 15 Grosvenor Square. The *Yorkshire Post* reported breathlessly that 'every room of their new home is a period room, the drawing room and boudoir being furnished from the antiques which Lady Forrest has collected assiduously over many years. There are more old pieces in the dining room, which is in the Adam style; Sir Walter's library has Chinese lacquer furniture.' I suspect Munca's hand in the décor too. Chinoiserie was a favourite of hers. The Forrests had also left Pudsey and bought a home in Harrogate instead. He remained an obsessive Yorkshireman, President of every Yorkshire Society you can think of. At the Yorkshiremen of the Year lunches, he hobnobs with the Duke and Duchess of Norfolk, who still own quite a slice of Sheffield.

Some of his interests were overseas: OK Bazaars, the largest chain of department stores in Africa, and Atkinson-Oates Motors, the biggest chain of motor importers and distributors in Africa. As you would expect, some of his interests were in Yorkshire and other parts of the north: David Scholes, wool

manufacturers of Morley; Sterlings, boot and shoe factors of
Pudsey; the North British and Mercantile Insurance Company;
the Harrogate Hydropathic Co.; the Thames and Mersey
Investment Trust. But quite a few were grouped in the West
Country around Bristol: J. Moore and Sons of Frenchay, Charles
Newth and Sons of Kingswood, and ... Lennards.

Walter had been chairman of Lennards for years. It is the
only company whose shares are mentioned in his will. In
the final clause of the codicil to it, which he signed only two
months before he died, he declared that 'My Trustees shall
retain my shares and interests in Lennards Limited without
being responsible for loss so long as they in their uncontrolled
discretion think that such shares and interests can be retained to
the present or future advantage of my estate.' In other words,
they were to hang on to the shares until and unless it would be
suicidal to do so. If he did not quite die with 'Lennards' graven
on his heart, the company remained in his thoughts and his
affections to the last.

As did his family. He had been married when he was barely
21, in an almost dynastic Pudsey marriage. His bride was
Katie Stillings, the daughter of a local boot and shoe merchant,
James Stillings, who came to live with them after his own wife
died. Walter and Katie had one son, Harold Stillings, born in
1893. The sad but, for our purposes, crucial event occurred in
March 1913, when Katie died at the age of 47, of peritonitis
following ulcerative colitis. She died at Meadowhurst with her
husband by her side. There was a huge funeral for one who
had been three times Mayoress of Pudsey and a popular one.
The town came to a halt on the day. Hundreds of townspeople
filed past her open coffin to catch a final glimpse of her.
Hundreds more sheltered from the incessant rain in Walter's
enormous conservatory or queued in the extensive grounds
of Meadowhurst.

Walter and Katie Forrest as Mayor and Mayoress of Pudsey

Then and now, when a widower makes a relatively quick second marriage, it is often thought of as a tribute to the first wife, and not a betrayal. By most people's reckoning, a decent interval had been observed when Walter Forrest married for the second time, two and a half years after Katie's death.

His second wife was Mary Macduff, widow of John Willie Macduff of Sheffield.

Here then is the last link in the chain, obscured all these years until now by the hand of Time and the hand of Munca. W. F. is Munca's stepfather. Her sugar daddy and her foster-father too, but what he is first and foremost is her stepfather, and he remains her stepfather for 24 years until his death. He joins the long list of people in Munca's life who are not who she says they are.

It was a very quiet wedding, the *Pudsey and Stanningley News* tells us. He is 46 and she is 45. Widow and widower are married in Sheffield, in the Burngreave Road Wesleyan Chapel, down the road from where Mary now resides at 171 Shirecliffe Lane with Alfred and Doris and the infant Denis, who was born in the house. The chapel is a stone's throw too from Munca's convent school on the other side of Burngreave Road. The *Sheffield Daily Telegraph* has only a brief paid-for announcement describing her as 'Mary Macduff of Pitsmoor', which is pretty much the same as Burngreave. The *Telegraph* is too full of pictures of Sheffield lads in the Hallamshires and the Yorks and Lancs who have been killed or wounded in Flanders or on the beaches of the Dardanelles to have room for a wedding photo of a widower from Pudsey and a widow from Pitsmoor. She may in fact still be working for the Walshes and so really living at 15 Ranmoor Park Road, but it is more fitting to be married from a family address than a place of employment. But though she may be married from her home, they are wed in the nearest chapel of his faith. Walter, like his father before him, is a devout Wesleyan Methodist, while she was brought up C of E and married John Willie in the great parish church of All Saints, which towers above the smoky bit of Brightside. The wedding venue is the first sign of how her new married life will be.

After the ceremony, there is a lunch at the Grand Hotel, Sheffield, followed by a motoring tour that takes in the Midland Hotel, Manchester, and ends up at the Imperial Hydro, St Anne's, on the Fylde coast. In the marriage notice in the *News*, the newlyweds announce that on their return there will be an At Home at Meadowhurst on 14 and 15 October. I presume that anyone is welcome to come along and take a first look at the second Mrs Forrest, just as they were welcome to come along and take a last look at the body of the first Mrs Forrest. A quiet wedding it may be, but certainly not a hole-and-corner affair.

So Walter comes into all our lives, even into the lives of myself and my sister half a century later. For all those treats in the West End, those dinners at the Causerie, those nights in the suite at Claridge's, all Munca's homes that we stayed in over the years, with their Rouaults and Dufys on the walls, all of it derived ultimately from the fortune Walter inherited and multiplied. As so often in the past century, the brass that was made in the north was spent in the south. Munca's jewels, Buster's motors and marriages, Unca's Roller and the open Merc, and of course the majority shareholding in Lennards – they were all made possible by Walter Forrest, a name never mentioned by Munca, a man whom I have never heard of, except as a pair of initials on an old suitcase.

Walter died just before the outbreak of the Second World War and just before his seventieth birthday, on 18 July 1939. He left £226,383. In today's money the equivalent of about £40 million, and roughly twice what his father had left ten years earlier. It is probable that both men had a lot more than that to leave. Death duties were already biting hard in the 1930s, harder than at any time before or since; they then accounted for a tenth of all government revenue (in comparison, by the 1990s inheritance tax was providing less than a hundredth of the government's revenue). The top rate was 50 per cent, so any provident plutocrat who was on speaking terms with his heirs would be offloading the major portion of his loot to them well before he died. In those days, the qualifying period for full exemption from death duties on gifts to your loved ones was only 12 months, as opposed to seven years today. So it took only a tremor of mortality to remind a rich man to start giving it away, and we know that Sir Walter, as he now was, had been seriously ill for some time. Judging by their lifestyle before he died, I am sure that his heirs had been benefiting from his benefactions all through the 1930s. Who paid for the little hunting box in Gloucestershire, after all?

And we know who his heirs were from the evidence of the will he made three years before he died. He left a life interest in the whole estate to his wife Mary. That included all his houses, the jewels, trinkets, plate, glass, pictures, books, musical instruments and motor cars, plus the income on the residuary estate, after the cash legacies to his other nearest and dearest had been paid, viz:

Twenty thousand pounds to my wife
Twenty thousand pounds to my son Harold
To my stepdaughter Doris Parkinson five thousand pounds
To Denis Macduff Burke the son of the said Doris Parkinson ten thousand pounds
To Archibald Alastair Baring the son of my stepdaughter Eileen Constance Page one thousand pounds

And then in a separate clause, the sum of £10,000 is put into trust for the said Eileen Constance Page and the said Archibald Alastair Baring. The residue, too, is to go into trust: four-fifths of it for the ultimate benefit of Harold and the remaining fifth to be shared between Doris and Denis, and Munca and Buster.

Here, for the first and only time in all my researches, the true relationships between all the *dramatis personae* are set down in cold print, or rather in the fading typescript of Messrs Allen and Drury of 3 Finch Lane, Threadneedle Street. It is a Dickensian denouement, *Jarndyce v Jarndyce* with a happy ending.

Yet even here, in the ultimate candour that is necessary for the distribution of serious money, we cannot miss the sense of strain. Notice, for example, the difference between the treatment of Doris and Denis, the reliable pair, and that accorded to Munca and Buster, the fly-by-nights. Not only are the fly-by-nights to receive less cash, a total of £11,000 as against £15,000, but their money is to be held in trust because neither of them is a safe pair of hands. We must also note the remarkable thing: at this final moment, Walter simply does not know what to call Munca. He settles for Eileen Constance

Page, a combination of her old Christian names and her new surname, making up a moniker that she has never gone by before and never will again. For by the time that the will is signed and dated, on the last day of 1936, it is already out of date. Dallas Page died three months earlier, and Eileen Constance, as she now isn't, is married to my uncle. As always, it is hard to keep up with her.

How can she have recovered so quickly from the shock of Dallas's death and arranged a full-blown trad wedding in time for Christmas? Even for a quick operator like Munca this is some sledding. I have already suggested that she might have been on holiday in the South of France with Greig while Dallas was watching Walter Hammond's immortal innings before taking his last fatal spin back home over the Cotswolds. Now, late on in this tortuous odyssey, I come across a fragment that would not have made sense before I knew about Walter Forrest and his connection to Munca. In the *Desert Sun*, a news sheet established to serve the gilded clientele of Palm Springs, California, there is an item in the issue for 25 January 1935, which lists the celebrities then in residence at the Palm Springs Hotel. Among them are 'Mrs Forrest and the G. R. Mount party, Santa Monica'. Mary is still Mrs Forrest, because Walter has been knighted only in that New Year's Honours List and won't yet have been to the Palace, though he may be waiting for the call, which is why he is not fleeing to the winter sun with the rest of his family. So nearly two years before their marriage, Greig and Munca know each other well enough to go on holiday together with her mother. It sounds as though he had organized the trip, which is not so unlikely, because he has been training at a hotel school in Switzerland with a view to going into the profession. So Greig is already well in with the Forrests. You sense that even if Dallas had not been killed, his days as Munca's husband would have been numbered.

You might think that an upright Wesleyan Methodist like Walter might disapprove of Munca's in-and-out running. You would expect him to express his disapproval in the most unmistakable manner open to him, by cutting off the supply of funds to her and her disavowed son. At the very least, as the latest details of what the two of them have been up to trickle into the sickroom at 15 Grosvenor Square, you might expect that there would be some alteration to the terms of the will.

And so there is. It is as late as 19 May 1939, only two months before his death, that Walter adds a codicil. Although there is optimistic talk of his making a full recovery and he has been moved back from the nursing home to Grosvenor Square, he must be well aware of the more likely outcome. He is housebound now, and the codicil is witnessed by the butler Arthur James Clements and Mary's maid Elsie Blackburn.

What the codicil says is not quite what you would expect. It does change the proportions in which the residue of the estate is to be distributed, but it changes that distribution *in favour* of the stepdaughters and stepgrandsons. Formerly Harold, Walter's only child, was to get four-fifths and the steps only one-fifth. Now the cash legacies are reduced or abolished, and two-fifths of the residue is to go to the steps, only three-fifths to Harold. 'Eileen Constance Mount (formerly Page)' has her new marriage acknowledged, again by a hybrid name she will never hear again. And though she and Buster are still to receive a smaller share of the kitty than Doris and Denis, about half as much in fact, they are to receive exactly the same as they would have received under the original 1936 terms: 13.3 per cent of the total estate, or £30,000, something like £5 million in today's money.

After my own painstaking calculations, I can only take my hat off to Walter's scrupulous insistence that the redrafting is not to injure his original intentions. I think that the real purpose of the codicil is radically to reduce the size of the cash legacies that would fall victim to death duty and to shovel more money into the residuary Trust, which would be exempt. This only strengthens my belief that he has already given Munca and Doris and their sons substantial dollops of cash. They are in no immediate need of further lump sums. Doris isn't anyway, because since 1936 she has been married to one of the richest men in England, described in the popular press as 'reputedly England's shyest millionaire' – although he doesn't sound all that shy to me. I suspect that she actually met Frank through Walter. Both men are Leeds born and bred and devoted to their native county, and anyway tycoons stick together. On that marriage certificate where Walter makes his first appearance in the story, Doris gives her address as 20 Grosvenor Square. So after divorcing Alfred, she is living only a few doors away from her mother and stepfather. There was always something a little protected, not to say pampered about Doris, certainly according to her elder sister. After Walter's death, her mother comes to live with Doris and Frank down at Charters, and Denis, now aged 25, is there too at the outbreak of war, according to the National Register, so this side of the family sticks together.

When we look closely at the terms of the will, we can see straight away why, 20 years later, there is something equivocal in the attitude of my uncle and aunt towards both Doris and Denis. There's really no mystery about it. To put it bluntly, they were left twice as much. For his part, Denis has reason to feel aggrieved too. A few months after Walter's death in July 1939, he is made a director of Lennards at the age of 24. No doubt, being family, he hopes to become chairman in due course. But he is overtaken by the interloping Greig, and has to plod on under him for years, long enough to be deputed to dance with the teenaged Georgie at the Lennards Christmas dance. He might also be more than a little miffed that Munca should refuse to recognize him as her only nephew by blood, while there am I, 25 years younger and no real relation, the apple of her glittering eye.

Yet Walter has not forgotten the Parable of the Prodigal Son. His strict Wesleyan upbringing has not eclipsed either his instinctive charitableness or his affection for his wayward elder stepdaughter and her son. Loyalty and generosity seem to come naturally to him. Appended to his obit in *The Times* there is a tribute from 'A Correspondent' who obviously knew him well and speaks of 'that kindly gentleness of spirit which made him outstanding' and of 'his peaceful outlook'. 'When difficulties arose, the quiet, wise and tolerant counsel of which he seemed to have an abundance quickly smoothed them away.' Just the sort of counsel you would need an abundance of when dealing with Munca and Buster. The correspondent adds that Sir Walter was greatly helped by Lady Forrest and that the two were an ideal couple. After expressing sympathy to her and the family in their loss, he concludes by saying that 'the country is the poorer by the passing of one who was indeed the perfect gentle knight'.

Not a tribute often paid to a millionaire Yorkshire mill owner. Far from grinding the faces of the poor, Walter appears to have been a *chevalier sans peur et sans reproche*. What lucky stepchildren. A real-life fairy tale, and not the usual sort in which the step-parent is the cruel and heartless villain.

Stepfathers do become fond of their stepdaughters, for all sorts of reasons, not least because they may remind them of their wives when young. I can imagine, too, how beguiling and spirited Munca must have been when Walter first met her in her late teens. And later on, when she blew into Meadowhurst to see how Buster was getting on or to take refuge from her latest scrape, she must have seemed like a breath of life. Walter was not going to forget either her or Buster at the last. Even so, these huge legacies and the perhaps even larger transfers during Walter's lifetime do make me pause. For stepfathers usually become that fond of their new wives' daughters only if they first meet them when they are little girls, and by the time Walter marries Mary, both Munca and Doris are themselves already married, each with a baby son. Perhaps it is the baby sons, Buster and Denis, who catch Walter's heart.

It is only as I am puzzling through Walter's will and codicil for the second or third time that I realize something else too. Or rather, I remember where I have come across No. 1 Great Cumberland Place and the village of Churt before. It was in Kathleen's petition to be rid of Buster that they featured as two of the places they lived in during their brief, frantic marriage. Gorse Cottage, Churt, was within walking distance of the Old Barn. So the newlyweds, neither of them yet 20, continued to live under the close supervision of Walter and Mary, and in London actually in the same house. The Forrests have brought up Buster as their son and he remains part of the close family even now he is married. It seems that he needs protecting against the world, not least against the wayward carry-on of his real mother.

In later life, though, we have seen how close he keeps to her. Just before the war, he and Esmé are living around the corner from Unca and Munca in Lancaster Gate, and they are all working together in the furniture business. During the war, he runs a garage on the Wentworth Estate; after it, he farms at Warfield, Berkshire, which is about the nearest farmland to the Munca/Doris haunts; he courts and marries a married woman in Angmering who lives round the corner from Blue Waters; his tortuous life on and off the track with Jean and Charles Mortimer, all of it takes place within a 20-minute drive of Munca, probably less if you are driving at Buster's pace. Yet how seldom my sister and I catch a glimpse of him, and when we do, there is an impatient irritability about him and about Munca too, as though she doesn't want him there when we are there, suggesting that she needs to keep her two lives separate as far as she can. She must have wanted to separate her blood family from her invented family, to prevent inconvenient thoughts being stirred up. When we weren't there, Buster may well have popped in and out, ready to be chided about his latest entanglements and disentanglements as a price for touching the nearest thing he had to a home base in his life. My impression was that even Georgie had not seen very much of him, so his visits may have been timed when she was away at school, or in the holidays when she was having her riding or dancing lessons. Anyway, far from being excluded and roaming the world in pursuit of fast cars and fast women, Buster was as much caught up in Munca's web as everyone else. In its strange secretive way, Munca's side of the family, like Doris's, sticks together more than you might think.

Surely we are there now. The journey's over. I know the whole saga. And yet, and yet.

There is still one question that we have not begun to answer. How exactly does Mary Macduff make her escape from the worst part of Sheffield where she is more or less destitute, without a roof of her own, her husband dead and her daughters scattered? How does she get from that very bad place to a place where she is courted by the richest widower in Leeds, without, it seems, leaving her modest home in Sheffield where she is huddled with Doris and her family? How does she come to meet the perfect gentle knight?

Is there perhaps a link between Walter Forrest and the two households where we know Mary lived for a time: that of Sydney Hudson, the East India merchant on the outskirts of Manchester, and then, 20 years later, Walter Walsh, the department store king of Ranmoor Park Road? Both her employers were leaders in the great Northern textile world. What is more likely than that at either of these places, or even at both, she should meet the textile magnate of Pudsey, another Walter? As a lively girl in service, she might have caught the eye of an energetic young man away from home and perhaps fretting under the constraints of Pudsey Nonconformity. As a mature widow, still attractive and perhaps more attractive because she was so in control at 15 Ranmoor Park Road, she might have offered a refuge to the distraught widower. Now at last we can see why the fact that Mary had once been a lady's maid hung in Munca's mind and once popped out in our hearing. It was the crucial factor in Mary's life, and in her children's too, the turning-point that transported all three of them upstairs.

From Mary's point of view, the drapery connection offers an escape route from the fatal grind of Sheffield's heavy trades, from the hellish belching of Brightside, into refinement and a purer air. The soft fall of felt and flannel, the swish of drapes, the fresh feel of newly ironed cotton and linen, the hushed atmosphere of the soft furnishings department – all this is a world away from the screech and clang and blare of the furnace and the rolling mill. Doris has already started on that route, with her position in the mantle trade. For all we know, she may be working on the floor at Walsh's, calling the customers Madam and herself entitled to be addressed as Miss Macduff, though perhaps she may have to wait a bit for that. At any rate, Mary is already on her way out from the back streets and the grim pubs along the canal from which her uncle Joseph went out to drown himself.

Only a few years after she married Walter, we can glimpse the two of them at one of the Queen's debutante balls in May 1923. Mrs Walter Forrest is wearing 'a gown of vieux rose and silver mesh mounted on silver lamé with a girdle of self-coloured jewels and a train of transparent vieux rose and silver mesh bordered with silver lamé, from Isobel of Maddox Street'. It sounds as if she outshone the Hon. Nancy Mitford, then aged 18, who was there with her mother, Lady Redesdale, and wearing a gown of white and gold brocade with a train of old lace. Mary's outfit was probably a cut above anything she had ever had to get ready for Mrs Hudson of Chorlton-upon-Medlock. Yet perhaps even in her new splendour she kept up the old habits of plumping up cushions and instinctively dusting piano lids, and perhaps she passed that on to her daughter, who at the time of the debutante ball was living at some unknown address in bigamous bliss with William Anderson.

Walter has his funeral at the Wesleyan Chapel in Pudsey. Mary is there (she is later buried beside him in Pudsey cemetery, just next to Tofts Road), and so are 'Mr and Mrs F. Parkinson (step-daughter)'. No sign of Munca. At least not in person. But among the floral tributes there is one from 'Greig, Buster and Betty'. At last her new name begins to override all the Eileen Constances in Walter's will.

The following week, as befits Walter's status as a former MP, there is a memorial service at St Margaret's Westminster, attended by the cream of the Liberal party plus the above family members, this time including Mr D. M. Burke. All these are listed in the first paragraph of *The Times* notice, the family pew so to speak. Down in the next paragraph, with the rest of the congregation, comes the name of Mrs Greig Mount. Even in death, they are divided.

I still feel that there is something darker here, darker than anything I have uncovered yet, one final shroud smothering the truth. And after reading Walter's *Times* obit, I think I know what it is, although there is no hope of my ever proving it, or for that matter disproving it.

Halfway down the column, there is a photograph of Sir Walter Forrest. A mugshot, as we say in the trade, just wide enough to fill the column. And I look at it, then I look away, and then look at it again in a sort of primitive test to make sure that I am not imagining things. But the longer I look, the surer I am.

Obituary

SIR WALTER FORREST

POLITICS AND BUSINESS

Sir Walter Forrest, who was Liberal M.P. for Pontefract from 1919 to 1922 and for Batley and Morley from 1924 to 1929, died yesterday at his London home in his seventieth year. In 1931 he joined the Conservative Party, and in a letter to Mr. Baldwin he stated that his belief in free trade had gradually weakened and it was his conviction that the well-being of the nation demanded safeguarding at home and the widest possible extension of inter-Imperial trade. Later he became identified with the Liberal National Party, and at the time of his death was treasurer of the London Liberal National Party, and a member of the National Executive of the Liberal National Council.

Walter Forrest was the son of the late Sir William Forrest, of Aldringham, Roundhay, Leeds, and his career was very similar to that of his father. For many years he was interested in the woollen manufacturing industry of Yorkshire and like his father was a member of the firm of W. C. Forrest and Co., Limited, of Pudsey. The business was sold in 1917. Both he and his father were original members of the Pudsey Corporation. Sir William was mayor seven times and Sir Walter was mayor for three years. In 1922 Sir Walter was Parliamentary private secretary to the Postmaster-General and it was in 1935 that he received his knighthood for political and public services.

As far back as the nineties Walter Forrest was President of the Pudsey Liberal Association, and he also took part in local government work as a member of the West Riding County Council for Pudsey and Farsley. He first entered the House of Commons in 1919 when he won a by-election at Pontefract as a Coalition Liberal. In 1922 he lost the seat in a three-cornered contest, and the following year was unsuccessful in the Batley and Morley division; but he was returned for the latter division in 1924, and continued to sit

Sir Walter Forrest, *Times* obituary, 19 July 1939

238

It is an arresting face that stares out of the unwieldy bound volume of *The Times* for July 1939. The eyes are dark and piercing. If this was an oil portrait hanging on the wall of a gallery, the eyes would follow you around the room. The strong dark eyebrows droop down at the temples, which is what gives a hooded, concentrated quality to the gaze, the gaze of a falcon perched on the falconer's glove: contemptuous, watchful. That look follows you down the raptor's nose, a short, strong-bridged nose, flared and a little flattened at the end. Nothing droopy about it and not squashed like a boxer's nose either; more like that of a proud impassive Native American chief. And then the upper lip, proud too, with the same acerbic aspect. The lips themselves thin and turned down, strangely flat as if they had been painted on the skin, a thin stain that widens only a little in the middle under the flared nostrils. His chin is strong but it has a certain delicacy too. This is only a head-and-shoulders shot, but you can still see how erect Walter holds himself, the way that short men carry themselves. I do not know what height he is, but I am sure that he is not a tall man.

I know this face. It is Munca's face, or Eileen's or Betty's or Liz's or whatever you want to call her. If I curl my fingers round the mugshot to block out the no-nonsense businessman's haircut, what I see is Munca just as I knew her when she was the same age as Walter must be in the photo, the early sixties. I know this face as well as any in the world. Munca is a shortish woman, 5 ft 3 ins I should say, and even before I am in my teens I am tall for my age. So when we are sitting down to one of Olive's roast-beef and apple-pie lunches at Blue Waters or Castlewood or Holthanger, I am on her level and I study her face very closely because it is such an arresting face, quite unlike the face of anyone else I know, much older for one thing, although quite how much older I then have no idea.

I must be careful. Philosophers used to tell us that what they call our 'sense impressions' are the only reliable perceptions that we can have of the world. All we can truthfully say of something is that this is what it looks like to us. But even this claim is itself unreliable, because so often we see what we want to see. It is our brain, not our eyes, that is filling in the report. If for some ulterior motive we are eager to detect a resemblance between A and B, then detect it we will and continue to maintain its existence, just as Munca used to maintain that Georgie looked exactly like my sister and me.

I am now playing the same trick back on her. To me, the resemblance between Walter and Munca is not eerie or uncanny or any of those other words we use to describe a resemblance that has taken us by surprise. To me, this resemblance is too precise in every detail to have anything other than a straightforward physical explanation. It cannot mean anything but a blood relationship.

For me, Walter has to be Munca's father. As I eagerly scan pictures of him in the *Pudsey and Stanningley News* or the *Yorkshire Post* opening bazaars, chatting to the Duke and Duchess of Norfolk, presiding at the committee to consider the gift of the Meadowhurst estate, the resemblance jumps out at me every time. It would take a full-scale DNA test to shake my conviction, and it is extremely unlikely that any such test will ever be taken. We are, after all, not dealing with a cold crime case or trying to prove that Anna Anderson is or is not Anastasia, the last of the Romanovs.

If I am right, this would explain several things. It would explain why this upright Wesleyan should stay loyal to his twice-divorced, triply bigamous, four- or five-times-married stepdaughter and her seven-times-married illegitimate son. It might explain why Walter's father should leave £250 in his will to the Leeds Unmarried Women's Benevolent Association. It would also explain the desperate secrecy that enshrouded the whole family. Walter was anything but a nobody. He was uncrowned king of Pudsey, indeed a political and religious leader of the West Riding. That he should have fathered a child by another man's wife would have destroyed him if the news got out. Everything possible had to be done to keep the whole story blacked out for ever.

If I am right, then Harold Forrest, Walter's son by his first marriage, his only legitimate child, is not Munca's stepbrother but her half-brother. He is only a year older than she is, and for a quarter of a century his father is married to her mother. Yet we never hear a word of his existence. Is it perhaps because they look too unnervingly alike, because Walter's strong features have come down to both of them and they must not be seen together or people will draw the inescapable conclusion?

What it would certainly explain is how and why Walter and Mary come together from their totally different backgrounds and get married within a relatively short period after Katie's death. They do not need to go through the rigmarole of courtship because they have been through it all before, 20 years earlier. It might even explain why Munca went to Leeds rather than stay in Sheffield during the time when her legal father was dying. Even if she did not know in precise terms that Walter was her father, Mary might have told her that there was this friend of the family in Leeds, a kind man she had known slightly years ago and who might help her because he was rich as well as kind.

But these explanations only prompt a fresh question: how exactly had Mary come to know Walter all those years ago, in the early 1890s? He was, after all, already married to Katie in

1890, four years before Munca was born. And Mary herself had married John Willie in 1893, only eight and a half months before she gave birth. Was the affair a brief encounter, or did it last several years, beginning perhaps when Katie was pregnant with Harold and continuing until the eve of Mary's marriage, if not beyond? Either way, not exactly the conduct of a pillar of Yorkshire Methodist society. But Walter was still in his early twenties and a man of great energy and spark. At that age, men like that may find that their desire overwhelms their principles.

So where on earth did Walter and Mary first meet? The only possible place is the house of the East India merchant in Chorlton-upon-Medlock, on the outskirts of Manchester, where Mary was a housemaid in 1891. Sydney Hudson's mansion with its nine indoor servants was a classic location to incubate a romance between a coming young textile magnate from Leeds and a pretty girl below stairs, both playing away from home.

When Mary had to go back to Sheffield because her mother had been killed jumping from a cart full of vegetables, it would not be surprising that the affair should continue. Sheffield is, after all, no further from Leeds than Manchester is and just as plausible a destination for a business trip.

Sceptics may object that there is something too neat, too symmetrical about this pattern of illegitimacy. Perhaps I am in danger of seeing illegitimacy and adultery everywhere, even in the most upright and moral households. Yet if you find the timing hard to credit, then consider the case of Justin Welby. All his life, the Archbishop of Canterbury had believed that he was the son of his legal father, the louche alcoholic adventurer Gavin Welby. Only in the spring of 2016 did a DNA test confirm the lurking rumour that he was in fact the son of Anthony Montague

Browne, the long-serving secretary to Sir Winston Churchill. Justin's mother, Jane Portal, had worked for Churchill alongside Montague Brown, and they had a quick fling just before she married Gavin Welby, which was why the future archbishop was born 8 and a half months after the wedding, just as Munca was. A scientific survey from Liverpool John Moores University in 2005 suggested that a similar 'Paternal Discrepancy', as it is politely termed, might account for no less than 3.7 per cent of all births.

Besides, such strayings and such accidents do run in families. The hero of Arabia, T. E. Lawrence, was famously agonized by having been born illegitimate, one of five sons born to his father's governess, Sarah Lawrence. What is less well known is that Sarah herself was illegitimate, the daughter of Elizabeth Junner, a servant in the household of an insurance surveyor in Sunderland, probably by the surveyor's eldest son John. What's more, Elizabeth Junner had been born illegitimate too. To rephrase Philip Larkin, woman hands on misery to woman, or did then.

Those days of shame are over now. People do not cover up like that any more. We are proud of where we have come from, whatever sort of place it was. The journey we make is what shapes our life. For any woman now it would itself be a shameful thing to be ashamed of having been destitute or of having borne a child without being married. It would be unthinkable for her to invent a new past for herself for any such reason, and to ruin the lives of other people by that invention. Although the old 1861 Act is still in place, judges these days take a kinder view of bigamy too. Those found guilty often get off with a suspended sentence: in other words, go away and don't do it again (which might not have deterred Munca). Most of us lead untidy lives, after all.

We are better now, aren't we? Yes, I think we are. Our private lives are our own. There are no public pressures not to follow our desires. In fact, there are laws and codes of practice now to protect those desires from insult or obloquy. Deviancy is a thing of the past, because there is no sexual orthodoxy to deviate from. And you would need a stony heart not to welcome most of this. Stigmas belong on flowers and not on human beings. But we are the conscripts of posterity, and we have a duty to pity first before we condescend. And we find it difficult to imagine how people could ever have felt obliged to behave like that or how society could have been so harsh and unforgiving.

Anyway, it won't do to leave Munca on any mournful or hesitant note. She was not made for threnodies. It is hard to think of anyone less like her low-spirited neighbour in Crawford Mansions. 'This is the way the world ends / Not with a bang but a whimper': for T. S. Eliot possibly, but not for Eileen Constance Sylvia Macduff Ridge Clark Anderson or, come to that, for Patricia Elizabeth Baring Page Mount. She came in with a bang, not the approved sort of bang perhaps, and she kept on banging. Those of us with a more nervous disposition had better tiptoe away and leave her clicking her fingers in time to the music of Harry 'Tiger' Roy and his Mayfair Hotel Orchestra.

I'm gonna kiss myself goodbye,
Oh goodbye, goodbye
I'm gonna get my wings and fly
Up high, up high

You went and broke my heart in two
Oh yes you, yes you

And when I'm gone, you'll be so blue
'Cos who you gonna doublecross, you rascal you

A good man's mighty hard to find
Better hurry up and change your mind
Before I hold me close, say farewell
And kiss myself goodbye.

9

Brightside Revisited

As you walk along Savile Street, you see a huge black thing that from a distance looks like a brutal sculpture by Eduardo Paolozzi. A sign tells you that you are entering Brightside and this monstrous object is a Firth Brown five-ton steam hammer. It used to take five men to manoeuvre the red-hot ingot onto the anvil. The infernal clanging of those hammers was the heart-thump of Brightside in its heyday. You don't hear it now. For the most part, Savile Street is as silent as, well, the grave, for this is the main avenue in the cemetery of Sheffield steel. The enormous Atlas works of Firth Brown lies idle. Aetna and Hecla erupt no more. Mile after mile of fine red-brick works stand empty and quiet, the yards and sheds behind them rusting deserts of smashed cars, wrecked pallets and bundles of industrial waste. The odd forklift truck moving idly across the scumbled asphalt seems to have no discernible purpose. In the back streets here and there you see the glow of a small furnace or catch the whirr of an old lathe – a couple of 'little meesters' still grinding out a living. The only steel concern still going strong seems to be EMR Scrap Metal Dealers on East Coast Road – 'largest stock of ferrous and non-ferrous metals in the UK'. At least John Willie Macduff's business survives, even if he didn't.

Every now and then you pass spanking car showrooms – Ford, Vauxhall, Land Rover. Instead of the biggest rolling mills in the world, there is the largest Tesco store I have ever seen. All cathedrals of consumption rather than manufacture, demanding plenty of steel but not much of it made here.

Cross the river at East Coast Road and go on down to the desolate canal once jostling with coal and iron-ore barges, and there is the Bacon Lane Bridge where Joseph Vail threw himself in the water, and beyond it the Woodbourne Hotel where he had his last drink. The canal's dark waters still invite oblivion, but the Woodbourne is shut for the duration, and so is the Norfolk Arms at the bottom of precipitous Sutherland Street, where Mahala Crabb's cart came to grief. It's not just because the mills have gone that the pubs have closed too. Brightside is to a great extent an Asian district now (primarily Pakistani and Bangladeshi), and its new residents move gracefully about the quiet streets in sari and shalwar kameez without a thought of the saloon bar.

The old inhabitants just aren't there any more. Those thousands of families who flocked in from Ireland and Scotland and the Midlands — the Burkes, the Macduffs, the Crabbs and the Vails — are all as vanished from this hillside as the lost tribes of Israel.

I begin to look for the places where they all lived: the terraced hovels in Greystock Street and round the back of Savile Street where Sam and Mahala Crabb brought up their two daughters, 39 Catherine Street where Matilda Macduff raised her family, 111 Grimesthorpe Road where Mary and John Willie lived when Eileen and Doris were small, 31 Nottingham Street where Doris lodged and her mother came to stay when John Willie was dying, 171 Shirecliffe Lane at the top end of Brightside where Doris and Alfred Burke lived when they were first married and from which Mary married Walter — all gone, every one of them. Before and after the war, and on into the 1960s and 1970s, Sheffield Council had one of the largest slum clearance programmes in Europe. The whole hillside has been cleared and the old back-to-back terraces replaced by pleasant small semi-detached homes, often with a patch of front lawn and solar panels on the roof. The air is clear and there are slivers of green space carved out on the steeper slopes. Foul, smoky old Brightside is scarcely even a memory. George Orwell would not recognize the place. Only the silent empty steel works are still preserved down along the riverside, desolate shells of bygone industrial glory.

The churches have been demolished too: All Saints, Ellesmere Road, where Mary and John Willie were married, with its heroic spire built at the expense of Sir John Brown, is as vanished as the John Brown Company (parts of the John Brown empire were subsumed in later combines and survive, just, today in Sheffield Forgemasters at the far end of Brightside Lane, although Forgemasters has come close to the brink in recent years). Gone is the Methodist Chapel at the top of Sutherland Road where Mahala would have started her fatal descent. Gone too is the splendid Wesleyan Chapel in Burngreave Road where Mary married Walter and changed the fortunes of her whole family. Town planners seldom have much respect for the temples of the poor.

The only buildings I can find standing that Munca would have recognized are her old convent school, 'Underwood', at 152 Burngreave Road, a little dilapidated now but still serving as St Catherine's home for patients with dementia; and over to the west of the city, the Walshes' mansion, 'Ranfall', at 15 Ranmoor Park Road, still commands its wonderful views of the whole city.

And the house where she was born? Even Thorndon Road no longer exists, let alone No. 53. The whole area between Lyons Street and Sutherland Road is now a thicket of hawthorn and hazel with a scruffy football pitch in the middle of it. At the Lyons Street end, only a spray of cobbles indicates where

Thorndon Road began before expiring into the scrubby bushes. The houses for hundreds of yards in every direction have disappeared. Cobbles, that's all that's left. Cobbles and scrap. With its tumult of hills and its fast-flowing rivers, Sheffield has as exciting a site as any great city in England, and it is somehow a noble place still, but it is a great place for demolition. The past never gets much of a look-in here. There's no trace left of Mary, Queen of Scots, and no trace of Munca either. If you want to see what Joseph Schumpeter meant when he said that 'capitalism requires the perennial gale of creative destruction', come to Brightside.

I sit down on a surviving kerbstone and take out my tattered Orwell paperback and my Ordnance Survey reprint of Sheffield in 1911, and I look again at what Orwell wrote about Brightside. Then I look at the map. And I suddenly see for the first time that the patch of waste ground that Orwell pinpoints as the most frightful spot in the most frightful city in the world must have been about ten yards from where Munca was born. This isn't

just a fancy, because Thorndon Road is the only half-street on that blighted hillside, the only one that had a vacant lot at the end of it.

As I turn to go back down the hill, I notice for the first time behind me a smart new grey industrial building, proudly proclaiming on its pediment in bright blue letters 'Yorkshire Fabrications Ltd'. What a perfect title for the one-woman business that Munca kept going all her life, only without the limited liability. It is nice to think that, here at source, the business carries on.

Seven Hills

Georgie died on 24 September 2015. At least that was the date established by the autopsy. She may have been dead for some time when she was found by Janice, her devoted cleaner, friend and carer. She was cremated at the new Seven Hills crem just outside Ipswich. You could hear the hum of the Ipswich ring road beyond the trees. There were twelve of us there. From her earlier life, her teenage best friend Fiona Annesley, and her childhood friend Vicky Stead, whom we hadn't seen for 50 years, and my sister and me. As we were waiting on the terrace outside the crem, a rather charming timber building like a model farm in Holland, Vicky told us that she too had been adopted and had only been told by a friend at a party when she was 21. 'We're all adopted here,' she said gaily. But she was shocked when we told her that Georgie hadn't known until she was nearly 50.

The rest of us at the crem were friends from her Suffolk years. Georgie had first got to know two of them when they were all working at the charity in Fulham. There was a brief service: the Lord's Prayer, 'I know that my Redeemer liveth' over the sound system, and a few short tributes. My sister spoke about growing up with Georgie. Her friends from her days in Hurlingham Court, Joyce Aspland and her executor Olive Quinton, described a later life that we didn't know anything about: quiet evenings of music and crosswords, decorating the Christmas tree when she lived in a former pub, the Swan at Bramfield, and walking up the hill to see the Christmas lights reflected in her window. Olive said that Georgie had opened her eyes to literature and music and encouraged her daughter Justine to work her way into university. Justine was there too, a pretty, dark girl with a lively look. She said she thought of Georgie as an aunt – one last invented relationship in Georgie's life, but this one born of love, not a lie.

It sounded like a quiet, secluded sort of existence. Olive said that after her cancer and brutal radiotherapy Georgie's life had turned more reclusive. Not at all like the old Georgie. But then who could be sure what the old Georgie was really like after Munca had finished with her? Perhaps she was really closer to happiness in those later years. But that may be only wishful thinking, and there has been too much wishful thinking in this whole story.

That at least seemed to be the end. But it wasn't, quite. At Easter 2016, I happened to ring my sister and she mentioned by the way that she had just heard from Lyn, the eldest of Munca's four grandchildren. It was the delightful Lyn who had triggered off my quest in the first place ten years earlier, and it was only fitting that she should add a final footnote to it. Lyn said she was now in touch with Celeste, who lives in Edmonton, Canada, in fact has lived there all her life after leaving Angmering and being adopted by a family called Ireland. I do not know if this was a legal re-adoption, but at any rate Edmonton is where she has stayed and lived her life.

What Celeste had told Lyn was that in the last weeks of her life Georgie had got in touch with her. The one person she wanted to talk to at the end of her life was the person who had so briefly been her adoptive sister 60 years earlier. Talk about orphans of the storm. The original *Orphans of the Storm* is in fact a story about two adoptive sisters. D. W. Griffiths made it into a famous film starring Lilian and Dorothy Gish, who were sisters in real life (almost exactly the same age as Munca and Doris, as it happens).

In our early teens, Georgie and I liked many of the same books: P. G. Wodehouse, Agatha Christie, Noel Streatfeild, especially *Ballet Shoes*. This is about no less than three orphaned girls – the eldest was rescued from the *Titanic*, the parents of the middle one died in Russia, and the third was abandoned by her callous mother, a dancer 'who had no time for babies'. I loved *Ballet Shoes* too, though I could not have cared less about the ballet. What we both adored was the way the girls danced on through every disaster, Georgie then not having the least idea of her own situation.

How seductive it is, this idea that you do not need parents to make you happy, or to make the best of yourself. On the contrary, to be a heroine, it is better to be free of these nagging, fretting figures in charge of you, and to forge on through life unencumbered. Far from orphanhood/adoption being any sort of handicap, it's actually a launch-pad.

Consoling, that's what fiction does, though we like to think it does all sorts of other things for us too. And this is one sort of consolation it provides: it whispers to us that we can do it all on our own, that the loss of our birth parents leaves no wounds and bequeaths no resentments. But is that enforced solitary path through life guaranteed to ensure our happiness, or to enrich our souls? Or is it sometimes only a comforting fancy, a delusion even, which for some may turn into an even more piercing sense of abandonment and loss? From Tom Jones, through Pip in *Great Expectations* and Oliver Twist, to Kim and Anne of Green Gables and Pollyanna, the novel tells us that the foundling is more resolute, more cheerful, ultimately *stronger*. But what if she isn't?

Not long ago, I happened to catch the TV adaptation of *Ordeal by Innocence*, a late Agatha Christie starring Bill Nighy and Anna Chancellor. The plot is both ominous and preposterous. The mysterious Dr Calgary comes to Sunny Point to tell the Argyle family that their brother Jacko was wrongly convicted of killing their mother. Jacko could not have done it, because at the time of the murder Calgary was giving him a lift into Drymouth. Calgary is startled to find that the family are upset by the news of Jacko's innocence. 'You should be pleased – thankful,' he says. 'Your own brother is innocent.' To which one of them, Micky, replies, 'he wasn't my brother. And she wasn't my mother. Hasn't anyone told you? We were all adopted. The lot of us.' Virtually all the suspects were taken in by Mrs Argyle, who couldn't have children. And it turns out in the end that one of these adoptees, it is in fact Jacko after all, is guilty of conspiring to commit the murder – an example of A.C.'s not infrequent trick of the original suspect turning out, after many a twist, to have been the murderer all along.

I was intrigued by this weird plot, and trawling the internet, I discovered to my surprise that in half a dozen Agatha Christies the murderer turns out to be a secret adoptee, for example, in *Mrs McGinty's Dead*, published six years earlier. The plot here is even more fantastically complicated, involving a string of assumed and mistaken identities. In the end, we learn that it is the flamboyant theatre director Robin Upward who has murdered his adoptive mother. Mrs McGinty is merely the cleaner who is murdered by Robin Upward after she recognizes the photo of his real mother, a bad lot who had inspired her lover to murder her husband. Here the message of the dangers of adoption are even more glaring. Not merely may the adopted child grow up to loathe his adoptive mother, but the secret of his or her true identity is so toxic that he will kill anyone who is capable of revealing it.

In *The Mirror Crack'd from Side to Side* – a Miss Marple mystery – the film star Marina Gregg believes that she is unable to bear children and so adopts three, before conceiving one of her own, who is born mentally disabled because she had German measles while pregnant, and Marina consigns her to an institution. Marina goes on to murder three people. One of the suspects turns out to be one of the children she adopted and then 'got tired of' and now fails to recognize. Here then we have the other side: the adoptive mother may be a vicious and faithless woman (Marina is on her fifth marriage), with no real loyalty to any of her children, whether by blood or adoption.

I only skimmed the other three books on the list, but the underlying message of them was pretty much the same. The link between the adopted child and his or her new parents is an unstable and potentially poisonous connection. The illegitimate and/or abandoned child grows up either resentful or resented or both, liable to kill or be killed by his supposed carer. If there is an example of reciprocal love in an adoptive relationship in any of these books, I failed to spot it.

In real life, thousands, in fact millions, of adoptions work out brilliantly. A huge number of adoptive children retain a lifelong fondness for their new parents who have so deliberately chosen to cherish them. For them, there is no unease at all about the relationship, no sense of not fitting in, of feeling alien – just a warm and loving kinship, no less intense for having been sought out. As a dedicated fan, Georgie must have read some if not all of the Agathas I have mentioned. If so, she must have found them intensely painful, perhaps recognizing in them, as I now recognized, echoes of her own life and the way she came to hate her mother, distorted memories no doubt but piercing all the same. It was no good to dismiss the books as trashy thrillers. If they were bestsellers, that was because millions of ordinary readers picked up those same echoes, for this was part of what they really thought about adoption, although they pretended they didn't. It's a prejudice too that the law, no doubt with the best intentions, conspires to reinforce, by treating adoption as a dreadful secret, the details of which can be revealed only after the most exhaustive precautions. After all, as I discovered later, this was what Dame Agatha herself thought: her own mother's life had been a miserable one, because she couldn't get over being adopted, and she managed to pass on a share of that misery to her daughter. When Agatha fled from her faithless first husband, she took a false name and hid out in a hotel in Harrogate. One answer to wretchedness, it seems, is to kiss yourself goodbye.

———

Celeste Ireland had been Celeste's name ever since she came to Canada, so she still had the first name Munca had given her when she took her in. This meant I could google her, which I did, though I don't know what I hoped to find out. I certainly had not expected to discover that Celeste was on a quest of her own. She was looking on Ancestry.com for her birth mother and for the brother she hadn't seen since she was a baby.

All at once the whole ether seemed to be overwhelmed by the anguish of the lost and separated. What a strange thing it is – and I think mostly a blessing – that the internet should allow us to share our private desolations. It disturbs some people, mostly older people, that the digital revolution should so amplify the throbbings of our hearts. But there are times — and this is one of many — when the message on the screen offers an unprecedented solace, and a solace that is as moving, even to total strangers like me, as any film or romance.

I hope Celeste will forgive me if I reproduce here some of the threads just as they came up on the message board at Ancestry. com. I don't trust myself to rewrite them, and this story badly needs a happy ending.

Posted 4 Oct 2002 1.59 PM GMT

CELESTE.IRELAND: Looking for birth mother or half brother:
I am looking for either my birth mother or half brother … My birth mother's married name is Susan Elizabeth Giacomini. My records indicate I was born Marguerite Giacomini and I was originally placed with Mr and Mrs G. Mount from Blue Waters, Angmering on Sea, Sussex … My brother's name is Rene Marc Giacomini. Thank you for all your help. If you come up with anything I would love to hear.

And then — posted 23 Feb 2016 5.12 PM GMT— a full *fourteen* years later:

SEANJEN26: re Brother:
I realise this is an incredibly old thread and the odds of this reaching the original poster are slim, but … my father in law is the brother you are looking for!!! We've been looking for you for a few years now, which is all the time that he's even known about you. I was incredibly excited to find this post! If you get this or if anyone knows how to contact Celeste please, please let me know …

And then – posted 24 Feb 2016 2.17 AM GMT – nine hours later:

SEANJEN26: re Brother:
Happy news! We've found Celeste and gotten in touch with her. It's been a crazy wonderful day! Anyone looking for family don't give up hope. You never know what each new day might bring. Best of luck!!

Thanks

My first thanks for this little book go to Lyn Baring Gregory, whose revelations set me off on such a strange adventure. It is a great sadness to me that she died a few months before the first draft of the book was finished and was not able to read it. I very much hope that her siblings at least may enjoy this account of their grandmother's remarkable life. I dearly hope also that, if Celeste reads it, she may be intrigued by the story of the years before and after her all too brief appearance in our lives.

I am abidingly grateful to my sister Francie, who shared the years with Munca and Georgie and who has been helpful in so many ways.

I must also thank the unfailing staff of the General Register Office and of the National Archives at Kew, and the Sheffield Archives and Libraries, in particular to Clea Carroll, and to Roger Gibbons of the Gloucestershire County Cricket Club Heritage Trust for finding the photographs of Bev Lyon and Dallas Page. My great thanks too to Gill Lamprell for the fascinating tour of Charters. And to Fiona Annesley, David Dimbleby, Ian Dunlop and Max Hastings for their help and encouragement.

Finally, I would like to send my warmest wishes to all Georgie's friends in Suffolk who lit up her later years as we could not.

PICTURE AND TEXT CREDITS

The following images are reproduced by kind permission of the copyright holders.

Page 12: The staircase at Holthanger: Architectural Press Archive / RIBA Collections

Page 42: Bev Lyon at the crease: Roger Gibbons

Page 43: The 1930 Gloucestershire team: Roger Gibbons

Page 67: The Healey Silverstone: Brian Snelson / CC BY 2.0

Page 89: Charters exterior: Frank W. Westley/ *Country Life* Picture Library

Page 92: Frank Parkinson by Howard Coster: © National Portrait Gallery, London

Page 98: The Morning Room at Charters: Frank W. Westley/ *Country Life* Picture Library

Page 111: The Windsors at Charters, May 1947: British Pathé

Page 122: View of Brightside: Reproduced by kind permission of Amberley Publishing

Page 132: All Saints, Ellesmere Road: Sheffield Local Studies Library, www.picturesheffield.com

Page 134: Thorndon Road: Sheffield Local Studies Library, www.picturesheffield.com

Page 134: Thorndon Road 2: Sheffield Local Studies Library, www.picturesheffield.com

Page 148: Walter Walsh: Sheffield Local Studies Library, www.picturesheffield.com

Page 149: John Walsh and Co, 39 High Street: Sheffield Local Studies Library, www.picturesheffield.com

Page 154: Two photographs from the wedding of Denis Burke and Philippa Cunliffe-Owen: Barry Swaebe Archive

Page 155: Sunningdale Park: Choice/ Alamy stock photo

Page 161: Scavenging for coal on Burngreave Bank: Sheffield Local Studies Library

Page 163: Buster's birthplace, 66 Lofthouse Place: Reproduced with permission from WYAS Leeds, LC/ENG/CP/29, no. 76

Page 206: Dallas at the crease: Roger Gibbons

Page 210: The Immortal Dallas: Roger Gibbons and the Gloucestershire CCC Trust

Page 222: Meadowhurst in Pudsey: Betty Longbottom / Meadowhurst House - off Tofts Road / CC BY-SA 2.0

Page 238: Sir Walter Forrest obituary in *The Times*, July 19, 1939: *The Times* / News Licensing

All other images are from the author's private collection or in the public domain.

The following extracts are reproduced by kind permission of the copyright holders

Page vi, quote from *Sweeney Agonistes* by T. S. Eliot: Faber & Faber

Pages 88, 93 and 95, various quotes from *Country Life*: Christopher Hussey/ *Country Life*

Page 104, quote from *Berkshire* by Geoffrey Tyack, Nikolaus Pevsner and Simon Bradley. Reproduced with permission of The Licensor through PLSclear

Page 116, quote from *The Road to Wigan Pier* by George Orwell: A. M. Heath

Page 175, quotes from *The Letters of T. S. Eliot*: Faber & Faber

Pages 176 and 221, quotes from *The Waste Land* by T. S. Eliot: Faber & Faber

Page 244, quote from *Collected Poems 1909–62* ('The Hollow Men') by T. S. Eliot: Faber & Faber